THE
MYTHOLOGY
OF
Richard
III

The
Mythology
of
Richard
III

John Ashdown-Hill

AMBERLEY

History will be kind to me, for I intend to write it.

Sir Winston Churchill

History is always written by the winners.

Dan Brown, *The Da Vinci Code*

In memory of my dear mother, Joan, who wrote to me that 'your love of history must stem from me as I always loved the subject at school'.

First published 2015

Amberley Publishing
The Hill, Stroud
Gloucestershire, GL5 4EP

www.amberley-books.com

British Library Cataloguing in Publication Data.
A catalogue record for this book is available from the British Library.

ISBN 978 1 4456 4467 7 (hardback)
ISBN 978 1 4456 4473 8 (ebook)

Typesetting and Origination by Amberley Publishing.
Printed in the UK.

Contents

Introduction 7

Part 1 The Geography of Richard III 13
 1 York – or Leicester – or ...? 14

Part 2 The Path to the Throne 19
 2 Richard, the Abnormal Prince 20
 3 Sorcery and the Supernatural 29
 4 Richard, the Serial Killer 39

Part 3 Richard's Religion 61
 5 Catholic or Anglican? 62

Part 4 The Monster King 73
 6 Richard, the Usurper 74
 7 Richard, the Tyrant 86
 8 Marriage Mythology 91

Part 5 Legends of Richard's Last Days 109
 9 The Inn and the Bed 110
 10 The White Horse and the Sleepless Night 117
 11 The Last Mass and the Last Battle 122

Part 6 Richard III's Dead Body 127
 12 Burial Myths 128
 13 The Body in the River 135

14 The Mythology of Rediscovery   140
15 The DNA Link   146

Part 7 Kudos, Fantasies and Profit   151
16 The post-2012 Leicester Edition of Richard III   152
17 Images   159
18 The Tourist Trade   163

Conclusions   167
Appendix 1: Potential candidates for identity with the
Leicester Greyfriars bones   171
Appendix 2: The Plantagenet Y-chromosome (email
correspondence between the author and Dr Turi King of the
University of Leicester, September 2012)   177
Appendix 3: Suggested amendments proposed by the
Looking For Richard Project Team to the article 'The King
in the Car Park', as published in the journal *Antiquity*   180
Appendix 4: Correspondence with the editor of *Antiquity*
regarding the amendments proposed in Appendix 3 (above)   183
Appendix 5: Misleading interpretations from Leicester   184
Notes   186
Acknowledgements   204
Bibliography   205
List of Illustrations   213
Index   216

Introduction

No man should be judged by another.
The Cloud of Unknowing (written by an anonymous English
priest, possibly from the East Midlands, *c.* 1390)[1]

Richard III's life story was rewritten – and in a thoroughly slanted light – by the propagandists of his victorious opponents after his defeat and death at Bosworth in August 1485. Should anyone harbour the slightest doubt that such things still happen today, in the real world, they have only to look at how the story of the rediscovery of the king's remains in 2012 has been edited since that discovery was made. The authentic and true story of this search – which was not led by anyone based in Leicester – is revealed in *Finding Richard III – The Official Account*.[2] But editing of this true story seems to have been chiefly manipulated by the University of Leicester Press Office and its associates in order to claim maximum kudos in respect of the discovery, firstly for the university itself, and secondly for the city of Leicester. Evidence of this activity is presented in part 7 and the appendices (see below). As for the possible motivation for such conduct on the part of an academic institution in the somewhat unfavourable context of the modern world, that is examined in this book's final chapter ('Conclusions').

Attempts have also been made to edit the true story of the rediscovery of Richard III's remains by certain *soi-disant* 'professional' historians, archaeologists and writers. Curiously, not one of the individuals in question was responsible for a single significant revelation, or for the discovery of any new evidence, relating to King Richard or his burial site. Nevertheless, these individuals presumably hoped that it would prove financially rewarding for them to cash in on the discovery once it had been made. It is also intriguing that one of them is a Fellow of the Society of Antiquaries. His selective use of the terms 'amateur' and 'professional' appears to show remarkably little knowledge of the history of the Society of Antiquaries, or of the hugely valuable work done by its 'amateur' Fellows in the past.

One forthcoming book on Richard III, due out in April 2015, has been written by 'the Grey Friars Project Team' (that is to say, the team as currently defined by the University of Leicester), together with Lin Foxhall, head of archaeology and ancient history at the university, and journalist Maeve Kennedy of *The Guardian*. Professor Lin Foxhall is basically a classicist. She is a reputable scholar in her specialist field – though her reading and interpretation of medieval Latin can sometimes be questioned slightly (see below, chapter 2). Nevertheless, neither she nor Maeve Kennedy carried out any research on Richard III that contributed to the search project for his long-lost remains, or to the eventual setting in motion of the archaeological excavation of August 2012.

In precisely the same sort of way, the government of the usurping and essentially non-royal King Henry VII rewrote history from August 1485, in order to improve the standing of the new head of state. Henry VII had no valid blood claim to the English throne. The true Lancastrian claimant to the English throne in 1485 was either the King of Portugal or the Earl of Warwick.[3] But Henry seized power by means of a foreign-backed invasion which culminated in the battle of Bosworth. He then legitimised his power seizure by causing Parliament to recognise him as king. His conduct in respect of his accession contrasts notably with that of his predecessor, Richard III, who, as we shall see, was not legitimised as sovereign *post hoc factum*, but rather was offered the crown in advance by the three estates of the realm. Full details of the true nature of Richard III's claim to the throne are offered below, in chapter 6.

One of the earliest and most obvious rewritings of history was, in fact, Henry VII's repeal of the Act of Parliament which had recorded and confirmed the offer of the crown to Richard. That 1484 Act was repealed unquoted – an unprecedented move – in an ultimately vain attempt to ensure that no one in the future would ever be able to access the evidence which had led to Richard being offered the throne. To airbrush this evidence out of history even more effectively, Henry VII also forbade any copies of the original Act to be kept, under the threat of severe penalties.

Of course, the actions of Henry VII and his government were in no way unique. It would be naïve to suppose that any ruler, of any historical period, who has been violently ousted by a political opponent, is, or has ever been, favourably reviewed subsequently by the incoming regime. After all, both the political role and the authority of the new regime are entirely based upon the predecessor's downfall.

Examples of such rewriting of history can be found in every period of recorded history, from the ancient world to the present day. Indeed, in my own lifetime we have witnessed a number of examples, such as the ousting of the Perón government in Argentina (more than once), the overthrow of the Shah of Iran, and the fall of a number of other Middle Eastern regimes, not to mention the political controversy in Myanmar (Burma) and the way in which the government there has portrayed the opposition leader, Aung San Suu Kyi. In all such cases the fallen regimes, or the outlawed political leaders, have been negatively portrayed by those who replaced them, or excluded them from power.

It is interesting to consider what these modern examples of the rewriting of history reveal. For example, the reign of Mohammed Reza Shah Pahlavi definitely had what can be seen as positive points, including the Shah's support of education and of women's rights. Of course, it also had what can be seen as negative points, such as the Shah's transformation of Iran into a one-party state. Problematically, however, many of his policies could potentially be viewed either positively or negatively depending upon the viewpoint of the observer or commentator. Policies which fit into this equivocal category include the Shah's support of modernisation and secularism, foreign support for his regime, and his recognition of the state of Israel. Another curious point is the fact that, during his reign, the Shah was criticised for holding political prisoners. Ironically, however, after his overthrow the number of political prisoners vastly increased. 'According to official statistics, Iran had as many as 2,200 political prisoners in 1978, *a number which multiplied rapidly as a result of the revolution*'.[4]

Recently, the Shah's reputation has experienced something of a revival in Iran, with some people looking back on his era as a time when Iran was more prosperous and the government less oppressive. Journalist Afshin Molavi reported that some members of the uneducated poor – traditionally core supporters of the revolution that overthrew the Shah – were making remarks such as, 'God bless the Shah's soul, the economy was better then', and found that 'books about the former Shah (even censored ones) sell briskly', while 'books of the Rightly Guided Path sit idle'.[5]

In a similar way, the government led by Juan and Eva Perón in

Argentina can be said to have done some bad things and some good things. For example, the Perónist regime was also extremely active in promoting womens' rights. Probably most political regimes in history are, in reality, a mixture of good and bad. But if they suffer a downfall, their reputations, as promoted by those who replace them, become exclusively bad.

It is therefore in no way surprising that history as written under King Henry VII and his immediate successors should have represented Richard III as a secretly malicious, ambitious prince, motivated by a hidden lust for the crown – a lust which allegedly led him to become both a serial killer and a usurper. All of the stories relating to this Tudor depiction of King Richard will be examined in detail in the course of this book.

What is even more curious, however, is the fact that, in spite of his official political image as monster and murderer, Richard III has, for many centuries, also been viewed on another level as a kind of money maker and potential tourist attraction. One modern example of a somewhat similar phenomenon is the reputation of Eva Perón. Eva was initially represented by political opponents in Argentina, as a socially unacceptable, money-grubbing harlot. After the overthrow of her husband in the 1950s, and during the rule of the military dictatorship of 1976–83, such accounts of her were disseminated much more widely. Nevertheless, at that same period Evita's 'story' was seen as a source of income by many writers. For example, the musician Andrew Lloyd Webber produced a slanted, and somewhat inconsistent, version of her life history in the form of a famous money-making musical in 1978. In a similar way, Richard III has been perceived by some people as a possible source of income. Ricardian parallels of the musical *Evita* began in the sixteenth century, with the Richard III plays written by Shakespeare and others.

This phenomenon has generated, or disseminated, some very intriguing stories about Richard and his alleged local links with certain areas. And while many examples of this phenomenon date from the past, it is also a fact that, as we shall see later, the profit motive is a feature of Richard's 'history' which remains very much alive today. For example, there can be very little doubt that, since the discovery of his remains in August 2012, Leicester City Council has perceived Richard III as a potentially huge source of income, leading the mayor of Leicester to announce that only over his dead body would the king's bones be removed from the city. At the same time, people in York have also attempted to claim ownership of Richard. The effects of such phenomena are quite worrying from the viewpoint of those who were and are in quest of the *real* Richard III and his story. It has already been noted that another outcome has been that many authors who had absolutely nothing to do with the research which led to the quest for Richard III have, since the discovery of his bones, produced books and articles about him, some of which contain inaccurate material. Accounts in other media, including television, also tend to be more interested in sales and rating than in focussing on historical truth.

The problem is that the accounts which result, both from political propaganda and from the desire for profit, include myths and legends presented as reality. Even though serious and unprejudiced historical research can generally reveal the errors – and the alleged accounts have absolutely no genuine evidence to substantiate them – many people seeking to learn about Richard III will find themselves easily misled. What is even more alarming is the fact that a surprisingly large number of serious academic historians appear to allow themselves to be easily misled by such mythology. For example, in his well-known study of Richard III, Charles Ross accepted without question – and, sadly, without doing any research on the matter – the traditional version of the 'body in the river' story (for details of which, see chapter 13).

By contrast, the present writer was recently described by members of the West Mercia Group of the Richard III Society as a 'mythbuster'! In addition the Looking For Richard Project, led by Philippa Langley, of which I was a founder member, and which, in reality, was responsible for the 2012 search for Richard III's physical remains, always had two objectives. One of these, of course, was to find Richard III's lost grave and body, but the other was to get behind the myths and legends to the true and authentic Richard III. It was the fervent hope of the Looking For Richard Project members that the discovery of Richard III's lost remains would be accompanied by the setting of the king in his real historical context – a real context upon which myself and other members of the project (notably Annette Carson), together with our predecessors in the Richard III Society, had been trying to shed new light for a number of years.[6]

Sadly, the new Richard III Visitor Centre that opened in Leicester in 2014 appears to take little account of such research. For example, Eleanor Talbot (the key figure upon whom Richard III's legitimate claim to the English throne depended) is not mentioned there. Yet my detailed research on Eleanor – a lady who had been long neglected by historians – together with Annette Carson's important work on Richard III's marriage plans of 1485, and a great deal of other significant material which has been ignored by the Richard III Visitor Centre, play a vital role in this book. Here I shall do my best to explore and expose every key aspect of both the traditional and the modern Ricardian mythology.

As we shall see, the outcome of this approach is not always that the true story then becomes crystal clear. Particularly in terms of the past, the picture that emerges may be somewhat cloudy. But in the end, it is always far better to be left with an open question to which we know that we can offer no simplistic answer, rather than to be palmed off with an easy 'answer' for which, in reality, there is absolutely no historical basis.

PART 1

The Geography of Richard III

Rex Richardus tercius – born in the Castle of Foderyngay a myghti prince in his days speciall gode to the town & lordship of Warrewyk wher yn the castel he did gret cost of byldyng In the which his most noble lady & wyf was born and at gret instance of her he of his bounteous grace with owt fee or fyn graunt to the seyd borowh frely by charter as kyng William Conquerour his noble progenitor a fore tym gret previlagis.

John Rous, *The Rous Roll*, 1483–84

1

York – or Leicester – or ...?

Richard Plantagenet, and the other children of Richard Duke of
Yorke, were brought up in Yorke-shire and Northampton shire.

George Buck[1]

Richard III is well known for having been a northerner.

Amy Licence[2]

Richard III and his elder brother, Edward IV, tend to be seen as
essentially English in terms of their nationality – unlike many
monarchs who have worn the crown of England, but who have
been perceived as half French, or mostly German. However, we
should perhaps take note of the fact that Richard and Edward were
both one-eighth Spanish. Their great-grandmother, Isabel, Duchess
of York, was the daughter of Pedro (Peter) 'the Cruel', King of
Castile.

That ancestry is perhaps significant. King Pedro's popular
appellation 'the Cruel' might, perhaps, at first sight, appear to
imply that England's murderous and tyrannical king (as Richard
III is traditionally described) had inherited his wickedness from
his Spanish ancestor. But in my view, Richard's descent from King
Pedro is significant in quite another way.

Popular memory generally views Peter as a vicious monster.
Much but not all of Peter's reputation comes from the works
of the chronicler Pero López de Ayala, who after his father's
change of allegiance *had little choice but to serve Peter's usurper*.
After time passed, there was a reaction in Peter's favour and an
alternative name was found for him. It became a fashion to speak
of him as *El Justiciero*, the executor of justice (the Lawful).[3]

Richard, too, has suffered from the writings of those who later had to serve *his* usurper, Henry VII. But in schools in Yorkshire, Richard is referred to as Good King Richard.[4] Perhaps one day both Richard's reputation, and Pedro's, will be fully reassessed.

One popular image of Richard III is that he was a northerner. It is certainly true that his mother's family – the Nevilles – had strong connections with the north of England. Also his father, Richard, Duke of York, had been brought up for part of his childhood as a ward of the Neville family. As a consequence of this, he too had therefore established certain northern connections. However, the Duke of York's royal ancestors had been based in the south of England, while his Mortimer forebears had held territory in a variety of locations, including East Anglia and Ireland.

As for Richard III himself, the surviving evidence seems to show that he was neither conceived nor born in the north of England. His conception may well have taken place at Ludlow Castle, since that is where his parents had spent the Christmas season of 1451.[5] Subsequently, it was in October 1452, most probably at the York family's castle of Fotheringhay in Northamptonshire (but just possibly at Berkhamsted Castle in Hertfordshire), that the Duchess of York gave birth to her last son, the future King Richard III. In fact his birthplace is usually stated to have been Fotheringhay, as though that was the only surviving account. The later versions of the York genealogy in William Worcester's *Annals* state that Richard was born at Fotheringhay and so does a note in Richard's Book of Hours. However, Sir George Buck, descendant of a Yorkshire family whose ancestors had served the house of York, said that Richard's birthplace 'was the Castle of Fotheringhay, or as some write, the Castle of Birkhamsteed'.[6] Buck's source for Berkhamsted as Richard's birthplace was probably Stow's *Annales*. The fact that one seventeenth-century account names Berkhamsted as Richard's birthplace means that, if we are trying to avoid simplistic answers (which could lead to possible errors), the question of where he was born needs to be examined.

Fotheringhay Castle was certainly held by the Duke of York. As for Berkhamsted Castle, a claim has been advanced that it, too, was a hereditary possession of the Dukes of York, having been granted by Richard II to Edmund of Langley, 1st Duke of York.[7] However, other sources assert that this castle belonged to the duchy of Cornwall from 1356. This version of the story would clearly imply that in 1452, Berkhamsted would effectively have been in the hands of Henry VI.[8] But even if this is correct, that would not necessarily have made it impossible for Richard to have been born at Berkamsted Castle. The surviving evidence indicates that several of the other York family children were born at properties which were not actually owned by their father.[9]

It is true that records show that the *Duke* of York was certainly at Fotheringhay in both August and December 1452.[10] Unfortunately, however, the more significant location of his wife, the duchess, is nowhere specifically recorded. Nevertheless, the note, apparently written later by Richard III in his own Book of Hours, states clearly that he was born at Fotheringhay. It seems, therefore, that the king himself did think of Fotheringhay as his birthplace.

A recent scientific report on Richard III's remains states that

> We applied multi element isotope techniques to reconstruct a full life history. The isotopes initially concur with Richard's known origins in Northamptonshire but suggest that he had moved out of eastern England by age seven, and resided further west, possibly the Welsh Marches.[11]

But of course this does not prove scientifically that Fotheringhay was Richard's birthplace. It merely indicates that the early years of his childhood were spent in Northamptonshire, probably in the nursery at Fotheringhay Castle.

Geographical connections are not established only by the conception and birth of an individual. During his childhood Richard probably travelled about the country a good deal. In 1459, for example, he stayed with his family at Ludlow. But on 12 October the Lancastrian forces defeated the Yorkists at the battle of Ludford Bridge. The Duke of York then fled to Ireland, while his eldest son, Edward, Earl of March (together with his uncle and cousin, the Earls of Salisbury and Warwick), made his way to Calais. Meanwhile Ludlow was sacked by the Lancastrians, and Cecily Neville, Duchess of York, and her younger children, Margaret, George and Richard, were captured and carried off to Coventry. There, a Lancastrian decision was taken to consign Cecily to the custody of her elder sister, Anne Neville, Duchess of Buckingham. Following this decision, it has traditionally been reported that Cecily and her three youngest children were then taken to one of the Buckingham family manors in Kent.[12]

It is certain that in the following year (1460) Richard, together with his elder brother, George, and their sister, Margaret, stayed for several weeks in Southwark, at a property, located immediately to the north of the site where the Shard now stands – a property which then belonged to the Paston Family, but which had been built earlier in the fifteenth century by Sir John Fastolf. It was the Duchess of York who requested this accommodation in Southwark for herself and her younger children. Soon afterwards the duchess left to join her husband. But the children remained in Southwark for some time.

Subsequently, following the deaths of his father and his elder brother, Edmund, Earl of Rutland, at the battle of Wakefield, Richard had the traumatic experience of being sent, with George and a few family servants, to the Low Countries. Obviously their mother was alarmed for their safety. Thus the two little boys had to cross the North Sea in winter, at a time when weather conditions were not good.[13] When they landed, Philip the Good, Duke of Burgundy, did not wish to compromise himself politically by receiving them. They therefore found themselves forwarded to Utrecht, where they were the guests of Philip the Good's illegitimate son, the Prince Bishop. The two young Yorkist princes spent a couple of months in Utrecht, until the success in England of their brother, Edward (IV), encouraged the Duke of Burgundy to recognise their presence – and their status – and receive them with honour in the town of Bruges. After the duke's princely reception, the two boys returned home via Calais and Margate.

Back in England, the new king, Edward IV, then established a household for his three youngest siblings, Margaret, George and Richard, at the Palace of Pleasaunce (Richmond). Later, however, Richard, now Duke of Gloucester, was consigned to the guardianship of his older cousin, the Earl of Warwick. Richard then spent a brief period of his life at Middleham Castle.

This episode is often misrepresented by those who wish to see Richard as a northerner. For example it was suggested to me by a friend who lives just outside York that 'at the age of nine Richard was put in the care of his uncle the Earl of Warwick and so began his lifelong association with the north when he went to receive the knightly education worthy of a King's brother at Middleham Castle'.[14] This is an interesting story, which accurately reflects how things are perceived by many who live in and around York. However, the phrase 'at the age of nine' implies that Richard was assigned to Warwick's guardianship in 1461, when he returned to England from his first brief exile in the Low Countries. There is no evidence to substantiate that assumption.

As we have seen, in 1461 Edward IV based Richard (together with his brother George and his sister, Margaret) at the Palace of Pleasaunce (Richmond), near London. It was not until 1465, just after his thirteenth birthday, that Richard was assigned to Warwick's care and went to live at Middleham Castle.[15] Since by 1469

Warwick and George, Duke of Clarence, were at odds with Edward IV – who was accompanied and supported by his youngest brother, Richard, Duke of Gloucester – Richard's sojourn at Middleham lasted three years at most. Moreover, he certainly did not spend the whole of those three years in the north of England. In 1467 he seems to have been visiting Sir John Howard (later Lord Howard, Duke of Norfolk) in Colchester, Stoke-by-Nayland, Lavenham and other towns and villages in Essex and Suffolk, followed by a trip to Cambridge.[16] In 1468 he travelled from London to Canterbury as part of the escort of his sister Margaret, who was then setting off on the journey to her marriage with Charles the Bold of Burgundy.

Although Richard's teenaged visits to Middleham did not constitute continuous residence at that castle, and comprised only a relatively short period of his growing up, he later returned to the north as Edward IV's effective 'viceroy'. Richard does seem to have felt some kind of affinity for the northern counties and, particularly after the execution of his brother, George, Duke of Clarence, he appears to have preferred to stay away from London – where the Woodville family were then dominant, and in a position of power.

But of course, Richard continued to travel. He appears to have visited Gloucestershire on occasions, and he also visited his mother from time to time, at Clare Castle in Suffolk, and later at Berkhamsted.

Curiously, although the king's dead body is now known to have spent the last 500 years or more in Leicester (and will apparently now remain there for ever), during his *lifetime* Richard was only a very infrequent visitor to that East Midlands town. He stayed in Leicester from Sunday 17 August until Wednesday 20 August 1483, while he was on his way to Nottingham, and again on the night of 22 October. The records specify that on Monday 18 August the king was at Leicester Castle, and maybe he stayed at the castle for all four nights. The following year he paused briefly at Leicester Abbey on Saturday 31 July when he was travelling from Nottingham. However, there is no evidence that he spent the night at the abbey. Probably, therefore, his visit on this occasion merely represented a short rest break on his journey. In the last year of his life Richard seems to have spent two nights in Leicester, from Friday 19 August until Sunday 21 August.[17] There is no contemporary record which states precisely where he stayed on this occasion, so serious historians are obliged to report that the venue is unknown. However, the traditional mythology surrounding the king's Leicester visit of August 1485 (recently rather worryingly reinforced by the University of Leicester and the Richard III Visitor Centre in Leicester) will be examined in detail later (see chapter 9).

PART 2

The Path to the Throne

It was shown by means of a supplication contained in a certain roll of parchment that King Edward's sons were bastards on the basis that he had previously married a certain Lady Eleanor Boteler,[1] before he took Queen Elizabeth to wife; furthermore the blood of his other brother, George, Duke of Clarence, was attainted, so that now no certain and uncorrupted blood line of Richard, Duke of York, could be found except in the person of the said Richard, Duke of Gloucester. Therefore, at the end of this roll, he [Gloucester] was begged, on behalf of the lords and commons of the kingdom, to assume his rights.

Crowland Chronicle Continuations, 1486 (trans. J. A-H.)[2]

Richard, the Abnormal Prince

Shakespeare ... made Richard two men in one, that's what I complain of. One of 'em's a wormy, plotting sort of fellow and the other's a bold, bustling sort of chap who chops people's heads off and flies into tempers. It doesn't seem to fit somehow, eh?

Dorothy L. Sayers, *Have His Carcase*, 1932

According to the nineteenth-century historian James Gairdner, 'Richard III was ... a military commander before he was nineteen, usurped the throne when he was thirty-one, and was killed at Bosworth at the age of thirty-three. Precocious, therefore he certainly was'.[3] Gairdner was a scholar, yet this curious statement of his contains interpretations which can be questioned in almost every respect. The use of the verb 'usurp' in relation to Richard III's accession will be examined in detail later (see chapter 6). As for Richard's age at the time of his accession, thirty-one was by no means young for mounting the throne (though in reality at the moment of his accession Richard III had not yet attained his thirty-first birthday, but was only thirty years and six months old). Edward III had become king at the age of fourteen; Richard II, at the age of ten; Henry V, at the age of twenty-six; Edward IV, at the age of eighteen; Edward V, at the age of twelve; Henry VI at the age of eight months; Henry VII at the age of twenty-eight. Even Henry IV had only been thirty-two years and five months old when he became king. Thus, of all the fifteenth-century monarchs, Richard III was actually the *second oldest* when he mounted the throne. Similarly, nineteen was not a notably young age for exercising military command. Nor was thirty-three a young age for dying.

Sadly, despite his in many ways serious and logical approach to the matter of sources, Gairdner evidently found himself so deeply embroiled in traditional mythology as received by historians of the nineteenth century that sometimes he could not escape. Thus he reports that Richard is said to have spent two years in his mother's womb, and 'came into the world feet foremost, with teeth in his jaws and with hair down to the shoulders'.[4] Yet, despite the existence of very curious and contradictory later rumours, there is no real evidence that Richard's birth was in any way unusual.

One intriguing – and warning – feature of certain aspects of the traditional Ricardian mythology is that often, conflicting accounts exist. Thus, while Richard III is frequently described as having been a monster from birth,[5] an alternative version of this mythology describes the onset of his alleged deformities as late in origin, and in some narratives, it is said to have been due to sorcery. We shall return to this account of sorcery in the next chapter. Meanwhile, chronologically, the first significant feature of the traditional mythology of Richard III obviously comprises tales of his conception and birth. Here, too, we encounter two divergent accounts of the boy's supposedly abnormal gestation. Thus, in respect of his period in his mother's womb, as in other aspects of the traditional Richard III mythology, we find ourselves confronted by conflicting and mutually incompatible accounts of Richard's alleged abnormality.

Assuming that Richard's birth occurred a standard nine months after his conception (but see below), he was probably conceived at Ludlow Castle, as we have already noted. Moreover, if the standard timescale for human gestation applies in his case, he must have been conceived under the sign of Capricorn. This in itself may potentially have represented a rather bad start. According to *The Joys of Hymen* (published in the eighteenth century, but based on earlier writings), parents were well-advised to avoid conceiving a child under certain zodiacal signs, for fear of producing a monster, and late December and January was definitely one of the times to be avoided if possible, since

> Capricorn – to Saturn near ally'd,
> Curs'd by the vig'rous fire and teeming bride,
> Deforms the face, and blisters all the skin,
> And fills the mind deprav'd with lechery and sin.[6]

However, Richard III's gestation narratives, which represent a prime example of how mutually contradictory myths about Richard have been perpetuated in defiance of all logic, suggest that the length of his mother's pregnancy was abnormal. The fifteenth-century Warwick historian John Rous (*c.* 1411–91), writing after 1485, reported that Richard III was 'retained within his mother's womb for two years'. In factual terms, this is self-evidently nonsense. On this basis, Richard would have been conceived in 1450. Since the Duchess of York gave birth to another son, Thomas, (who died young) early in 1451, Thomas and Richard would then necessarily have been in their mother's womb simultaneously. But, curiously, the two boys were born more than eighteen months apart. Such a parturition event would surely have been unique in the annals of gynaecology.

A later writer – the sixteenth-century playwright, William Shakespeare – flatly contradicts Rous. Shakespeare claims that, far from spending two years in the womb, Richard was born as a premature infant. In Shakespeare's play *Richard III*, the character of Richard is made to describe himself as having been 'Sent before my time into this breathing world, scarce half made up'. Elsewhere, in *Henry VI part 3*, King Henry is made to tell Richard,

> The owl shriek'd at thy birth, an evil sign;
> the night crow cried, aboding luckless time;
> dogs howled, and hideous tempest shook down trees,
> chattering pies in dismal discords sung.
> Thy mother felt more than a mother's pain,
> And yet brought forth less than a mother's hope,
> to wit an undigested deformed lump,
> not like the fruit of such a goodly tree.
> Teeth hadst thou in thy head when thou wast born,
> to signify thou cam'st to bite the world.[7]

Shakespeare's Richard himself later confirms, 'I have often heard my mother say I came into the world with my legs forward. ... The midwife wondered, and the women cried "O! Jesus bless us, he is born with teeth".'

It is clear, in fact, that Shakespeare wishes to present Richard as both monster and prodigy. 'For sixteenth-century Christians a prodigy was a disturbing and unusual event, one apparently contrary to nature and therefore attributable directly to God. It served to warn of divine displeasure and future misfortune'.[8] In the prodigy tradition unnatural births were fully expected to be associated with other significant manifestations of disruption in the natural world, such as comets, floods and earthquakes. Though strong winds and bad weather are not, in fact, necessarily so very untoward in England, in October, Shakespeare's 'hideous tempests' coinciding with Richard's birth were clearly perceived by the writer as falling within the prodigy tradition.

Moreover, while Rous and Shakespeare may be at variance over the duration of Richard's gestation, they are at one on the fact that he was born with teeth and hair. Rous, indeed, goes further than Shakespeare, claiming that at birth Richard already had 'hair to his shoulders'. The symbolism of teeth, and of a birth feet-first hardly require explanation. Teeth are used to bite, while coming into the world feet first would be taken as a sign of the child's overpowering ambition. Long hair, however, is perhaps rather more arcane in its symbolism. In the biblical story of Samson, we find that long hair was a sign of great physical strength. Later, for the early Frankish kings, long hair had been the distinguishing mark of the sovereign.[9] Presumably, therefore, Rous' intended message is to the effect that the little monster, Richard, was destined to throw his weight about and seize the throne. But of course, his canny prophecy that Richard would reign was penned with the inestimable advantage of hindsight. Richard was the eleventh of the twelve children – and the youngest of the eight sons – of his parents. Since his father never reigned as king, Richard was therefore born at quite a considerable distance from the throne.

After briefly alluding to the reports that Richard had spent two years in his mother's womb, and was born with teeth and hair, the nineteenth-century historian Gairdner then goes on to report of Richard's childhood that 'it would seem that Richard ... was slender and sickly'.[10] However he cites no evidence in favour of his use of the word 'slender'. As for Richard's supposed childhood sickness, Gairdner mentions his contemporary Mr Sharon Turner, whose book, *History of England during the Middle Ages*, claimed that Turner had 'found evidence somewhere, as he believed, that Richard had serious illness as a child, *but was not able to refer to the source of his information*'.[11] As for Gairdner himself, he based his own assessment of Richard's childhood sickliness upon the sentence 'Richard liveth yet' in a poem (see below), adding that 'we have distinct testimony to the fact that in after life he was a small man of feeble bodily powers'.[12]

In reality there is absolutely no real evidence that Richard was a sickly child. Indeed, all the rumours of Richard's sickliness appear to be based solely on the poem cited by Gairdner. This was written in 1456 (when Richard was only three or four years old) by Friar Osberne Bockenham OSA, of Clare Priory in Suffolk. The poem is entitled 'The Dialogue at the Grave of Dame Joan of Acres', and it lists all the children of the Duke and Duchess of York, who were patrons of Clare Priory, and owned the neighbouring castle of Clare. The English version of the poem merely states that Richard 'liveth yet'. From the structure of the poem, it is clear that it says this, not because Friar Osberne (who may never have seen the little boy) knew that Richard's life was precarious, but merely in order to contrast the living Richard with those of his siblings who had died young. What is more, the Latin version of the friar's verses lack this particular phrase. This suggests that it was probably a product of the English poem's metre and bore no special significance. The relevant Latin verse runs

> Margret post proles hinc Willelmusque Iohannes,
> Quos raptus seculo statuit Deus almus Olimpo.
> Inde Georgius est natus Thomasque Ricardus,
> Thomas in fata secessit sorte beata.
> Ultima iam matris proles fuit Ursula, regis
> Que summi voto celesti iungitur agno.[13]

There is some dispute as to whether the original version of the poem was the English or the Latin text.[14] However, the English text also applies the phrase 'Richard which yet liveth' to the Duke of York, father of Edward IV and Richard III, and no one has ever deduced that *he* was sickly. In this matter, as in all questions relating to Richard III, one must therefore be very wary of crediting unsubstantiated later mythological explanations and interpretations.

The discovery of Richard III's body in August 2012, on the site of the Franciscan Priory (Greyfriars) in Leicester, has proved conclusively that legends about Richard are still rampant and have to be treated with scepticism.[15] For example, Rous's statement that Richard as a grown man was small and feeble is also disproved both by recent analysis of the king's physical remains, and by the active role that Richard took in warfare, hunting and other activities.

According to the traditional accounts, Richard III was said to be physically deformed in various ways. This point will be examined in detail in the next chapter. But regarding Richard III's overall physical appearance, we have a traditional myth which contrasts a tall, fair, handsome Edward IV with his small, dark, twisted and deformed younger brother. It is difficult to trace the origin of this story (though Shakespeare has Richard remark how little his brother, Edward, resembled their father, the Duke of York). The widespread modern dissemination of the alleged physical contrast between Edward IV and Richard III seems to owe a great deal to the writings of historical novelists. However, its underlying significance is transparently obvious, for dark colouring has always been associated with evil, and with the Devil,[16] while, as we shall see in the next chapter, low or misshapen stature suggests links with witches.

Factually, in respect of hair colour, this story is entirely false. Richard and Edward had hair of similar colour (mid brown), as is shown in their earliest surviving portraits (the pair of 'Paston' portraits of Edward and Richard held by the Society of Antiquaries of London) and likewise in fifteenth-century miniatures. The general opinion seems always to have been that the adult Richard did not have fair hair. As for Edward IV, it is incontrovertible that he had brown hair, as can easily be seen from surviving hair samples taken when his tomb was opened in the late eighteenth century.[17]

In respect of their respective physiques, all that can be said with confidence is that Edward was undoubtedly fatter in later life than Richard. He was also taller. It is known from his skeletal measurements that he was six feet two inches in height.[18] As for Richard III we now know from his bones that, at around 5' 8", he was shorter than Edward. But his height would probably have been slightly above the average for the period.

Despite this, as we have seen, Rous's account, written not long after Richard's death, suggested that he had been 'small of stature'. Of course, low stature, particularly when associated with deformity, had undesirable connotations at that period. However, documentary evidence relating to 1461 shows clearly that at that point Richard was of at least average height for his age group.

Evidence from the same source also indicates that the middle brother of the York family – George, Duke of Clarence – may have been of below average height. When George and Richard were in exile in the Low Countries in 1461, George was about eleven and a half years old and Richard was about eight and a half. But the chronicler Jehan de Wavrin,[19] who met them, assumed that they were nine and eight years old respectively.[20] Therefore it seems that George appeared to be at least two years younger than his real age, and only about one year older than his brother. Richard, on the other hand, was clearly of about the correct average height for his chronological age.

George might perhaps have inherited his height genes from his mother, for Cecily Neville was described as 'a woman of small stature but of moche honour and high parentage'.[21] Although some modern historians have tried to suggest that George's *father* was 'short and small of face',[22] no genuine evidence has ever been cited to support this assumption. Indeed, the only evidence we appear to have regarding the appearance of the Duke of York states that in 1460 he was 'manly and myʒtfulle'.[23] This seems to imply that he was of above average height and build.[24]

Some features of George's somewhat unpredictable character were later (and unjustifiably) misattributed by Tudor propagandists to Richard III.[25] It may therefore be that the Tudor claim that Richard III was short is also derived from true reports and memories regarding the stature of his brother George.

Richard III's height has now been approximately established, and it is now considered that his scoliosis would have had very little effect upon this. 'Experts now know he would have had a slightly curved spine which would not have affected his prowess in battle'.[26] Nevertheless, the legend that he appeared short still seems to be very powerful. Thus Leanda de Lisle, who admits that she finds it hard to sympathise with Richard, stated (incorrectly) in *The Spectator* that 'although Richard III was five foot eight, his spine was so twisted he stood a foot shorter'.[27] Similarly, it has also been alleged that, in a talk about the king, Dr Richard Buckley suggested that, owing to his deformed back, Richard III's height was only 'about 4ft and some inches'.[28] It was also reported that on that occasion a member of the audience interrupted and said he had scoliosis very similar to Richard's and he was 5ft 8ins tall. Would Buckley like him to take his shirt off? He went on to do just that. Buckley's reported response was that he had said 'what he had been told to say'.[29] He did not identify who had given him that advice. However, one possible source for such opinions regarding the effect of the king's scoliosis upon his height will emerge shortly, when we explore the somewhat controversial translation and interpretation of Rous's Latin text produced by one of Buckley's colleagues, employed by the University of Leicester (see below).

As for the actual text in which Rous suggests (incorrectly) that Richard was small in stature, its original, Latin version runs as follows:

> *Attamen si ad eius honorem veritatem dicam ut nobilis miles licet corpore parvus et viribus debilis ad ultimum anhelitum suum modo defensorio clarissime se habuit.*[30]

These words were employed in a worrying way by Professor Lin Foxhall of the University of Leicester in her presentation at the university's famous, televised 4 February 2013 press conference, when the identity of Richard III's remains was formally announced.

She was inspired, apparently, by earlier remarks made by Dr Jo Appleby, an osteologist from her university department who had examined the bones, and who had commented on camera in autumn 2012 on the gracile nature of the limbs and the feminine nature of the sciatic notches. Referring (without naming him) to Rous, Dr Appleby had stated that 'there is actually one of the historical sources – and I'm afraid I forget which one – that refers to him [Richard III] as fighting surprisingly well in battle considering that he was lacking in masculinity. So there is actually some historical back-up for that theme'.[31] Possibly at that stage Dr Appleby (or whoever had translated the passage for her) had erroneously misinterpreted *viribus* as an inflection of the noun *vir* (= man). In fact it is derived from *vis* (= strength or might), and when used in the plural form, e.g. *viribus*, this word has a more specialised meaning in a military context, when it is usually taken to refer to military forces, i.e. troops. It is interesting to note that, given the meaning which Appleby attributed to the Latin term, Philippa Langley, who was present for the filming, was unable to recognise her source.

At the press conference on 4 February 2013, Professor Foxhall suggested that Rous's text implied that Richard III was rather effeminate. She cited the Rous quotation as a piece of fifteenth-century documentary evidence which supported Dr Appleby's conclusion that he was 'gracile'. Professor Foxhall's words on that occasion ran as follows:

Now, Jo [Appleby]'s discoveries about the delicate, gracile character of the skeleton, which is unusual in a man of this period [*sic!*], might encourage us now to see these historical descriptions in a new light and to read them rather more literally than I suspect scholars and translators have done in the past. In Latin the word *vis*, 'strength' or 'vigour', is often a characteristically masculine quality, and of course Rous describes Richard as *viribus debilis*, 'weak in vigour or strength'.[32]

Due, perhaps, to her reported special interest in masculinity,[33] Professor Foxhall continues to imply that Rous was describing Richard's appearance as not notably masculine. Her current translation of Rous runs as follows:

However, if I might speak the truth to his honour as a noble soldier, though he was slight in body and weak in strength, to his last breath he held himself nobly in a defending manner.[34]

In the view of the present writer, Professor Foxhall's rendition of the word *viribus* remains open to question. Also, as a classicist, she may be unaware that in medieval Latin the term *miles* means 'knight'. Personally I should prefer to translate Rous's Latin text into English as follows:

> However, if, in honour of him as a noble knight, I speak the truth, although his body was small, and his military forces, weak, to his last gasp he held himself illustriously in a defensive manner.

This reflects the fact that the word *viribus*, being a plural form of the noun *vis*, and occurring here in the context of a battle, is much more likely to mean 'military forces' or 'resources'.

My colleague Annette Carson would also prefer to translate *viribus* in this manner, pointing out that

> this clearly makes much more sense in view of the defection of the Stanley forces to the opposition (and also Northumberland's lack of intervention in Richard's support). There is also the very important report of Salazar as quoted by de Valera [stating that Richard] 'began to fight with much vigour, putting heart into those that remained loyal, so that by his sole effort he upheld the battle for a long time'.[35] Appleby and Foxhall would of course lack access to this medieval eyewitness report, which clearly indicates that Richard in his person was observed to exhibit 'much vigour' – not 'feeble strength'![36]

From their surviving portraits, and from Richard's modern facial reconstruction, there is evidence that in terms of facial features, both Richard III and his elder brother George, Duke of Clarence, resembled their father, the Duke of York, while their eldest brother, Edward IV, more closely resembled his mother, Cecily Neville.[37] This could account for the kind of comment made by Shakespeare's Richard III, to the effect that Edward IV did not look like their father (see above). However, as we have seen, while Cecily Neville was reported to have been a short lady, the Duke of York was probably tall. Thus it seems that in terms of their height both Edward IV and Richard III more closely resembled their father – unlike their brother George.

Sorcery and the Supernatural

Plots have I laid, inductions dangerous,
By drunken prophecies, libels and dreams.
                    Shakespeare, *Richard III*, act 1, scene 1

We know now, from his physical remains, that Richard III suffered from scoliosis, and that the effect of this would have been to make his right shoulder appear slightly higher than his left. This point was first recorded by John Rous in about 1490. And beholding it in the flesh – or, at least, the bone – had a great impact on me personally (and I imagine also on my colleagues Philippa Langley and Annette Carson) when I first saw the king's remains fully exposed, but still lying in their grave, in September 2012. It was immediately apparent that the curve in his spine would have produced precisely the effect which Rous described. However, the subsequent, strongly emphasised story of Richard III's alleged hunch-back, seems basically to be Tudor in origin.

Curiously, the Society of Antiquaries 'Paston portrait' of Richard, painted probably in about 1520, shows a slightly higher *left* shoulder. However, this portrait may be a mirror image copy of a lost earlier (and possibly contemporary) portrait of Richard. Other evidence that it is a mirror image comprises the fact that the king is playing with a ring on the third finger of his *left* hand, and that, as I have suggested previously, this was possibly a portrait painted originally in connection with Richard III's negotiations in 1485, for a royal marriage with the Infanta Joana of Portugal.[1] At this period wedding rings were actually worn on the third finger of the *right* hand.[2] We may therefore assume that the putative original portrait, now lost, would have correctly shown Richard's right shoulder slightly higher.

As for the hump shown in later paintings of Richard III, that has been proved by X-ray examination to have been added to the next earliest painting of Richard – the one in the royal collection at Windsor – having apparently formed no part of the original artist's work. Nevertheless, two late fifteenth-century Tudor sources do refer to Richard as having had a crooked back. As we have already noted, John Rous, writing within six years of Richard's death, said that he had 'unequal shoulders, the right higher and the left lower'. In addition, in May 1491, an altercation took place in York, as a result of which some of those involved appeared before the mayor and council. The surviving records reveal that during a heated exchange one of the antagonists had claimed that 'Kyng Richard was an ypocryte and crocheback'.[3] Clearly, from the fighting which took place, this was possibly viewed generally as an inappropriate overstatement of the situation. This statement was hotly contested by the man's adversary and described by another witness as 'unfyttyng langage',[4] even though vilification of the late king was well entrenched at the time when it was made.

In the modern western world, talking of the physical abnormalities of a living individual would generally be considered politically incorrect. Of course, 'the phrase "political correctness" was born as a coded cover for all who still want to say Paki, spastic or queer, all those who still want to pick on anyone not like them, playground bullies who never grew up. [Nevertheless,] the politically correct society is the civilised society, however much some may squirm at the more inelegant official circumlocutions designed to avoid offence. Inelegance is better than bile'.[5]

But even in the modern, politically correct world, 'bullies remain bullies, and they do not curb their actions merely because a new word is now commonly used to refer to the characteristics that they wish to use as a basis for insulting people. A bully who formerly used the word "retarded" as a term of scorn can just as easily use the euphemism "differently abled" as a term of scorn by using a malicious tone of voice. Indeed, as feminist author Germaine Greer notes, "It is the fate of euphemisms to lose their function rapidly by association with the actuality of what they designate, so that they must be regularly replaced with euphemisms for themselves" (1971, 298)'.[6] In other words, if Richard III was alive today, and suffering from scoliosis, it would almost certainly be considered absolutely outrageous to employ a term such as 'crookback' to describe him. Nevertheless, there would probably still be people around who would simply find another term for insulting him.

But in actual fact, since Richard III is a dead man, there seem to be some people who feel that there is therefore no reason why they should not apply to him the traditional kind of derogatory terminology. After all, he is not available to take action against them. Thus a recent scientific article on Richard had the heading 'Infected [*sic* for Infested?] and Hunched [*sic*]: King Richard III was crawling with roundworms'.[7] It is very doubtful whether the writer of this article would have described a *living* celebrity sufferer from scoliosis – for example, Sarah Michelle Gellar, the star of the television series *Buffy the Vampire Slayer* – as 'hunched'. It is also curious that the modern discovery that Richard III suffered from intestinal parasites – at a period when most of the population of Western Europe probably had them – should apparently be considered significant enough to warrant a headline. And it is even more curious that this fact should then be linked, in the title of the article, with Richard's alleged (but incorrectly designated) spinal deformity. Indeed, the title of the article appears to suffer from terminological inexactitudes. Parasites do not 'infect', while the spinal deformity should have been correctly characterised as scoliosis. The point should also have been made that while the occurrence of intestinal parasites was probably quite common in the late fifteenth century, scoliosis was a problem from which the majority of Richard's contemporaries would not have suffered.

Incidentally, when the bones discovered on the Greyfriars site in Leicester were being analysed by a scoliosis specialist during the filming of the Channel 4 documentary *Richard III: The King in the Car Park* (4 February 2013), the specialist described the remains as being those of a 'hunchback'. This greatly surprised Philippa Langley, who was present at the time, because it had then already been confirmed that the skeleton did not suffer from kyphosis. Later it was also confirmed that scoliosis patients should never be described as 'hunchbacked'.[8] When such patients lean over there is a 'prominence' in the back on the side, in the ribs, but this does not push the head forward and onto the chest, as in the case of kyphosis, to create a 'hump'.

Another point worth noting in connection with possible modern mythology relating to Richard III's scoliosis is the fact that, in the Channel 4 TV documentary *Richard III: The New Evidence* (17 August 2014) Dominic Smee was chosen to act as a living representation of Richard III, since he has the same scoliosis. After putting Dominic through rigorous physical tests, one misleading conclusion reached by the programme was that, when he was unhorsed at Bosworth, Richard III would not long have survived, because his scoliosis would have affected his levels of aerobic fitness. This conclusion was based upon the effect of strenuous activity on Dominic Smee. But unfortunately it was not made clear that, apart from his scoliosis, Smee also had other underlying health issues, which meant he had been unable to undertake any previous physical activity.

However, there was another potential candidate for the documentary. Mark Kydd, the body double used in the film at the Richard III Visitor Centre in Leicester, is an actor from Edinburgh. Kydd also has the acute scoliosis of King Richard but, unlike Smee, he has no other underlying health issues. He is physically fit and active, having trained as a ballet dancer in his early years and now regularly undertaking Bodypump classes. As a result, Kydd (currently in his mid-forties) suffers from no aerobic difficulty. It is probable, therefore, that Kydd would have offered a more realistic representation of the king and his battlefield potential.

The origin of descriptions of Richard III's supposed physical deformities must, of course, be understood in the context of the period in which they were disseminated. Medieval thinking was based upon the twin foundations of Judeo-Christian theology and Classical philosophy. In the Judeo-Christian tradition deformity and sickness were associated with sin, and constituted potential manifestations of divine retribution.[9] At the same time, the complex concept of archetypes,[10] and of the regression of likenesses, which the medieval world derived from the neo-Platonists,[11] inferred a connection between a deformed human body and a perverted social system. Let us explore these two basic approaches to deformity a little further.

To the medieval and early modern mind a physical deformity could be both the punishment for, and the unmistakable sign of, a twisted and evil mind. Alternatively (and perhaps even more horrendously) the physical deformity might be diabolical in origin – the visible sign of a pact with the Devil. The Devil frequently manifested himself 'as a degenerate or deformed person with a physical ugliness that inspires terror. ... In token of his favor, and to set them forever apart as his own, the Devil signs his followers with a visible mark, just as Christian baptism sets a person apart for God with an invisible mark ... there is great diversity in the size and shape of the Devil's mark it might be a withered finger or other deformity'.[12]

At the same time, from neo-Platonism the medieval world derived the concepts of man as a 'little world' (microcosm), and of his relationship to the universe as a whole (macrocosm). As a result, a twisted body and a sick society could be perceived as linked. This correlation would have seemed particularly potent if the deformed body was that of the sovereign. Accounts of Richard III's physical abnormalities were therefore deliberately intended to convey clear messages about both his character, and the society in which he lived – and for which, as sovereign (*de facto*, even if not *de iure*) he bore responsibility.[13] It is therefore a moot point whether what appeared to be physical descriptions of Richard III were ever seriously intended to convey accurate factual information about his appearance. What mattered was not what he actually looked like, but the fact that 'the transgressions of the body's natural boundaries through disease or deformity constitute ... a kind of denial of the systems modelled on it, rendering vulnerable the principle of order'.[14]

Both Classical and Christian traditions had long associated physical deformity with the Black Arts. A Greek black-figure-ware cup made in about 400 BC depicts the witch Circe with her victim, Odysseus. Both are shown as stunted and malformed.[15] A lekythos of the same date bearing the head of Medea portrays an ugly woman with a long, pointed nose, features found much later in witch depictions.[16] A sixteenth-century Flemish painting now in Bilbao Museum shows witches served by dwarfs and hunchbacks.[17] The latter is particularly interesting, given that both diminutive stature and a crooked back form a significant part of the standard Richard III mythology.

Richard was also reported to have had a withered arm. Although it has now been established by the examination of Richard III's physical remains that there was never any truth in this, the story nevertheless needs to be considered. We find the following scene described both in Holinshed's *Chronicle*, and in Thomas More's *History of King Richard III*.[18] The setting is a council meeting in the Tower.

> Then said the protector: 'Ye shall all see in what wise that sorceresse [Elizabeth Woodville], and that other witch of hir councell, Shores wife [*sic*],[19] with their affinitie, have by their sorcerie and witchcraft wasted my bodie'. And therwith he plucked up his dublet sleeve to the elbow, upon his left arme, where he shewed a weerish withered arme, and small; as was never other.[20]

On the basis of this account, Richard was evidently supposed to have been born with a normal left arm, which suddenly became 'weerish' in the summer of 1483 due to witchcraft. But according to Holinshed, the members of the royal council knew 'that this matter was but a quarrel. For they well wist that the queene was too wise to go about anie such follie'.[21] Moreover, according to this account, all of them were also well aware that Richard had, in fact, been suffering from a withered arm since his birth,[22] – though, as we have already noted, his remains have now proved that such was not, in fact, the case.

Twenty-first-century western man may experience some difficulty with the idea of witchcraft, but fifteenth- and sixteenth-century people did believe in this, and it is a recorded fact that Richard III levelled accusations of witchcraft against his enemies, including Elizabeth Woodville. It was in Richard's act of *titulus regius* of 1484 that Elizabeth Woodville was accused of witchcraft. However, this real accusation said nothing of any sorcery practised against Richard himself. Rather, it accused Elizabeth Woodville (together with her mother, the Duchess of Bedford) of having used sorcery to induce Edward IV to marry her. Perhaps later Tudor concern to ensure that the relationship between Edward IV and Elizabeth Woodville was never questioned, led to the creation of the new – and invented – sorcery account published by Holinshed, which claimed that Richard III accused Elizabeth Woodville of using sorcery to disable him. For Henry VII and his dynasty it was vitally important to maintain the validity of the Woodville marriage (see chapter 6). Thus, if people remembered that Richard had accused Elizabeth Woodville of witchcraft, Henry VII would have been anxious to confuse and mislead them, regarding the true nature of that accusation.

While we have no further surviving evidence to prove that Elizabeth Woodville had attempted to seduce Edward IV by sorcery, that story itself is not completely implausible. Richard III's genuinely made accusation to that effect needs to be understood in a wider context. Elizabeth Woodville's mother, Jacquette, dowager Duchess of Bedford, had been accused of sorcery in 1469, when Thomas Wake, a member of the Earl of Warwick's affinity, brought his lord a damning piece of evidence against her. The evidence comprised an 'image of lede made lyke a man of armes, conteynyng the lengthe of a mannes fynger, and broken in the myddes, and made fast with a wyre'.[23] If events in the country at large had gone differently at that period, Jacquette might well have been imprisoned for this, just as her sister-in-law, Eleanor Cobham, Duchess of Gloucester, had been earlier. The evidence produced against Eleanor Cobham had also included an image employed for the working of magic. All this is significant, because the Duchess of Bedford was said to have been present at her daughter's secret marriage to Edward IV in 1464. Thus she apparently had knowledge of her daughter's relationship with the king at a time when this was still hidden from the rest of the world.

Witches, from time immemorial, were quintessentially female. There are Classical prototypes such as Circe and Medea. Indeed, the latter is credited by Euripides with the opinion that 'we were born women – useless for honest purposes, but in all kinds of evil, skilled practitioners'.[24] The Middle Ages kept up this anti-feminine tradition, and there had been earlier accusations of witchcraft against women closely associated with the royal family. Alice Salisbury (Perrers), mistress of Edward III, was tried for witchcraft before Parliament in 1376, as was Henry V's stepmother, Joanna of Navarre, in 1419. Later, as we have seen, Henry VI's aunt, Eleanor Cobham, Duchess of Gloucester, was similarly accused, and in 1469 Edward IV's mother-in-law likewise – all prior to Richard's accusation against Elizabeth Woodville and her mother. And while Joanna of Navarre had eventually been pardoned, the unfortunate Eleanor Cobham had been imprisoned for life.

However, the fact that Richard was male did not, in itself, automatically exclude him from any possible involvement in the black arts. Alice Salisbury and Eleanor Cobham had both been associated with male as well as female sorcerers. Male 'necromancers' were also involved with Richard's brother George, Duke of Clarence, in 1476. Mancini reported in 1483 that 'the Duke of Clarence was accused of seeking the king's death with magic and sorcerers'.[25] According to the rather strange account of the Crowland chronicler (1486),

A certain Master John Stacey, called the Astronomer, though he had rather been a great necromancer, examined together with one Burdet, a squire in the duke [*of Clarence*]'s household, was accused, among many charges, of having made lead figures and other things to get rid of Richard, Lord Beauchamp, at the request of his adulterous wife and during a very sharp examination he was questioned about the use of such a damnable art; he confessed to many things both against himself and against the said Thomas [*Burdet*]. He and Thomas were therefore arrested together. Sentence of death was eventually passed upon them both in the King's Bench at Westminster in the presence of almost all the lords temporal in the kingdom along with the justices.[26]

The Crowland account is very odd because it focusses only on the alleged murder of Lord Beauchamp, and says nothing about the much more important allegations against Stacey and Burdet of involvement in plots against the king and the Prince of Wales. However, these more serious charges were also brought against the accused, as other contemporary sources show.

Following his arrest, the 'necromancer' Stacey was questioned under torture, and admitted to having sought to bring about the death of Edward IV and his eldest son by the use of the black arts, and to having cast horoscopes to work out when they were likely to die. Stacey's confession also specifically implicated Thomas Burdet, who was then a member of the Duke of Clarence's household, but who had formerly been in the service of the Butler family of Sudley. This is significant, because the Butlers were the family of Lady Eleanor Talbot's first husband. As we shall see later, Eleanor Talbot was the woman who was responsible, in a way, for putting Richard III on the throne of England, since it was claimed that she had married Edward IV prior to his secret marriage to Elizabeth Woodville, thereby rendering the children of Edward's Woodville marriage illegitimate. It was on this basis that the young king Edward V was debarred from the throne in 1483. (For a detailed exploration of this story, see chapter 6.)

Burdet's connection with Eleanor Talbot's family therefore links the 1476 case with the fact that in that same year Burdet had been publishing verses in London, aimed at promoting the Duke of Clarence as the legitimate heir of Edward IV (instead of his Woodville children). Given his links with Stacey and other Oxford University astrologers, it is possible that these verses (none of which now survive) included elements which claimed to predict the future. Indeed, they may well have been the source of the famous 'prophecy of G'.

A later poem about Clarence, believed to date from about 1547, briefly tells the Tudor version of this prophecy in the lines,

> A prophecy was found, which sayd, a G
> Of Edward's children should destruction bee.
> Mee to bee G, because my name was George,
> My brother thought, and therefore did me hate.[27]

Of course, in the Tudor period, this prophecy was used against Richard (whose title of Duke of Gloucester began with the letter G). Thus, as Edward Hall's *Chronicle* (published in 1542), reported,

> The fame was that the king or the Quene, or bothe sore troubled with a folysh Prophesye, and by reason therof begâ to stomacke & greuously to grudge agaynst the duke. The effect of which was, after king Edward should reigne, one whose first letter of

hys name shoulde be a G. and because the deuel is wot with
such wytchcraftes, to wrappe and illaqueat [*ensnare*] the myndes
of men, which delyte in such deuelyshe fantasyes they sayd
afterward that that Prophesie lost not hys effect, when after kyng
Edward, Glocester vsurped his kyngdome.[28]

However, if the origin of the prophecy of G was indeed Burdet's
poems, published in 1476, and inspired by the Oxford University
'necromancers', the reference to someone whose name began with
'G' was not to Richard III, but to George, Duke of Clarence. The
purpose of the poems would then have been to inspire popular
support for George to be accepted as the rightful heir to the throne.
And Edward IV and Elizabeth Woodville would then have been
correct in perceiving the Duke of Clarence as the person responsible
for this campaign.

Although Burdet's published verses have not been preserved –
and the source of the 'prophecy of G' is therefore not now precisely
verifiable – the existence of this prophecy had been attested more
than half a century before Hall's *Chronicle* and the Clarence poem
appeared. The earliest surviving reference to it dates from shortly
after the death of Richard III, when the existence of the prophecy
– and its connection with the fate of the Duke of Clarence – were
mentioned by John Rous (*c.* 1490) as follows:

> Because there was a prophecy that after E., that is, after Edward
> the fourth, G would be king – and because of its ambiguity –
> George Duke of Clarence (who was between the two brothers,
> King Edward and King Richard) on account of being Duke
> George, was put to death.[29]

Since Rous's reference to the 'prophecy of G' cites it as one of the
reasons underlying George's execution, this clearly implies that the
prophecy had indeed been current in 1476–77.

Before the king's body was rediscovered in 2012, rationalisations
had sought to explain the story of Richard III's withered arm by
suggesting that military exercise might have resulted in it being less
strongly developed than the right. But if such had been the case,
Richard would hardly have been unique in this respect. Moreover
such a condition would not have arisen suddenly and unexpectedly.
We now know that Richard's left arm was not deformed. However,
it would probably always have been better not to handle such
material as though it were literally true, but to bear in mind
its essential character as a fictional construction built upon the

tradition of deformity myths. Curiously, although the Coventry Tapestry shows no hump on Richard's back, it does depict a strange left hand. Might Richard III have had a natural tendency to be left-handed? As the words themselves reveal that characteristic was once perceived as sinister!

There are other elements of Richard's story which may bear a dark gloss. For example, there is no doubt that Richard chose, as his personal emblem, a white boar, but it is also the case that the Devil was said sometimes to appear in the form of a wild boar (though appearance as a large goat seems to have been considered more common).[30] The famous rhyme

> The Catte the Ratte and lovell owyr dogge
> Rulyn all Engeland undyr an hogge[31]

refers to Richard and his close associates, William Catesby, Robert Ratcliffe and Francis, Viscount Lovell. Interestingly, however, it also focusses upon animal forms which were later commonly believed to be assumed by the familiars of witches.[32]

Essentially, the world view which originally engendered the 'Richard the Monster' myth is long-since *passé*. It is no longer generally assumed that those human beings who suffer from some physical deformity are, of necessity, evil, nor that corruption in society mirrors and is mirrored in the corporeal malformation of its leading members. In this sense, accounts of Richard's physical abnormalities are now robbed of their original *raison d'être*. Thus, apart from the fact that human curiosity naturally leads us to want to know the truth, one is tempted to ask why it should now matter one jot whether or not Richard III had some physical deformity.

Hopefully, even a modern writer who wished to argue that Richard was evil, or that late fifteenth-century England was a corrupt and ill-governed society, would not consider statements about Richard's birth and physique to be of any relevance. Sixteenth-century writers, by contrast, had been led to believe that such statements were both indispensable evidence of Richard's evil disposition and symptomatic of the distressed state of the earlier England which he had ruled. To the sixteenth-century mind it was largely irrelevant whether or not accounts of Richard's deformity were objectively true. What mattered was that they represented a perceived psychological truth. Thus a sixteenth-century writer who believed that Richard and his regime were evil would have described the king as deformed even if, in modern terms, he had no evidence for such physical deformity.

4

Richard, the Serial Killer

... it is a great principle of English law that every accused person
is held to be innocent unless and until he is proved otherwise.
                    Dorothy L. Sayers, *Strong Poison*, 1930

According to the Tudor accounts of Richard III, he was a killing
machine, the most famous of his alleged crimes being the murder
of his nephews and potential rivals for the crown, the so-called
'princes in the Tower'. In this context, it is an interesting point
that his successors, Henry VII and Henry VIII, can be shown
to have systematically killed surviving members of the house of
York. As a result they have been categorised as strong kings! It
would therefore surely be legitimate to expect that if it could be
proved that Richard III had murdered his nephews he would also
be categorised as a strong king. Yet, curiously, this has never been
the case. The playing field of history appears not to be composed
of level ground.

The list of Richard's numerous alleged victims is wonderfully
– and very completely – summarised by the succession of ghosts
who prevent his sleep on the last night of his life in Shakespeare's
famous play. These ghosts comprise Edward of Westminster (the
putative son of King Henry VI), Henry VI himself, George, Duke
of Clarence, Earl Rivers, Richard Grey and Thomas Vaughan, Lord
Hastings, the 'princes in the Tower', the Duke of Buckingham and
Queen Anne Neville.

However, the crime of murder is normally defined as the unlawful,
premeditated killing of one human being by another. The deaths of
George, Duke of Clarence, Earl Rivers, Richard Grey, Thomas
Vaughan, Lord Hastings, and the Duke of Buckingham were not
murders, but executions – an execution being the culmination of a

legal process of some kind, the carrying out of a sentence of death upon a condemned person. Moreover, the execution of George, Duke of Clarence, was carried out not by Richard's government, but by the government of King Edward IV. What is more, no writer has ever suggested that Richard personally killed his wife or his two nephews. Thus, the only two deaths on the list in which the fatal weapon was actually alleged to have been wielded by Richard himself were those of Edward of Westminster and Henry VI.

Even this simple and basic introductory analysis has therefore already raised several questions about the alleged 'crimes' of death attributed to Richard. And when we examine the 'crimes' individually, we shall see that there are many more questions to be asked. For example, one intriguing factor common to the alleged killings of Henry VI, and of Rivers, Grey, Vaughan and Hastings, is the fact that the dates and processes of all these deaths have been questioned.

Stories suggesting that Richard was a killer generally only refer to a period relatively late in his lifetime. Curiously, perhaps, no one but Shakespeare has ever suggested that Richard was a murderous child or adolescent, or that he was responsible for the deaths of any of his child siblings. Shakespeare, however, does depict Richard as having killed the Duke of Somerset at the first battle of St Albans in May 1455 – at a time when the real Richard had not yet reached his third birthday! This occurs in *Henry VI Part II* act 5, scene 2.[1] With this one exception, Richard's reputed killings begin with reports that he took part in the slaughter of Edward of Westminster, the putative son of King Henry VI, and thus the Lancastrian Prince of Wales. At the time of Edward of Westminster's death, in 1471, Richard, Duke of Gloucester, was approaching nineteen years of age.

As for Edward of Westminster, he was about a year younger than Richard, having been born to Margaret of Anjou at the Palace of Westminster on 13 October 1453. At the time of his birth, King Henry VI was suffering from mental problems, and although he later recognised the boy as his son, the child's paternity was questioned at the time, and has subsequently been debated.[2]

In 1470 this exiled Lancastrian Prince of Wales had been married to Anne Neville, the younger daughter of Richard, 'the Kingmaker', Earl of Warwick. Richard, Duke of Gloucester, had spent some time under the guardianship of Warwick at Middleham Castle, and he must have known Anne. Indeed, it is possible that he loved her and already aspired to marry her himself (for more on this, see chapter 8). Thus Anne's marriage to Edward could well have been a cause of personal animosity on Richard's part towards the Lancastrian prince. Interestingly, however, none of the accounts of

Richard's involvement in the death of Edward of Westminster make any use of this possible motive!

The seventeen-year-old Edward returned from France with his mother and his young bride in 1471, in the wake of his father-in-law and new supporter, the Earl of Warwick. They landed at Weymouth in Dorset on the morning of Easter Sunday – 14 April. Unfortunately, unbeknown to them, this was the very day on which the Earl of Warwick had been defeated and killed at the battle of Barnet. Thus, when they landed, the Lancastrian cause in England was already foundering.

Nevertheless, when he heard the news of the defeat at Barnet, Edward of Westminster urged his mother not to give up their cause. He himself hoped to join up with his uncle Jasper, Earl of Pembroke, so he and his mother and his young bride pressed on in the direction of Wales. However, the Yorkist army prevented them from crossing the River Severn at Gloucester. Instead the Lancastrians were forced to turn in the direction of Tewkesbury. By this time Edward IV and his army were in hot pursuit of them. The Yorkist king and his brothers finally confronted Edward of Westminster and his party just outside Tewkesbury. Although Queen Margaret of Anjou would have preferred to avoid combat at this stage, both the young titular Duke of Somerset and Margaret's own son were keen to fight.

The outcome of the battle of Tewkesbury was disastrous for the Lancastrian cause. 'Somerset' and Edward of Westminster both died as a result of the battle. In the case of 'Somerset', we know for certain that he did not die in the fighting. He was captured alive, and then executed after the battle. However, accounts of the death of Edward of Westminster vary. For example, Philippe de Commynes wrote that 'the prince of Wales was killed on the battlefield, together with several other great lords and a very large number of ordinary soldiers. The Duke of Somerset was captured; next day he was beheaded'.[3] Commynes' contemporary and countryman Jean de Roye also reported: 'there died, and was killed the said Prince of Wales, which was a great shame, for he was a handsome young prince'.[4]

But later accounts began to suggest that, like 'Somerset', Edward of Westminster had been captured alive, and was then put to death after the battle had ended. Such accounts also report that it was King Edward IV and his two brothers who killed the young Lancastrian prince. Thus, more than a century after the event, in 1577, the *Chronicle* of Raphael Holinshed gave the following account of Prince Edward's demise:

After the field was ended, proclamation was made, that whosoever could bring foorth prince Edward alive or dead, should have an annuitie of a hundred pounds during his life, and the princes life to be saved if he were brought foorth alive. Sir Richard Crofts, nothing mistrusting the kings promise, brought foorth his prisoner prince Edward, being a faire and well proportioned young gentleman; whom when king Edward had well advised, he demanded of him, how he durst so presumptuouslie enter into his realme with banner displaied?

Whereunto the prince boldlie answered, saying: 'to recover my fathers kingdome & heritage, from his father and grandfather to him, and from him after him to me, lineallie descended'. At which words king Edward said nothing, but with his hand thrust him from him, or (as some saie) stroke him with his gantlet; whom incontinentlie, George duke of Clarence, Richard duke of Glocester, Thomas Greie marquesse Dorcet, and William lord Hastings, that stood by, suddenlie murthered.[5]

Such graphic later versions of the story of Edward's death are contradicted by a surviving letter, contemporary with the battle, written by Edward IV's middle brother. In that letter, George, Duke of Clarence, states specifically that 'Edward, late called Prince ... [was] slain in plain battle'.[6] There is therefore absolutely no contemporary evidence that Edward of Westminster was killed after the battle, let alone that Richard, Duke of Gloucester, was in any way involved in the young man's death. It is also noteworthy that even Holinshed's sixteenth-century account merely alleges that Richard was one of a group involved in the death of the Lancastrian prince. It does not suggest that Richard himself was the murderer.

The second murder which is attributed to Richard is that of Henry VI. It is claimed that, in the immediate aftermath of the battle of Tewkesbury, Richard killed ex-king Henry in London. Thus, according to Holinshed's *Chronicle* (1577), 'in the Tower ... Richard duke of Glocester (as the constant fame ran) ... (to the intente that his brother king Edward might reign in more suertie) murthered the said king Henrie with a dagger'.[7]

King Henry is usually reported to have died, or been killed, on the night of 21 May 1471.[8] This date is based on an account written by John Warkworth, which states that Henry 'was putt to dethe the xxj day of Maij, on a tywesday night, betwyx xj and xij of the cloke'.[9] Warkworth then goes on to report that 'the Duke of Gloucester, brother to King Edward and many other' were then at the Tower.[10] It appears that Warkworth's decision to name only

Gloucester out of the 'many' can hardly be accidental. Moreover, Warkworth also states that 'on the morrow he [Henry VI] was chested and brought to Paul's, and his face was open that every man might see him. And in his lying he bled on the pavement there; and afterwards at the Black Friars was brought, and there bled new and fresh'.[11] The bleeding of the dead body was apparently thought to be significant – a kind of supernatural public proclamation that Henry had died a violent death.

In point of fact, however, Warkworth's alleged date for the death of the Lancastrian ex-king cannot be regarded as a proven fact. For example, in his biography of Henry VI, Betram Wolffe proposed that the former king may actually have died early on the morning of Wednesday 22 May,[12] while Polydore Vergil's account suggests that Henry VI died after Edward IV had pacified Kent and dealt with Fauconberg. Thus, although Vergil's version of the story mentions no specific date, it appears to suggest a death date either very late in May or early in June.[13] As for Sir Clements Markham, he 'made use of the Exchequer *Issue Rolls* (detailing expenditure during Henry's final days in residence in the Tower), to demonstrate that the deposed king was still alive up to 24 May at least'.[14]

Some other writers have taken issue with Markham's conclusion, suggesting that 24 May merely represented a convenient date at which to end the accounting period. But despite their argument, other contemporary documentary evidence does clearly suggest a death date quite close to that proposed by Markham. The *Arrival of Edward IV* states that Henry died on Thursday 'the xxiij day of the monithe of May'. It also states in black and white that Henry died from natural causes.[15] We also have a poem written by Dafydd Llwyd of Mathafarn, shortly after the battle of Bosworth. This Welsh poem gloats at the news of Richard III's death. But at the same time, like the *Arrival*, it implies that Henry VI died on Thursday 23 May.[16] Of course, unlike the *Arrival*, Llwyd's anti-Richard poem does claim that Henry VI had been killed. The logical conclusion to be drawn from all this varied – and sometimes conflicting – evidence is that, while most modern accounts continue to state baldly that Henry died on 21 May, the real date of his demise could well have been at least a day or two later.

The belief that the government of the new king, Edward IV, was behind the death of his Lancastrian predecessor is probably one of the factors which caused later Lancastrian accounts to deliberately adjust the date of Henry's death to match one of the two days when Edward IV and his brother Gloucester were known to have been present in London. Edward had arrived in London on Tuesday 21

May, but he had left the capital again on Thursday 23 May, the Feast of the Ascension.[17] In reality, of course, if Henry VI's death was unnatural, King Edward IV might well have preferred to distance himself physically from this event. Thus, if Henry VI was put to death on his orders, logically, Edward would probably have arranged for the dispatch to take place *after* he himself had left the capital. Perhaps it is therefore not surprising that, as we have seen, some of the available evidence seems to suggest that Henry VI may well have died on 23 May or later.

There is certainly no solid evidence to support the traditional allegation that the death of Henry VI took place at the hands of Richard, Duke of Gloucester. Nevertheless, in his play *Henry VI Part 3* (inspired, no doubt, by Holinshed's account – see above), Shakespeare depicts Gloucester as speeding from the alleged post-battle gang-murder of Edward of Westminster, to the Tower of London.[18] There, Gloucester tells Henry that he has killed Edward of Westminster – 'thy son' – and after a lengthy prophesy from Henry on the subject of how many people will come to regret Richard's existence, the latter stabs the ex-king.

Obviously, once it has been established that the precise date of Henry's death is debatable, the supposed presence of Richard, Duke of Gloucester, in the Tower of London during the night of 21/22 May is meaningless, particularly since 'many other' people are also reported to have been there. An examination of the remains of Henry VI was carried out on 4 November 1910 by Professor Macalister. All the bones except those of the right arm were present, but Macalister makes no mention of signs of any wounds. He states in his report that 'the bones of the head were unfortunately much broken',[19] but once again he does not suggest that they showed any sign of damage inflicted by weapons.

Macalister is also said to have found remains of dark brown hair attached to some parts of the skull, and to have reported that 'in one place ... it was much darker and apparently matted with blood'.[20] Assuming that his interpretation of what he saw was correct, that certainly suggests that Henry VI's head may have suffered an injury shortly before he died. However, that does not prove that he was killed. If Henry was ill, he may have lost consciousness and fallen, wounding his skull. A very similar event occurred in the case of the present writer's mother, in the period leading up to her death. Moreover, a wound to Henry VI's head is not easily compatible with Holinshed's report that Richard of Gloucester stabbed him to death (see above). Thus, we have no clear evidence to show that the last Lancastrian monarch died from unnatural causes. Moreover, if he was killed, logically it would have been his replacement, the Yorkist King Edward IV, who would have been responsible for his demise. And of course, there remains a genuine possibility that Edward may have ordered Henry's death.

However, if Henry VI was put to death on the orders of Edward IV, then the killing would probably have been carried out by servants of much lower rank than the new king's youngest brother. In fact, Richard may well have disapproved of such action, as he certainly did a few years later in the case of the execution of his own brother, the Duke of Clarence. At all events, Richard III later seems to have shown signs of regret in respect of Henry VI's death. Subsequently he exhibited a personal devotion to the cause of Henry VI as a putative saint. And in 1484 it was Richard himself – then king of England – who ordered and paid for the exhumation of the remains of this erstwhile Lancastrian king (and budding saint) from the obscure grave at Chertsey Abbey to which Edward IV had originally consigned them. Richard III arranged for their reburial in a royal tomb in St George's Chapel at Windsor Castle, on the opposite side of the sanctuary from the burial site of Edward IV himself.

Of course, some have argued that practical considerations lay behind Richard III's reburial of the last Lancastrian king. Thus Griffiths suggests that Richard 'was wise to harness the dead king's reputation rather than try to suppress it as his brother had done, in view of the growing popular veneration and the miracles associated with Henry's name which are recorded from 1481'.[21] On the other hand it is also plausible that Richard's decision was inspired by a genuinely religious motive. He was a sincerely religious man, and the actions of human beings are not invariably inspired by cynical self-interest – even though that appears to be how some historians typically perceive all human motivation.

According to the traditional mythology, following his alleged murders of Edward of Westminster and Henry VI, Richard, Duke of Gloucester, then lay low until 1476–77. In that year he reputedly plotted his third violent death, namely the demise of his own brother George, Duke of Clarence. However, as we have already seen, no one can possibly claim that this was a murder, because there is absolutely no doubt that Clarence was put to death in the Tower of London, following a trial before Parliament, which had condemned him for treason. Thus it is impossible to put forward any credible claim that Richard *murdered* the Duke of Clarence. Nevertheless, the traditional story suggests that Richard lay behind the machinations which brought about Clarence's imprisonment, his trial, and ultimately his execution.

The most interesting evidence in respect of the death of Clarence probably comes from a letter written by Richard himself, as king. This letter was addressed to Thomas Barrett, Bishop of Annaghdown ('Enachden'), and comprised instructions for the bishop who was then acting as Richard III's messenger to James Fitzgerald, 8th Earl of Desmond.

The said bisshop shall thank him ... as remembryng the manyfold notable service and kyndnesse by therle's fadre unto the famous prince the duc of York the king's fader ... Also he shalle shewe that albe it the fadre of the said erle, the king than being of yong age, was extorciously slayne and murdred by colour of the lawes within Ireland by certain persons than havyng the governaunce and rule there, ayenst alle manhode, reason, and good conscience; yet, notwithstanding that the semblable chaunce was and hapned sithen within this royaume of Eingland, as wele of his brother the duc of Clarence as other his nigh kynnesmen and gret frendes, the kinge's grace alweys contynueth and hathe inward compassion of the dethe of his said fadre, and is content that his said cousyn now erle by alle ordinate meanes and due course of the lawes, when it shalle lust him at any tyme hereafter to sue or attempt for the punishment therof.[22]

Since the Desmond family believed that the then earl's father had been executed due to the maliciousness of Elizabeth Woodville,[23] Richard III's letter appears to show that he likewise believed that Elizabeth Woodville had been responsible for the execution of his own brother George. This interpretation is confirmed by the account written in 1483 by Domenico Mancini, who stated that in 1476–77,

The queen then remembered the insults to her family and the calumnies with which she was reproached, namely that according to established usage she was not the legitimate wife of the king. Thus she concluded that her offspring by the king would never come to the throne unless the duke of Clarence were removed.[24]

It seems that in 1476 George, Duke of Clarence, raised doubts about the validity of Edward IV's marriage to Elizabeth Woodville, and therefore also about the right of the couple's children to succeed to the throne. His campaign probably included the publication by his servant Thomas Burdet of the 'prophecy of G' (see chapter 3). As a result, Elizabeth Woodville urged Edward IV to arrest, to put on trial, and finally to execute the Duke of Clarence.[25] Thus, the responsibility for this death was in no way in the hands of Richard, Duke of Gloucester, who, indeed, protested at his brother's execution. Moreover, Richard later made arrangements in respect of the burial of George's body, the commemoration of his memory, the good of his soul and the future of his children.[26]

When Edward IV himself died in April 1483, his theoretical heir was his elder son, Edward, Prince of Wales (born in November 1470). Since 1473 the young Edward had been established in a household of his own at Ludlow Castle, where the little boy nominally presided over the newly established Council of Wales and the Marches. Actually, of course, given his very young age, the little Prince of Wales required a guardian. The person selected for this office was the senior brother of his mother, Elizabeth Woodville, namely the head of the Woodville family, Anthony, 2nd Earl Rivers. Despite his somewhat parvenu paternal line family background, Anthony Woodville seems to have been an intelligent and well-educated man. And, acting on the careful instructions supplied by Edward IV, he brought up the future Edward V in his own image, as a cultivated boy.

Following Edward IV's somewhat unexpected demise, Elizabeth Woodville (now the Queen Mother) ordered her brother to bring his ward, the boy king Edward V, to London, in order that preparations could be made for his early coronation at Westminster. Elizabeth and her family were, in effect, attempting a coup, whereby the Woodvilles would wield all effective power in the kingdom through their control of the new sovereign. But in England there was no legal precedent for such government during the minority of the sovereign. In fact, the closest thing to a precedent had been the seizure of power by Isabelle of France, 150 years earlier. Having ousted her husband, King Edward II, Queen Isabelle had then briefly ruled in the name of her young son, Edward III. However, Isabelle and her conduct were frowned upon, so this precedent would generally have been regarded as a very inappropriate and unacceptable model.

The norm, in England, was that, during the reign of a child king, authority rested in the hands of the boy's senior surviving male-line relative, the highest-ranking adult prince of the blood. That model had been followed a hundred years earlier, when the child king Richard II had assumed the crown. The government then lay in the hands of councils, with the young king's senior surviving uncle, John of Gaunt, as the chief figure of authority. In the fifteenth century, when the baby-king Henry VI mounted the throne, a similar pattern was followed, except that a new office, that of Lord Protector of the Realm, had been created for Henry VI's paternal uncle, Humphrey of Lancaster, Duke of Gloucester (and for his brother, the Duke of Bedford, when the latter returned from his post in France). On the basis of these two precedents, the rightful Protector of the Realm during the minority of King Edward V should have been the boy's only surviving paternal uncle, Richard, Duke of Gloucester.

But when Edward IV died, Richard of Gloucester found himself far away from London and the centre of power. He was based in the north of England, where he had been acting as his late brother's effective 'viceroy'. Moreover, when Edward IV died, the new boy king's mother did nothing to alert Gloucester of what was happening in London. It was left to certain key members of the nobility – Gloucester's cousin the Duke of Buckingham and the late king's friend Lord Hastings – to inform Gloucester of his brother's death.

Gloucester responded to this news in a very appropriate manner. He summoned the nobles of the north to the city of York, where they were required to take oaths of allegiance to the new king. Then, having received letters from the Duke of Buckingham and Lord Hastings apprising him of the fact that Lord Rivers was escorting the new king to London, Gloucester set off in the direction of the capital. *En route*, he met Earl Rivers at Northampton. Rivers had either left his nephew, the young king, at Stony Stratford, or had sent him on there with his escort. Initially the meeting between Gloucester and Rivers appears to have been harmonious. But a few hours later, 'eventually Henry, Duke of Buckingham, also arrived [when] … it was late'.[27] Once Buckingham had joined Gloucester, he apparently exerted considerable influence, and the situation in respect of Rivers and his nephew Sir Richard Grey seems to have changed (see also chapter 6, below).

However, Earl Rivers appears to have felt no initial anxiety about encountering Gloucester. Indeed 'his willingness in the previous month to nominate Gloucester to arbitrate a dispute indicates that they were on good terms and that Rivers did not perceive Gloucester as his enemy'.[28] Therefore it was perhaps Buckingham who, when he arrived, persuaded his cousin Gloucester to arrest – and later to execute – Lord Rivers, together with the earl's nephew Sir Richard Grey, and also Sir Thomas Vaughan, all leading figures in the household of the hitherto Prince of Wales.

Henry Stafford, Duke of Buckingham, is a very important figure in the story of King Richard III. A descendant of Edward

III's youngest son, Thomas of Woodstock (an earlier Duke of Gloucester), Buckingham was a cousin of the Yorkist kings and had a rather remote place in the line of succession. Although Buckingham had been married by Edward IV to one of the sisters of Elizabeth Woodville, he did not favour the prominence of his bride's parvenu family, and may have seen the meeting at Stony Stratford as an ideal opportunity to take firm action to remove the Woodvilles from their dominant position in the kingdom.

Thus, as we have seen, Anthony Woodville was arrested at Stony Stratford, together with his nephew Sir Richard Grey (half-brother of Edward V) and Sir Thomas Vaughan. All three were imprisoned in the north and taken for trial eight weeks later at Pontefract Castle, where they were executed in June 1483. As reported by John Rous (writing in the reign of Henry VII),

at the time of his death, Lord Antony Woodville, Earl Rivers, was found to be wearing sackcloth next to his bare flesh, as he had done long before that. Moreover, at the time of his imprisonment in Pontefract, he wrote a poem, which was shown to me, in English in the following words:

> Somewhat musyng and more mornyng,
> In remembring the unstydfastnes,
> This world being of such whelyng,
> Me contrarieng, what may I gesse?
> I fere dowtless remediles,
> Is now to sese my wofull chaunce.
> Lo in this staunce, now in substance,
> Such is my dawnce.
> Wyllyng to dye methynkys truly
> Bowndyn am I, and that gretly.
>   To be content.
> Seyng plainly that fortune doth wry
> All contrary from myn entent.
> Hytt is ny spent
>   Welcome, Fortune.
> But I ne went,
> Thus to be shent.
> But sho hit ment;
> Such is huz won.

and so the aforementioned lords were sentenced to death – and to a conspirators death – by Richard, Duke of Gloucester, then

Protector of England. Thus, innocent of all that had not been invented by their executioners, peacefully and humbly they submitted to the cruel torment of their enemies.[29]

Writing in the reign of Henry VII, who was married to Anthony Woodville's niece, Rous was doing his best to present Anthony's death in a saintly light. There is no doubt that Richard, Duke of Gloucester, must have agreed to his arrest and imprisonment – though he may not have taken the initiative in respect of these actions. The inspiration may have come from the Duke of Buckingham. It is also essential to remember that the context in which the arrest took place was an attempted coup on behalf of the Woodville family (led by Elizabeth) to illegally seize power. Subsequently, upon the failure of their coup, the Woodvilles pursued a course of rebellion rather than reconciliation. Thus, whether or not Gloucester *wanted* to punish Anthony Woodville, in the end he may have been left with little choice in the matter.

There is also no doubt that Anthony Woodville was subsequently tried and executed. But Gloucester was not directly responsible for the execution, since the trial and its sequel were carried out by the Earl of Northumberland. The latter was 'warden of the east and middle marches',[30] a post in which he had recently been confirmed by the boy king Edward V.[31] But although wardens of the Marches had the established right and authority to conduct treason trials relating to offences conducted within their own designated areas,[32] in this instance those circumstances did not apply. Therefore Northumberland was presumably deputized as Vice-Constable to conduct Anthony Woodville's trial under the Law of Arms. (If Earl Rivers had not been tried under the Law of Arms, he could potentially have insisted on the right to be tried by his peers.)

Incidentally, it has been alleged that the execution of Earl Rivers post-dated Richard III's accession to the throne (his so-called 'usurpation'),[33] but this may well be incorrect. Although some sources date the death of Rivers to 20 June,[34] according to the generally accepted account, he was executed on 25 June 1483, following his trial before the Earl of Northumberland. The Duke of Gloucester did not agree to receive the crown until 26 June.

There is no doubt whatever that Richard, Duke of Gloucester, Protector of the Realm for the then king, his young nephew Edward V, was responsible for the execution of Lord Hastings in the summer of 1483. William Hastings was a cousin of the royal house of York on his mother's side, and shared, more remotely, their claim to the throne (though he ranked much lower down the royal line than Edward IV and Richard III) for Hastings' mother was Alice Camoys, daughter of Elizabeth Mortimer and granddaughter of Philippa of Clarence. This meant that Hastings was a descendant of Lionel, Duke of Clarence, and of Edward III.

Hastings' second marriage had subsequently strengthened his Yorkist connection. His second wife was Lady Catherine Neville, sister of Warwick 'the Kingmaker', and thus a first cousin of both Edward IV and Richard III on their mother's side. These close family connections may be one of the reasons why, after executing Hastings, Richard (III) did not attaint his possessions, but allowed his own close relative Lady Hastings, and her children, the rights they would have enjoyed if Hastings had simply died from natural causes.

Like Edward IV's other friend John, Lord Howard (later Duke of Norfolk), Hastings was a good deal older than the first Yorkist king. But he was knighted on the field, immediately after the battle of Mortimer's Cross, after which his rise in Yorkist England had been rapid. 'By July 1461 his closeness to the king had been recognized by his appointment as chamberlain of the royal household'.[35] During the 1460s he had undertaken various military and diplomatic tasks for Edward IV, sometimes working alongside his brother-in-law Warwick.

'Hastings has usually been portrayed as a bluff military man, loyal to Edward through thick and thin, in wartime his trusted general, in peacetime hunting, carousing and wenching at his side'.[36] Mancini (who, however, never actually met either of them) reports that Hastings was 'the accomplice and partner of his [Edward IV's] privy pleasure'.[37] And as chamberlain, Hastings was a natural channel for requests to the king.[38] Thus it was probably through him that his distant relative Elizabeth Woodville had first approached Edward IV to seek a resolution to her land dispute with her mother-in-law. Hastings certainly knew Elizabeth Woodville prior to her secret 'marriage' with Edward IV, for on 13 April 1464 – eighteen days before the clandestine ceremony – he had agreed to a contract of marriage between one of Elizabeth's sons by her first husband, and one of his own daughters or nieces.[39]

Hastings may also have had knowledge of Edward IV's earlier marriage to Eleanor Talbot.[40] Eleanor's family connections were much more significant and influential in Yorkist England than those of Elizabeth Woodville, and Eleanor probably had her own means of access to the king, through her powerful relatives.[41] She would therefore have had no need to approach him *via* Lord Hastings, as Elizabeth Woodville later did. Nevertheless, a number of links can be substantiated between Hastings and Eleanor's family circle. Not only was Lady Hastings the Earl of Warwick's sister (Warwick's wife being Eleanor's aunt). In addition, William Catesby – who is best known as the 'Cat' of the famous doggerel rhyme against Richard III – was a well-established employee of Lord Hastings long before he entered the service of Richard, Duke of Gloucester.[42] And William Catesby also had a family connection with Lady Eleanor Talbot. His father (whose second wife was one of Eleanor's cousins) had also been one of her principal men of affairs, conducting business on Eleanor's behalf.[43] Moreover, in 1481 Hastings married his daughter Anne (then aged about ten) into Eleanor's family. Her husband was Eleanor's great-nephew George Talbot, 4th Earl of Shrewsbury.

Hastings also had connections with George, Duke of Clarence, who was reportedly associated with the sudden panic about the validity of her royal marriage experienced by Elizabeth Woodville in 1477. In March 1472 Clarence had appointed Hastings his chief steward and master of game at Tutbury, and steward of High Peak, producing a combined income for Hastings of £40.[44]

Following Edward's restoration, Hastings was appointed lieutenant of Calais on 17 July 1471, in which post he replaced Anthony Woodville, Earl Rivers. Soon after receiving this post, Hastings crossed to Calais, accompanied by his deputy, John, Lord Howard. On arrival he reduced the garrison to submission. Hastings was then to hold the Calais lieutenancy for the rest of his life. However, he spent little time there in person. Instead, he relied upon his brother Ralph to take practical care of Calais.[45]

As we have already noted, it was reported that towards the end of Edward IV's reign, Hastings had been the king's companion in various vices. Probably the two men partied together, for 'Hastings ... was also the accomplice and partner of [Edward IV's] private pleasures'.[46] Moreover, for what it is worth, Elizabeth Woodville seems to have disliked Hastings. Nor was she the only member of the Woodville clan to find herself at odds with him. In ways which are not entirely clear, faction rivalry flared up between Hastings and the the queen's eldest son, the Marquess of Dorset. Mancini reported that Hastings 'maintained a deadly feud with the queen's son ... and that because of the mistresses whom they had abducted, or attempted to entice from one another'.[47] It has been thought that their quarrel may possibly have had something to do with the last known mistress of the king himself, Elizabeth Lambert, whose favours Dorset is reputed to have shared with the king, or inherited from him. Elizabeth Lambert also 'seems to have been suspiciously close to the old warhorse Lord Hastings, for the report in the *Great Chronicle* states that ... [later] her goods were seized in order to return certain of them to Hastings' widow'.[48]

At the time of Edward IV's death, the late king's only surviving brother, Richard, Duke of Gloucester, was still in the north of England. As we have seen, Gloucester appears to have received no official notification of his brother's death from the queen, nor any other member of the royal family in London. By about 20 April, however, the news of Edward IV's demise had finally reached Middleham Castle. Gloucester's informant was none other than Lord Hastings. Disturbed by the course of events in London, Hastings now took it upon himself to acquaint Gloucester – the senior living prince of the Blood Royal – with what was taking place.[49] The Crowland chronicler attributes this decision on Hastings' part to the fact that 'he was afraid that if supreme power fell into the hands of the queen's relatives they would then sharply avenge the alleged injuries done to them by that lord [for] much ill-will ... had long existed between Lord Hastings and them'.[50] Moreover, the Crowland chronicler implies that Hastings may also have sent news of events to the Duke of Buckingham.

Leaving his wife at Middleham, the Duke of Gloucester then set off for York, where he exacted oaths of fealty to Edward V from the city magistrates.[51] Gloucester remained in York until St George's Day (Wednesday 23 April), though he probably left the city that same day, heading south.[52] According to the Crowland chronicler, despite having apparently received no message from Elizabeth Woodville or the government in London, 'Gloucester wrote the most pleasant letters to console the queen,' offering fealty to his nephew, the new sovereign.[53]

Meanwhile, that nephew remained at Ludlow to celebrate the feast of St George. However, the day after the celebration (Thursday 24 April), he too set out for London, accompanied by his maternal uncle Lord Rivers.[54] It was at Northampton and Stony Stratford that the Duke of Gloucester met them, took control of his nephew's party and, as we have seen (possibly on the suggestion of the Duke of Buckingham), imprisoned Lord Rivers, who was later tried and executed by the Earl of Northumberland.

Once Gloucester had established himself in London as protector, Hastings at first appeared to be in full favour with the new government. Indeed, he 'seemed to serve these two dukes [Gloucester and Buckingham] in every way and to have deserved favour of them'.[55] On Tuesday 20 May, Hastings was appointed master of the mint.[56] Perhaps at this stage Lord Hastings – who, like

Gloucester and Buckingham, was descended from Edward III – was perceived by the three of them as collaboratively representing the male members of the extended royal family, who now comprised the ascendant party in the King's Council.

The break in this unity appears to have come about as a result of the public announcement made by the Bishop of Bath and Wells to the royal council. Bishop Robert Stillington, a former minor government servant of Henry VI,[57] who rose to be Chancellor of England in the service of Edward IV,[58] reportedly precipitated a constitutional crisis by revealing to a royal council meeting that Edward IV had secretly married Eleanor Talbot, daughter of the Earl of Shrewsbury, several years before his secret marriage with Elizabeth Woodville. Since Eleanor survived until 1468, while Edward's marriage to Elizabeth took place in 1464, Stillington's allegation, if true, meant that the king's second marriage was bigamous.[59] Consequently all the children of that Woodville marriage – including Edward V – were bastards.

Once the question of repudiating the young boy who had hitherto been acknowledged as King Edward V had been raised, the ensuing debate revealed that the assembled lords were split. Two different viewpoints emerged. Some were in favour of setting the boy king aside as a bastard. Others opposed this move. It is equally evident that Lord Hastings, who had hitherto apparently been at one with the dukes of Gloucester and Buckingham, now differed absolutely with Buckingham over this issue. Hastings vigorously opposed any move against the young son of his old friend Edward IV, evidently even to the extent of threatening Gloucester's life.

On 10 June 1483, Gloucester wrote to the mayor of York:

> Right trusty and welbelovyd, we grete you well, and as ye love the wele of us, and the wele and sortie of your oun self, we hertely pray you to come unto us in London in all the diligence ye can possible, aftir the sight herof, with as mony as ye can make defensibly arrayed, their to eide and assiste us ayanst the Quiene, hir blode adherents and affinitie, which have entended and daly doith intend, to murder and utterly destroy us and our cousin, the duc of Bukkyngham, and the old royall blode of this realme.[60]

Subsequently a divided meeting of the royal council took place in two separate venues. This was either the protector's or Buckingham's response to the division which had emerged. The result was to deliberately segregate what seems to have been a minority, comprising those peers who favoured retaining Edward V as king, from the other (and presumably larger) group of lords whose views eventually prevailed. The latter had accepted Stillington's report of the Talbot marriage, in consequence of which they now considered that Edward V had to be set aside as illegitimate.

The date of Lord Hastings' execution has been even more seriously questioned than that of Earl Rivers (see above),[61] though the widely recorded date of 13 June is probably correct. An account by a London citizen, thought to date from 1487 or 1488, reports that 'in the mene tyme ther was dyvers imagenyd the deyth of the Duke of Gloceter, and hit was asspiyd and the Lord Hastinges was takyn in the Towur and byhedyd forthwith, the xiij day of June Anno 1483'.[62] Although this London citizen cannot possibly have been privy to the intimate detail of this affair, his account is valuable because of its probable near contemporary nature. The *Crowland Abbey Chronicle*, written up in about April 1486, also records the event, albeit bereft of background details. 'On 13 June, the sixth day of the week [Friday], when he came to the Council in the Tower, on the authority of the protector, Lord Hastings was beheaded'.[63]

Mancini states that when Hastings, accompanied by Bishop John Morton and Archbishop Thomas Rotherham, arrived and entered, 'it is agreed that the protector cried out that a plot was under way and they had come with concealed weapons'.[64] Such conduct, committed before eyewitnesses, would clearly have constituted an offence punishable by death, so that the subsequent execution of Hastings would have been legally justified.[65] Mancini's account, written later that same year, and basically hostile to Gloucester, also reveals that Hastings, Rotherham and Morton were known to have held secret meetings in one another's houses.[66] Several other conspirators were also arrested. Presumably they had been planning an attack on the legally appointed Protector because he was now permitting open discussion of Edward V's right to the throne. After this round of arrests Archbishop Rotherham and Bishop Morton were sent into custody in Welsh castles.

However, it is interesting to note that Gloucester's overall response was rather mild. Hastings was executed, but his co-conspirators were not. In spite of their episcopal status, Richard would perhaps have been better advised had he also arranged for Morton and Rotherham to be put to death in some way. Morton unquestionably stirred up problems for Richard himself, later in his reign, and also ruined the king's reputation after his death. But Richard was too gentle a man, and had too much respect for men of the cloth.

Incidentally, this raises a very intriguing wider point which cannot be ignored. How do we account for the survival of significant enemies of this alleged ambitious, serial-killer king? The people involved included obvious, known enemies whom, logically, Richard III should probably have put to death. Yet the truth is that these enemies outlived him, and contributed both to his own death and to his subsequent vilification. If Richard III had really been the ambitious plotter and murderer depicted by traditional mythology, surely he should have eliminated Bishop John Morton (the great supporter of King Henry VII, and subsequently his Chancellor and Cardinal Archbishop of Canterbury) not to mention other plotters such as Henry VII's mother, Lady Margaret Beaufort, and her third (or fourth) husband, Lord Stanley.

In each death which we have so far reviewed, the demise is known to have taken place, even if the precise death date can be debated. However, when we come to consider the true fate of the 'princes in the Tower' there is absolutely no certainty as to what became of them. Nevertheless, historians – and others – have regularly spoken of 'the murder of "the Princes in the Tower"' as though the fate of the two sons of Edward IV were known for certain. One amazing example of the kind of assumptions made on this subject was contained in a speech made by the then Dean of Westminster, Dr Foxley Norris, at the Society of Antiquaries in the 1930s, following the examination by Professor Wright and Mr Tanner of the bones in the urn at Westminster Abbey created on the orders of Charles II to house the remains of children found during work at the Tower of London in 1674.

The Dean

commented upon the startling fact that the tear ducts of the skulls were vastly enlarged, the suggestion being that the boys had undergone such a harrowing experience that they actually wore a groove in the bone by constant weeping! Dr Barton states that each tear duct must have long since perished, but the bony canal through which it passed from the eye into the nasal cavity could not possibly, under any circumstances, be affected. It would take, states Dr Barton, far more years than each child had lived to produce such a result.

I mentioned these tear ducts to Professor Wright, but the only explanation he could give for the Dean's statement was that a casual remark made to Mr Tanner about the position and size of the lower orifice of the lachrymal duct had been passed on to the Dean and misunderstood. All is mystery. Those casually mentioned ducts grew in some peculiar manner in the Abbey until the Dean produced the complete tale before the Society of Antiquaries.

And that is how traditions are made![67]

Curiously, when Henry VII seized the crown, and began systematically to characterise Richard III as a 'usurper', he made no mention of any accusation that Richard had killed his nephews. Only a very general and vague allegation was made to the effect that Richard had shed the blood of unidentified infants. Since the Devil and his devotees were said to murder children, this was presumably merely part of the general attempt of the new government to blacken Richard III's reputation.

It was only many years later – after the claimant 'Richard of England' (usually known as 'Perkin Warbeck') had contested Henry VII's tenure of the throne on the grounds that he was the surviving Richard, Duke of York, the younger of the so-called 'princes in the Tower' – that Henry VII's government seems to have produced a serious claim to the effect that Richard III had killed his nephews. We have no direct evidence in support of this claim. We have only Thomas More's subsequent story, and Francis Bacon's assumption that it emanated from the king. Whatever its precise source, clearly this claim was Henry's killing of two (or more) birds with one stone. It was a weapon against Richard III's reputation, but it also made it more difficult for any future pretenders to appear, since the 'princes' whose identity such claimants might wish to assume were now officially extinct.

I have recently set out in detail elsewhere what I think may have been the true fate of the 'princes'.[68] Briefly, it seems certain that in July 1483 at least one attempt was made to access the sons of Edward IV in the Tower of London. We do not know for certain either the precise motive or the outcome of that attempt (or those attempts). Pamela Tudor-Craig assumed that the attempt was not to extract the 'princes' from the Tower, but to murder them.[69] Other historians have assumed that, whatever the precise aim of the attempt(s), it (or they) failed. But there is no real evidence for either of these conclusions.

For example, Alison Hanham has argued that when Richard wrote that 'certain persons ... of late had taken upon them the fact of an enterprise' which is generally taken to have been in this matter, his sentence did not have the definite meaning which it appears to bear. Her argument was that the word 'had' was then a past subjunctive form of the verb 'have', bearing the medieval meaning 'would have', while 'fact' meant 'enterprise' or 'crime'.[70] In other words she concludes that an attempt to access the 'princes' in the Tower of London was merely plotted, not successfully carried out in the form of a murder, as Pamela Tudor-Craig had earlier suggested. But Hanham's conclusions are highly questionable.

The plural preterit form of the subjunctive mood was normally identical in Middle English to the plural preterit form of the indicative.[71] Thus the form of the word by itself does not entitle Hanham to conclude that in this instance it comprises a subjunctive. Indeed, if Richard meant 'had' to be read as a subjunctive he would very probably have stated the relevant condition which applied. Also, his use of the words 'now late' strongly suggests that something had actually happened.[72] Thus 'had', as used in Richard's letter, is probably an indicative preterit, meaning precisely what it means today.[73] Also, an examination of the *Oxford English Dictionary* suggests that medieval uses of the word 'fact' generally meant 'deed' or 'action carried out' (based, no doubt, on the word's Latin origin).[74] Richard was clearly talking about a criminal enterprise which had actually taken place, since he is asking the Chancellor to proceed to try men for it. In other words, once 'had' is restored to its indicative sense, the argument over the meaning of the word 'fact' becomes academic.[75]

Whatever the real outcome of the attempt(s) to remove his nephews from the Tower, Richard III may have believed, or been told, that the boys had died as a result. He was reported by the sixteenth-century French writer Martin du Bellay (1495–1559) to have given out that his nephews had been accidentally lost, 'having fallen from the bridge which leads into the Tower'.[76] On the other hand, Vergil merely reported that Richard allowed the story that his nephews were dead 'to go abrode'. He does not suggest that Richard himself made any specific statement on the matter.[77] However, Vergil's account of Richard's treatment of his young nephews (both the 'princes in the Tower' and the Earl of Warwick) is mostly unadulterated rubbish. Thus Vergil – relying no doubt on his master King Henry VII's success at suppressing the Act of Parliament of 1484 – wrote that 'there is a common report that king Edwards children were in that sermon caulyd basterdes, and not king Edward, *which is voyd of all truth*'.[78] His last phrase is a blatant lie. The Act of Parliament of 1484 (the text of which survived, despite Henry VII's attempts to destroy it), states very clearly that the evidence put forward in June 1483 – and which led to the crown being offered to Richard III – was based on the alleged bastardy of Edward IV's children.

Vergil's and du Bellay's accounts are the only surviving reports of any alleged response from Richard III regarding the fate of Edward IV's sons. But it seems possible that Richard considered that his cousin and former supporter, the Duke of Buckingham – who had subsequently become the leader of a rebellion against him, in the cause of Edward V – had been behind the attempt to extract the two boys. This may have been the motive for his handwritten statement that Buckingham was 'the most untrewe creature lyvyng'.[79]

As for Buckingham, his involvement in the plot appears to be substantiated by the fact that the Buckingham Rebellion of autumn 1483 had, as its first and openly declared objective, the restoration of Edward V to the throne of England. It seems that Buckingham had initially opposed the succession of Edward V merely because he wanted to remove the Woodville family from power. But once the Woodvilles had been thoroughly ousted, Buckingham may have found Richard III a less submissive partner than he had expected and hoped for. Apparently the duke therefore decided that, after all, he would prefer to accept one of Edward IV's sons on the throne – provided, of course, that the real power and authority then lay in his own hands. There is no doubt that, after the collapse of his rebellion, Buckingham was executed by Richard III's government. But since he had been leading a rebellion against Richard's regime, his punishment is merely what might have been expected.

There is one final murder allegation which we need to consider. In his famous roll, written during the reign of Richard III, the priest John Rous of Warwick praised the then-reigning monarch profusely, declaring specifically that he defended the common people against their would-be oppressors. However, in political terms, Rous seems to have been a precursor of the famous 'vicar of Bray'. Thus, later, when Henry VII was seated upon the English throne, Rous changed his portrayal of Richard, depicting him as a freakish individual who was born with teeth and shoulder-length hair, after having been in his mother's womb for two years. As we have seen, Rous wrote that Richard's body was stunted and distorted. Rous also now spoke of Richard as a killer. Not only did he attribute the murder of King Henry VI to Richard. He also claimed that Richard had poisoned his own wife, Queen Anne Neville.[80] Although there is absolutely no evidence that Richard ever did anything to bring about the death of his consort, whom he appears to have cared for, subsequent historians picked up Rous's accusation and gleefully ran with it. A fine example of the kind of groundless case which was later published in respect of this alleged murder is James Gairdner's version. Gairdner produces no evidence. Instead he begins by asserting that it is not unknown for medieval royal personages to have 'anticipated the speedy demise of a wife' and concludes that 'Richard was certainly not the man whose nature would have recoiled from such a stroke of policy', an appallingly partisan assessment.[81]

Despite the fact that there is not a shred of evidence to suggest that Richard really was responsible for Anne's passing from this world, there are certain significant sequels to his queen's demise. The allegation of manoeuvres on Richard's part to enable him to marry his bastard niece Elizabeth of York – together with authentic and valuable Continental evidence (which proves beyond question that, while the king's plans for Elizabeth's future were very closely linked with his own marriage plans, his intentions were not at all what has been alleged) – will be examined in detail later (see chapter 8).

Meanwhile, the conclusion of this review of the evidence against Richard the serial killer must surely be that there is nothing to show that he ever murdered anyone. He certainly executed a few political enemies, but the number of these was amazingly (and perhaps ill-advisedly) small. A further conclusion could well be that, had Richard taken the killing of political opponents more seriously, he might legitimately have expected not blame, but praise for his strong kingship from those writers who have produced similar evaluations of Richard's Tudor successors.

PART 3

Richard's Religion

... rogo te dulcissime domine iesu christe ut custodias me famulum tuum Regem Ricardum et defendas ab omni malo atque ab hoste maligno et ab omni periculo presenti preterito et futuro ...

... I ask you, most sweet Lord Jesus Christ, to preserve me, your servant King Richard, and to defend me from all evil, and from the Evil One, and from all danger, past, present and future ...
Extract from the personal prayer of King Richard III[1]

5

Catholic or Anglican?

'You have to ring the passing-bell for everyone that dies in the parish, don't you, whoever they are?'

'Yes, dissenter and church alike ... Why we even had to ring for that woman as lived up the Long Drove, as was a Roman Catholic. Old Hezekiah was rare put out.' Mr Godfrey chuckled reminiscently. '"What, ring old Tailor Paul for a Roman?" he says. "You wouldn't call the like o' them Christians, would you, Rector?" he says. "Why, Hezekiah," says Rector, "we was all Romans in this country once; this church was built by Romans," he says. But Hezekiah, he wouldn't see it. He never had much education, you see.'

Dorothy L. Sayers, *The Nine Tailors*, 1934[2]

Curiously, in view of his evil reputation, it has always been known that Richard III apparently had a sincere interest in and commitment to religion. Even Gairdner, in the nineteenth century, seems, in the end, to have accepted (somewhat reluctantly) that Richard was responsible for 'charitable and praiseworthy acts'.[3] More recent and more favourable writers have stated that 'when tested on his public piety Richard III seems to have passed with flying colours in the opinion of most of his judges'.[4] His Book of Hours, or personal prayer book, survives in the Library of Lambeth Palace. It is not one of the typical 'coffee table' prayer books which many affluent fifteenth-century aristocrats and princes commissioned in order to display their wealth and cultivation. Instead it is a practical Book of Hours, clearly intended for real use – and evidently used by Richard since he had additions made to the text.

Other evidence of Richard III's religious faith includes the daily worship rules he established for his household at Middleham

Castle (as Duke of Gloucester), his love of religious music, and his interest 'in the more old-fashioned mystical and religious literature of the north of England, tastes he shared with his mother and sister Margaret'.[5] He also went on pilgrimages to English shrines, and endowed chantry masses for the deceased members of his family. 'His foundations were, above all, his response to the demands placed on a prince to provide prayers for the living and the dead'.[6]

Even the king's enemies acknowledged that he would have wished to attend mass regularly. They made use of this point in order to fabricate a mythology regarding Richard III's last mass. We shall explore that story later (see chapter 11). It has also been noted that Shakespeare depicted Richard as reading his prayer book when the throne was offered to him.[7]

Hitherto, the denominational nature of Richard's religious faith had never been seriously questioned. His devotion to the feast of Corpus Christi is certain.[8] This feast was and is focussed upon the Real Presence of Christ in the Most Holy Sacrament of the Altar. In the words of a famous hymn written for that feast day by St Thomas Aquinas,

> The Word made flesh turns true bread into the Body and Blood of Christ.
> And if senses fail, faith alone suffices to confirm sincere hearts.[9]

It is also well known that Richard and his siblings were brought up by a mother who became an oblate of the Benedictine order in her later life. Richard's sister Margaret, Duchess of Burgundy, was subsequently a committed patroness of the Catholic Church in the land of her marriage. Curiously, however, implied questions about Richard III's Catholic identity appear to have been raised since the discovery of his remains in 2012. This issue surfaced in the context of the dispute regarding where his body should be reburied.

In that context, the Director of Communications for the Diocese of Leicester, stated on the internet that 'The Roman Catholic Church did not exist at the time [of Richard III], the state church was Catholic but there was no distinction'.[10] The implication of this very misleading statement appears to be that the 'Roman' Catholic Church was only created in the sixteenth century, in response to the Protestant Reformation.

In terms merely of terminology and geography, this may be true, for the term 'Roman' Catholic is not one which the Catholic Church normally uses to refer to itself. That name was certainly invented by Protestants in the context of the sixteenth-century, post-Reformation and somewhat xenophobic state of England.

But if the *name* 'Roman Catholic' was invented by Protestants in sixteenth-century England, that does not affect the fact that the Church to which that name was then applied had existed for centuries. And during his lifetime, Richard III was unquestionably a sincere member of that Church – a religious body which, in the world at large, still normally refers to itself as 'Catholic', but which non-Catholics, particularly in the English-speaking world, refer to as 'Roman Catholic'.[11]

Further to Leicester Cathedral's published statement on this point, the following was written in a letter by David Monteith, Dean of Leicester (the emphasis placed on certain key words and phrases is mine).

> Richard III was king of England at a time before the Reformation, and its separation of what *we* now call the Church of England from what *we* now call the Roman Catholic Church, *and neither of those names would have meant anything to his generation.* As the established church the Church of England is the *legal* successor of the *national* church which Richard belonged to, and so it is to that church *that the nation has turned* to arrange his re-interment.[12]

Here, the implication appears to be that, as a member of 'the *national* church' of his day, Richard III could possibly be regarded as a kind of proto-Anglican. And indeed, it also appears that the Dean may really believe that Richard III was possibly of reformist tendencies, for he has elsewhere emphasised Richard III's ownership of a copy of a book which is commonly (but rather inaccurately) called 'the Wycliffe Bible'. We shall return to consideration of that point later.

Meanwhile, the Dean's letter is misleading in several other ways. First, his statement that 'the nation' turned to the Church of England to rebury the remains of Richard III is inaccurate. Discussions with Leicester Cathedral were initially opened, not by the nation, but by the Looking For Richard Project, led by Philippa Langley, in 2010, before the archaeological search for Richard III's remains was begun. With a Leicester burial confirmed by the landowner (the City Council, who gave Langley permission to dig) the majority of the Looking For Richard Project team members then favoured the cathedral as the potential reburial site (though this decision was not unanimous). Subsequently, it was not the nation, but the University of Leicester (having assumed custody of the remains found in August 2012 over Langley's lead partner, the City Council) which ruled that the burial should take place at Leicester's Anglican Cathedral.

As for the term 'Church of England', that seems sometimes to have been used in Richard III's lifetime and before – but of course, with a different meaning than the one which it has today. In the fifteenth century the 'church of England' would merely have comprised the two English provinces which then existed of the universal (Catholic) Church. Only with the advent of King Henry VIII and his changes in religious policy did the meaning of this term undergo a change.

As we have seen, it is true that 'Roman Catholic' was not a term used in the fifteenth century. However, the term 'Catholic', which originally meant 'universal' or 'worldwide', had come to characterise the western church since the Great Schism of 1054, when the western and the eastern geographical areas of the one Church had split apart and the eastern church had become known as 'Orthodox' (= followers of the right path). While the hierarchy of the eastern church was centred upon the leadership of a group of successors of Christ's apostles, known as patriarchs, the chief of whom was based at Constantinople, the western, Catholic Church was led by the pope, as the successor of Christ's leading apostle, Simon Peter, in the capacity of Bishop of Rome – in which city the pope was normally based.[13]

In Richard III's lifetime, the church to which he belonged was unquestionably the western, Catholic Church, led by the pope, based in Rome. Ample evidence survives to show that Richard was an obedient servant of the papacy in respect of his religion.[14] It was only half a century or more after Richard III's death that the situation in respect of the church in England changed. Richard's great-nephew, King Henry VIII, wishing to ensure that he had a male heir, decided to end his marriage with Catherine of Aragon. Since the papacy would not annul this marriage, Henry achieved his aim by declaring himself head of the church in England. In terms of its administration, he separated the English church from Rome and from the papal authority. Obviously, had Richard III not lost the battle of Bosworth and been killed, Henry VIII would never have been king, and the English Reformation might never have taken place. There is some controversy on this point, but, for example, Duffy has argued that there is little evidence of any strongly reformative tendencies among the English populace in the 1530s.[15]

However, once Henry VIII had set the process in motion, deeper changes then followed. Henry VIII's motivation had been basically political and financial, not religious. But subsequently, under Edward VI and Elizabeth I, the nature of the new 'Church of England' changed considerably. Not only was the authority of the pope denied, but a number of traditional beliefs of the church were also opposed. The 'Thirty-nine Articles' of the Anglican Church, established in 1563, and still printed today in the Anglican Book of Common Prayer, contain elements which would unquestionably have shocked Richard III. Article 6 excludes from the Anglican list of canonical scriptures certain books of the Bible accepted by both Catholics and Orthodox. Article 19 states that the 'Church of Rome hath erred, not only in their living and manner of ceremonies, but also in matters of faith'. Article 21 declares that councils of the church may not be assembled 'without the command and will of princes'. Most shocking of all for Richard III (a pious pilgrim to such shrines as Walsingham, Canterbury and Caversham, a great founder of chantries to offer prayers for the dead in order to help their souls pass through purgatory and a man who had prayers to his favourite saints added to his own Book of Hours) would have been Article 22, which states that 'the Romish doctrine concerning Purgatory, Pardons, worshipping and adoration as well of Images as of Relics, and also Invocation of Saint, is a fond thing vainly invented, and grounded upon no warranty of Scripture; but rather repugnant to the word of God'.

In addition to the use of such terms as 'Rome' and 'Romish' in the Thirty-nine Articles, contemporary mid-sixteenth-century propaganda specifically refers to the expulsion of persons categorised as 'papists', and their religion, from England. Elizabeth I explicitly focussed her government's attention on penalising those who continued to recognise *papal authority*. And the leaders of the new, independent 'Church of England' coined the term 'Roman Catholic' to refer to the now opposed Catholic ('Romish') Church, while at the same time highlighting the fact that its English adherents were considered to be of dubious patriotic loyalty. The loyalty issue was further reinforced early in the seventeenth century by the invention of the anti-Catholic festival of 'Guy Fawkes Day' (5 November) – a celebration at which images of the Catholic Guy Fawkes, and of the pope, used to be burned.

Later in the seventeenth century the English government introduced the Penal Laws. The most significant of these were the Clarendon Code (1661–65), which required holders of public office to take Holy Communion according to Anglican rites, and the Test Act (1673), *which excluded from all public office, anyone who would not accept royal supremacy in respect of the church, or who would not explicitly deny belief in the doctrine of transubstantiation*. Obviously if we review the religious beliefs of Richard III in the light of such rulings, the government of Elizabeth would have condemned him for his acceptance of papal authority, while the seventeenth-century Test Act would have excluded Richard from state office because, while he most certainly did believe in the doctrine of transubstantiation, he did not believe that the monarch was the head of the church.

As for members of the Catholic Church, they do not, and did not, have any particular problem with being defined by the English (British) government and others as '*Roman* Catholics'. Nevertheless, this is probably not actually the term which most of them would normally, voluntarily select in order to describe themselves. It is also not a term which has ever been widely employed in other European countries which, unlike England, remained predominantly Catholic.

The reality, therefore, is that Richard III was undoubtedly a Catholic in terms of his religion. The church to which he belonged was unquestionably subject to papal authority (based in Rome), and one of its key doctrines was belief in the Real Presence of Christ in the Eucharist. Thus, Richard's was that church which later, in England and elsewhere, came to be called *Roman* Catholic. While there is no doubt that the appellation *Roman* Catholic would not normally have been used in Richard III's lifetime, it is equally certain that this term was invented in the post Reformation period, specifically to refer to the church to which Richard III had belonged. And the term has always subsequently been used, particularly by Anglicans and other reformed denominations, to refer to that church.

As for the term 'Church of England', if it was employed in Richard's lifetime, it would have had a completely different meaning than it acquired in the sixteenth century, and still has today, i.e. a faith group centred upon England, with a religious hierarchy headed by the Archbishop of Canterbury, and separated – both administratively and in terms of certain aspects of its beliefs (see above) – from the Catholic Church centred upon the authority of the pope in Rome.[16]

We must now consider a suggestion which has sometimes been advanced to the effect that maybe Richard III had a reformist tendency. His possession of a copy of the book known as Wycliffe's English translation of the Bible has been offered as possible evidence in support of this view. Of course, John Wycliffe (*c.* 1320–84) was ultimately condemned by the Catholic Church as a heretic, and two hundred years later he was adopted by Protestants as 'the Morning Star of the Reformation'. But in Wycliffe's lifetime Protestantism did not exist and Wycliffe was never a Protestant. In spite of his questioning of papal authority (in the context of a split Catholic church which had, in his lifetime, two rival popes), Wycliffe was close to, and was supported by, the Catholic mendicant orders, including the Austin and Franciscan Friars, whom the house of York later patronised.

As for the fact that Richard III owned a copy of the Bible in English, this was not particularly unusual. Even in Wycliffe's own lifetime, two centuries earlier, members of the English nobility often owned translations, or partial translations, of the Bible into either French or English. In fact it is clear that, in the fifteenth century, while Latin was still the normal language for church services and religious texts, there was absolutely no problem for Catholics regarding use of the vernacular in a religious context. This is shown by the surviving instructions for parish priests penned by the Arroasian (Augustinian) Canon John Myrc (or Mirk) in about 1450. For example, Myrc told his readers to teach their parishioners to say both the *Pater noster* ('Lord's Prayer') and the 'Hail Mary' in English, daily. Myrc's English text for the first of these two prayers ran as follows:

> Fader owre þat art in heuene,
> Halowed be þy name,
> Þy kyngdom be for to come
> In vs synfulle alle and some;
> Þy wylle be do in erþe here
> As hyt ys in heuene clere;
> Owre vche dayes bred, we þe pray,
> Þat þow ȝeue vs þys same day;
> And forgyue vs owre trespas
> As we done hem þat gult vs has;
> And lede vs in to no fondynge,
> But schelde vs alle from euel þynge. Amen.[17]

The most important point to note, however, is the fact that it is not certain how much (if any) of the translation of the Bible owned by Richard III really was the work of John Wycliffe – even though such translations usually carry Wycliffe's name. 'Long thought to be the work of Wycliffe himself, the Wycliffite translations are now generally believed to be the work of several hands. Nicholas of Hereford is known to have translated a part of the text; John Purvey and perhaps John Trevisa are names that have been mentioned as possible authors. [What is more] the translators worked from the Vulgate, the Latin Bible that was the standard Biblical text of Western Christianity, and the text conforms fully with Catholic teaching. ... Although Wycliffe's Bible circulated widely in the later Middle Ages, it had very little influence on the first English biblical translations of the reformation era'.[18]

Nevertheless, on 29 October 2014 Leicester Cathedral issued a statement that 'the reinterment of King Richard lll will be take place accompanied by music written by prize-winning composer, Judith Bingham. ... The text for this anthem will draw on verses from Psalm 42 in a translation by John Wycliffe who was Rector of Lutterworth in Leicestershire. ... King Richard III owned scriptures translated by John Wycliffe'. As we have seen, the last sentence is not literally correct, and either the possible intended implication behind it, or its potential interpretation as perceived by those who read it, could threaten to reinforce a piece of Ricardian mythology in respect of Richard III's religious faith. This is the myth that implies that Richard may have had links with religious reformers and proto-Protestants – people who, in the fifteenth century, would almost certainly have been categorised as heretics.

In fact, Richard III's devotion to the Mass and to the Blessed Sacrament (through the Feast of Corpus Christi) proves his sincere belief in the doctrine of transubstantiation. Also, although he was King of England for two years, he certainly never aspired to be the head of the church to which he belonged (as the English monarch is today). Any thought of claiming such a role would have deeply shocked him. As far as Richard III was concerned, the true and rightful leader of his church was the pope, and he never questioned that point. In terms of the anti-(Roman) Catholic English laws of the sixteenth and seventeenth centuries, Richard's belief in transubstantiation, together with his acceptance of papal authority, would have sufficed to condemn him as a member of the then unacceptable (Roman) Catholic religious denomination. The logical conclusion has to be that Richard III was not only undoubtedly a Catholic, but that he would have been identified as what today is generally called, by non-Catholics, in the English speaking world, a 'Roman' Catholic, had that terminology been in use during his lifetime.

This makes a personal communication from the Bishop of Leicester to the present writer sound extremely odd. The bishop stated,

As to your suggestion that Richard should be laid to rest in a Catholic Church, that would appear to discount the historic ties between the monarchy and the Church of England which *since the Reformation has been the inheritor of the Catholic Church in this country in terms of the monarch's role as head of the established church.*[19]

As we have seen, prior to the Reformation no English monarch (and this includes Richard III himself) ever aspired to be head of the Church. That being so – and despite the fact that modern Christians of various denominations may well have a different perception – one probably has to accept that having his body first placed in repose, and then interred, in a church building used by a religious group which officially denies both papal authority and key aspects of the Catholic faith, might well have appalled Richard III himself.

But the final decision regarding the place for Richard III's re-interment was made by the University of Leicester. It was a decision which had nothing to do with the controversy over whether Richard III should be reburied in Leicester or elsewhere, because Leicester has a very large Catholic Dominican Priory which functions as the university's Catholic chaplaincy, and which could have been used for the reburial. The choice of Leicester Cathedral also had nothing to do with the age of the building selected. Leicester does have large and significant medieval church buildings which existed in Richard III's lifetime, and which are still in use today by the Church of England. However, Leicester Cathedral is not a medieval cathedral, and the greater part of the cathedral building is nineteenth-century in date.

The Bishop of Leicester told the present writer that the cathedral was chosen because it represented the closest consecrated ground to the site from which Richard III's bones had been exhumed (see chapter 16). However, this statement is also not literally correct. In point of fact, the closest consecrated ground to the site from which the bones were exhumed would have been the original grave site itself. There is no evidence that Henry VIII had the Franciscan Priory in Leicester (or any other dissolved religious house) deconsecrated, before selling off the property.

Catholic doctrine teaches that the prime focus of the living, in respect of the dead, is based upon concern for the good of their souls. This was reflected even in the closing words of the epitaph for Richard III commissioned by his enemy King Henry VII. But based upon the evidence available, it seems that the modern choice of Richard III's reburial location – together with many other decisions made in respect of his reburial – has not been motivated by that belief, nor by any attempt to consider what the king himself would have wanted.

The logical conclusion is therefore that the decisions must have been reached on other grounds. Possible factors may have included a desire for increased tourism – with its consequential profit. The proximity of Leicester Cathedral to the former Greyfriars site and the new Richard III Visitor Centre probably means that visitors will tend to circulate between the two, and the vicinity has now been redesigned as a garden (containing a statue of Richard III, donated to Leicester in the last century by the Richard III Society) to encourage this. Further aspects of the profit-making issue, and its connections with the saga of Ricardian mythology, will be examined later (see chapter 18).

It is also interesting to note that although the remains of Richard III had formally been identified in February 2013, the university and cathedral authorities both apparently continued to regard the bones as a 'scientific specimen' right up to and including his coffining in a laboratory.[20] Had Richard belonged to some other religion (Jewish or Muslim, for example), this would hardly have been possible and he would, without question, have been given the honour of coffining in the context of his own faith. Is it therefore the case that Richard's traditional (mythological) reputation, as currently perceived in Leicester, does not make him worthy of recognition either as a human being or Catholic? Ironically, the period selected for Richard's reburial is the last week of Lent: a season which Richard himself would have observed as a time of strict fasting and abstinence. The planned eating of food after the services of compline on Sunday 22 March and reburial on Thursday 26 March – particularly if the food includes meat and eggs – would have deeply shocked the king, as would the planned 'celebration' (with fireworks) on Friday 27 March. It seems Richard III's wishes are either not understood or not respected.

PART 4

The Monster King

The moost mighty prynce Rychard [III] by the grace of god kynge of ynglond and of fraunce and lord of Ireland ... Rewled his subiettys In hys Realme ful commendabylly poneschynge offenders of hys laws specially Extorcioners and oppressors of hys comyns and chereschynge tho that were vertues by the whyche dyscrete guydynge he gat gret thank of god and love of all hys subiettes Ryche and pore and gret laud of the people of all othyr landys a bowt hym.

John Rous, *The Rous Roll*, 1483–84

6

Richard, the Usurper

Richard III usurped the throne from the young Edward V, who disappeared with his younger brother while under their ambitious uncle's supposed protection.

The Official Website of the British Monarchy[1]

Usurp – to seize and hold (the power and rights of another, for example) *by force or without legal authority.*[2]

Definitions of the verb 'usurp' include terms such as to seize power by force and without legal authority (see above). Henry IV seized the throne from Richard II by force in 1399. Edward IV took the throne from Henry VI in battle in 1461. Henry VII took the throne from Richard III at the battle of Bosworth in 1485. Therefore, if those three kings were described as usurpers it would be very easy to understand why. Yet, curiously, not one of them is normally called a usurper, either by modern historians, or by the general public, and none of the three is described as a usurper by the official website of the British Monarchy.[3]

On the other hand, Richard III did not mount the throne by fighting a battle. He did not seize the crown. He was offered throne and crown by 'the three estates of the realm' (the intended members of the Parliament of 1483, which, however, was never opened because it had become unclear who was on the throne – and therefore who should carry out the formal opening). Later, the decision of the three estates of the realm was formally enacted by the Parliament of 1484.

There are therefore three lines of exploration which need to be followed in this chapter. First, we need to reconsider briefly how Richard, Duke of Gloucester, came to power in 1483. Secondly, we shall examine the basis of his subsequent claim to the throne, evaluate it, and assess whether it can correctly be characterised as 'usurpation'. The third line is the historiography of the application of the term 'usurper' to King Richard III.

In chapter 4, we have already seen that what took place following the death of Edward IV, in April 1483, was an attempt at an illegal coup by his 'widow', Elizabeth Woodville. Her aim was that she and her family should hold the effective power in the kingdom during the minority of her son Edward V. Although there was no legal precedent in England for a queen dowager or queen mother to assume power as Elizabeth Woodville sought to do, her conduct, following the death of Edward IV, never seems to have been explicitly recognised by historians as an attempt at an illegal coup. Nevertheless, that is what it was. Elizabeth's attempted seizure of power contravened normal fourteenth- and fifteenth-century English practice during the reign of a minor. The fact that she did not inform the late king's surviving brother of what was being done, but sought to bring her son to London very quickly and arrange for his rapid coronation, demonstrates that Elizabeth herself was well aware of the illegal nature of what she planned to do.

Also, in the nineteenth century James Gairdner discovered evidence to show that the Woodville family was unpopular towards the close of Edward IV's reign.[4] This may help to explain why Elizabeth Woodville was especially anxious to consolidate her position. There were precedents warning her that when a powerful but unpopular woman lost the monarch through whom she derived her power and influence, she might well suffer the consequences.[5] Moreover, as we know, by the date of Edward IV's death in April 1483 Elizabeth was already well aware of the fact that the validity of their marriage could be questioned.[6]

Yet Richard, Duke of Gloucester, did not respond to the situation created by Elizabeth Woodville by embarking on some kind of civil war. He merely acted upon the information he received from Hastings and Buckingham, and marched southwards to meet his nephew Edward V. When they met, Gloucester simply took over charge of the young king's escort from Elizabeth Woodville's brother Lord Rivers and continued with the boy to London.

Significantly, however, when Gloucester and Buckingham were received in Stony Stratford by the young Edward V, he reportedly told them that 'as for the government of the kingdom, he had complete confidence in the peers of the realm and the queen ... On hearing the queen's name the duke of Buckingham, who loathed her race, then answered, it was not the business of women but of men to govern kingdoms, and so if he cherished any confidence in her he had better relinquish it'.[7] Subsequently, as we have seen, Lord Rivers and Sir Richard Grey (Elizabeth Woodville's brother, and her son by her first husband) were imprisoned, tried and finally executed, possibly at Buckingham's instigation. Meanwhile, when the royal party arrived in London, all that happened was that Gloucester was formally recognised as Lord Protector. Under his now legally recognised authority, the preparations for Edward V's coronation went ahead.

The reason behind the sudden subsequent change of plans, and the offering of the crown to Richard, was the fact that one of its leading church members informed the royal council in June 1483 that the young king Edward V was illegitimate, and that he could not therefore be crowned as King of England. The royal council member in question was Robert Stillington, Bishop of Bath and Wells.

There is absolutely no evidence (despite the colossal assumption to this effect made by generations of historians) that Richard, then the Lord Protector, was in any way responsible for Stillington's revelation. Nor is there any evidence whatsoever that he was delighted by it. In fact, he may have been shocked. However, he behaved absolutely correctly. He made public the evidence which had been put forward to the royal council, and he invited the unofficial 'parliament' (the three estates of the realm) to consider the case and come to a decision. Nothing was done secretly or behind closed doors.

The situation he suddenly found himself having to deal with impinged upon the reputation of his late elder brother, King Edward IV, as a ladies' man. Possibly this reputation has been somewhat over-stated.[8] Nevertheless, during his lifetime Edward certainly had several mistresses, and fathered some illegitimate children. In itself that was a matter of no great public importance in the fifteenth century. There was no press in those days seeking to make a profit for its newspapers from royal scandals.

However, the king's amorous conduct included one significant aspect which, prior to 1483, had generally been hushed up. In terms of marriage, Edward IV had behaved very oddly. He had certainly not followed the norms expected of a European monarch at that time. Although, on two occasions, attempts had been made to negotiate foreign royal marriages for Edward (in accordance with the normal practice of the period) neither of these planned diplomatic alliances ever came to fruition.

As an alleged husband, or potential husband, Edward IV's

name has been linked with a total of five (or possibly six) women. Considered in chronological order, these were

either Yolande or Jeanne of France 1440
Eleanor Talbot (Butler) *c.* 1460–62
Elizabeth Wayte (Lucy) *c.* 1461–63
Bona of Savoy 1463–64
Elizabeth Woodville (Grey) 1464–1483

Plans for Edward's marriage with one of the available daughters of Charles VII of France were explored by the English government in 1445, when Edward was just a little boy, only three years old. At that time his father had been based in France on behalf of Henry VI's regime. Young Edward's planned marriage with a French princess never materialised.

Later Edward became involved in a relationship with Eleanor Talbot, daughter of the Earl of Shrewsbury, and a noble woman of English royal descent. Although, as we shall see, Henry VII later tried very hard both to conceal the relationship and to airbrush Eleanor out of history, the *existence* of this relationship has never been contested. The only point at issue, therefore, is the *nature* of the relationship. This is a key issue in connection with the evaluation of whether or not Richard III was a usurper. The question is, did Edward secretly marry Eleanor, as the 1484 Parliament formally declared, or did the couple merely indulge in a brief, illicit relationship?

Edward's next partner was Elizabeth Wayte (Lucy). She was less well-born than Eleanor, being the daughter of a Hampshire gentleman. Elizabeth seems to have begun a sexual relationship with the king in about 1461–62 and probably bore him two illegitimate children, a son, Arthur, and daughter, Elizabeth. Edward's relationship with Elizabeth Wayte could have been completely ignored in respect of the marriage question, were it not for the fact that Tudor historians later invented (for the sole purpose of being able to deny it and dismiss it as rubbish) an alleged marital connection between her and the king. Significantly, this Tudor invention was part of the process by which Henry VII and his government hoped to confuse the question of Edward IV's relationship with Eleanor Talbot. They were clearly hoping that most people would not remember the real name of the lady whom the Parliament of 1484 had declared to be Edward IV's legitimate queen. This was indeed possible, since the key Act of Parliament had been repealed unquoted and an attempt had been made to destroy all copies of it. But – fortunately for posterity – the copy of the Act in the Rolls of Parliament survived.

Edward IV's fourth relationship was with Bona of Savoy. Bona, daughter of the Duke of Savoy, was the sister-in-law of King Louis XI of France. As far as we know, Edward IV never even met this lady. Certainly he never married her. Nevertheless, a marriage with Bona was negotiated on his behalf by his powerful cousin Richard Neville, the 'kingmaker' Earl of Warwick.

Edward IV's final alleged marital relationship had been with Elizabeth Woodville (Grey), the eldest daughter of Jacquette, Duchess of Bedford (a lady of European royal descent), by her insignificant second husband, Richard Woodville. Despite its secrecy, and what was generally considered its inappropriate nature, this was the relationship which had been accepted as a valid marriage during most of Edward IV's reign, and which had produced a number of supposedly legitimate children, including Edward IV's eldest son and putative successor, Edward V.

However, Edward's marriage with Elizabeth Woodville (Grey) had been strange in several respects. First, in terms of her paternal ancestry, the bride was neither royal nor a significant member of the aristocracy. Secondly she was a widow, with children. It was not completely unknown for an English king to marry a widow, but it was somewhat unusual. Third, the marriage had not been approved, either by Edward's family or by the estates of the realm. Fourth, the marriage had been celebrated in secret, and was then kept secret for several months. These points had all been public knowledge since September 1464. But the new information revealed to the royal council by Bishop Stillington in June 1483 was that Edward's secret marriage to Elizabeth had been invalid, since at the time when it was celebrated, Eleanor Talbot had still been alive, and he (Stillington) had secretly married Eleanor to Edward prior to the secret Woodville marriage of 1464.

It was probably in Warwickshire, either at Eleanor's manor of Fenny Compton or at her manor of Burton Dassett, that she had been privately married to the young king, on or around Monday 8 June 1461, by Canon (later Bishop) Robert Stillington.[9] Since Bishop Stillington claimed to have officiated at this earlier marriage, and since he was also an expert in the canon law of the church, his statement to the royal council in June 1483 had to be taken seriously.

Although Eleanor Talbot was the daughter of the celebrated John Talbot, Earl of Shrewsbury, and the granddaughter of Richard Beauchamp, Earl of Warwick, and was descended in more than one royal bloodline from King Edward I, sadly she has been very much maligned by generations of historians. They have spent some five centuries casting aspersions on her birth, her ancestry and her morals. Despite the very explicit wording of the offer of the throne to Richard III, dating from 1483, it used to be widely questioned whether Eleanor really was the daughter of the Earl of Shrewsbury (as the offer, and the subsequent Act of Parliament stated). For example, the *ODNB* article on Stillington says that 'historians have not even been able satisfactorily to identify Eleanor Butler [*sic*]'.[10]

The continued existence of such a statement in the *ODNB* is rather appalling. Although, for the most part, five centuries of historians had done absolutely nothing to seek the truth about Eleanor Talbot, the reality is that when I began researching her, in the 1990s, I found it a simple matter to identify both Eleanor and her family. I also found evidence relating to her nature and character, and relating to her ownership of land and other matters. All this evidence was highly significant. As a result I proved beyond any possible doubt that Eleanor's family was precisely as stated in 1483.[11] Moreover, I also established Eleanor's religious devotion and morality beyond any reasonable doubt. Unfortunately, as we have seen, the *ODNB* and a number of other historical writing have yet to be updated.

Moreover, the recently created Richard III Visitor Centre in Leicester also takes little account, either of my significant discoveries of evidence in respect of Eleanor, or of the impact of Eleanor and her true story on the subsequent status of Richard III. Sadly, although members of the Looking For Richard Project Team – including the present writer – were originally asked by Leicester City Council to contribute draft material for the Visitor Centre, much of this material was either subsequently discarded, or heavily edited by the University of Leicester – a body which sometimes appears susceptible to the influence of traditional Ricardian mythology, as we shall see in chapter 9.

To summarise the position at Edward IV's death in April 1483, his eldest son by Elizabeth Woodville was acknowledged as the new king by everyone – including Richard, Duke of Gloucester. There was an attempted Woodville coup whereby the boy's mother hoped that she and her birth family could seize and hold power during his minority, but this illegal move was prevented and the boy's paternal royal uncle was officially proclaimed Lord Protector of England. But it was shortly after Gloucester was accorded official recognition in this role that Bishop Stillington, former Chancellor to Edward V's father, precipitated a constitutional crisis by his amazing revelation.[12]

Due to two key points, namely, the fact that Eleanor Talbot had been still living at the time of Edward IV's marriage to Elizabeth Woodville, and the fact that the Woodville marriage had been celebrated in secret, Stillington's statement meant that the king's Woodville marriage was, and had always been bigamous and therefore invalid in the eyes of the Church. Since Stillington was a priest and claimed that he personally had married Edward and Eleanor, a statement by him, under oath, would, in itself, have comprised sufficient evidence, even if there were no other witnesses of the Talbot marriage living in 1483. The consequence was that all the children of Edward IV's Woodville marriage – including Edward V – had now to be categorised as bastards.

Ever since the truth of the Talbot marriage allegation was rescued, in the seventeenth century, from Henry VII's earlier attempts to conceal it for ever, generations of writers and historians have made ludicrous and completely groundless claims in respect of what took place regarding Edward IV's marital status in the summer of 1483. The first and most widely promoted claim is the allegation that Richard, Duke of Gloucester, had himself invented the allegation of Edward IV's bigamy. There is absolutely no evidence to support this claim. Indeed, as we have seen, there is evidence that suggests that the issue had been brought up earlier. Elizabeth Woodville had become anxious about the validity of her royal marriage in 1476–77 and appeared to associate her anxiety with George, Duke of Clarence, and his aspirations.

The second groundless claim made by historians was that we had no means of knowing who Eleanor really was, but that the claim in the Act of Parliament that she was the Earl of Shrewsbury's daughter was probably rubbish. The present writer's earlier research on Eleanor has proved incontrovertibly that Eleanor really was the daughter of the Earl and Countess of Shrewsbury; a lady of royal descent, and also a religious lady who is highly unlikely to have consented to become the king's mistress at a time when both he and she were free to marry.[13]

The nature of the claim put forward by Stillington has also been systematically misrepresented by repeated use of the word 'precontract'. This is a word which few historians appear to understand, and many of them carefully avoid defining it. However, their fall-back position, based upon this curious word, has been that Edward IV did not actually *marry* Eleanor, he merely made a 'precontract' (which they interpret as a kind of betrothal). Once again this is rubbish. The term 'precontract' can (and could) only ever be used retrospectively. In other words, one could never make something called a 'precontract'. The sole possibility was to make a contract – the contract in question being a contract of marriage. It only became possible to refer to such a marriage contract as a 'pre-contract' in retrospect, when one of the two contracting partners went on to make a second – and bigamous – contract of marriage. Thus, when the documents of 1483 and 1484 refer to Edward IV's 'precontract' with Eleanor Talbot, they definitely mean his contract of *marriage* (which later became 'pre-' due to his bigamy with Elizabeth Woodville).

As we have seen, the way in which Richard, Duke of Gloucester, handled the astonishing revelation made by Bishop Stillington was absolutely open and above-board. Nothing was done in secret. Since a formal Parliament had not yet been opened, the evidence was presented to 'the three estates of the realm', namely those members of the lords spiritual and temporal and the commons who had already gathered in London to form the projected 1483 Parliament at its planned opening.

After considering the evidence, the three estates of the realm set aside Edward V as king on the grounds of his illegitimacy, and offered the throne to the next Prince of the Blood in the legal line of succession, namely Richard, Duke of Gloucester. *This* was how Gloucester became King Richard III. Moreover, the decision of the three estates was subsequently endorsed by a full Parliament. It is extremely difficult to see how this can possibly be described as a 'usurpation'.

As a result of the decision taken by the three estates, while Richard, Duke of Gloucester, was advanced to the crown of England, 'Edward V' was removed from the list of kings. This was not a deposition. As surviving documentation clearly proves, the decision was that, as a valid king of England, Edward V had never really existed. All the legal acts dated to his reign had therefore to be re-enacted. By the same token, Elizabeth Woodville was demoted from queenship, for Edward IV's legitimate wife and queen had been Eleanor Talbot. Later, however, Richard's opponent, Henry VII – who had his own axe to grind – restored Elizabeth Woodville to her former queenship. At the same time Henry VII did his very best to write Eleanor Talbot out of history, for reasons which we are about to explore.

We now need to consider the third line mentioned in the introduction to this chapter, namely the historiography of the use of the word 'usurper' to describe King Richard III.

In December 1483, the Italian friar, Domenico Mancini submitted to his employer Angelo Cato, Archbishop of Vienne, a report of his visit to England. Mancini had arrived in England either late in 1482 or early in 1483, and had almost certainly been living there at the time of Edward IV's death. He was in England as a kind of spy for the French government, and therefore represents a viewpoint essentially hostile to England. This may account for some of the views he expresses.

Mancini was definitely in England during the succession problems which followed the death of Edward IV. He did not speak English. His native language was Italian (one of the closest fifteenth-century descendants of Latin). However, he was an educated churchman, so he was also familiar with the earlier form of the Latin language. His account of the state of affairs in England, was therefore written in Latin, and was submitted to Cato under the Latin title *De occupatione regni Anglie per Ricardum tercium*. This Latin title has been translated into English as *The Usurpation of Richard the Third*.[14] However, in Late Latin the noun usually employed for the English term 'usurpation' was *usurpatio*,[15] while the Italian word for this was *usurpazione*. Arguably, therefore, a more accurate translation of Mancini's title – and a more appropriate translation, given the nature and purpose of his report – would be something like *Richard III's take-over of the Kingdom of England*. Indeed, had Mancini written the report in his native Italian language, the word *occupazione* could be translated into English even more blandly, as 'tenure'. Mancini himself is therefore not really the earliest source for the accusation that Richard III was a usurper. Armstrong, the subsequent English translator of Mancini's title, is the person responsible for the choice of that heavily coloured English word. Naturally, the ongoing effect of Armstrong's translation of Mancini's title has been and is very considerable. Unfortunately, even the present writer finds himself forced to quote it when referring to Armstrong's published text!

The continuator of the Crowland Chronicle appears to have been no great friend to Richard III. Even so, he does not categorise Richard as a 'usurper'. Indeed, once Richard is on the throne, he treats him consistently as king. However, he states that 'on the 26th day of the same month of June, Richard, the protector, claimed for himself the government of the kingdom with the name and title of king; and on the same day in the great hall of Westminster he thrust himself into the marble chair'.[16] While not, perhaps, particularly friendly, this writer's use of the verb *intrusit* does not amount to an accusation of 'usurpation'. Moreover, he then goes on to narrate in fairly accurate detail the reasoning behind the offering of the crown to Richard, with full mention of Edward IV's alleged marriage to

Eleanor, his subsequent bigamy, and the consequences of this for Edward IV's Woodville children.

Unsurprisingly, the earliest written accusation that Richard III stole the throne was penned by the self-styled Earl of Richmond (later Henry VII) in 1484. In a circular seeking support in England, he called for assistance in the 'furtherance of my rightful claim, due and lineal inheritance of that crown, and for the just depriving of that homicide and unnatural tyrant which now unjustly bears dominion over you'.[17] This is the first known instance of any such public assertion of Henry's alleged 'rightful claim' to the crown worn by Richard III, and the first description of Richard in such malicious language. Further, in Henry VII's first Act of Parliament on seizing the throne he declared Richard (and all who fought for the royal cause) guilty of treason against the rightful 'King Henry' whose reign he cynically attempted to pre-date from the day before Bosworth.[18] As one might expect from such propaganda, from the very start of his reign use of the word 'usurper' to describe Richard III becomes routine. According to Henry VII's historian Bernard André, Richard 'usurped the crown and was elevated to the throne'.[19] Cardinal Wolsey called Richard III a usurper in May 1525 (see chapter 7). And unfortunately, since the sixteenth century it has become all too easy to uncritically apply this term to Richard III.

Meanwhile, ignorant of her true identity, her good family background, her royal descent, and her sincere religious faith, generations of historians have discounted the claim that Eleanor Talbot was married to Edward IV. Instead, they have simply assumed that she was merely the king's mistress. This conclusion was based on

a) ignorance and a total lack of research concerning Eleanor.
b) the assumption that the supposedly evil King Richard III's subsequent use of Eleanor's story was nothing more than a wicked lie, concocted for his own selfish political advantage.
c) the view that the later airbrushing of Eleanor out of history by the supposedly good and virtuous King Henry VII was entirely correct and disinterested.

This appears to be incredibly naïve and partisan. While one may *argue* that in 1483 Richard III merely used the story of Eleanor's marriage for his own advantage we have to recognise there is absolutely no clear proof that this was the case. Even the nineteenth-century historian James Gairdner (who, as we have already seen, was no great friend of Richard III) declared that there was no justification for making such an assumption.[20]

The further assumption that Henry VII's later actions were disinterested is also ridiculously naïve and obviously partisan. As Henry himself stated very clearly and explicitly, his concern was to ensure that Eleanor's claim to be Edward IV's wife 'maie be for ever out of remembraunce and allso forgot'.[21] What is more, while John Rous had apparently formerly been in favour of Richard III (based on the evidence of his Rous Roll), after Henry VII's accession he clearly found himself working under the very powerful jurisdiction of the official spokesmen for the new regime (based on the evidence of his *Historia Regum Anglie* of about 1487).

Thus, when describing the political marriage of Henry VII, Rous wrote that the new sovereign 'at once took to wife the celebrated Lady Elizabeth, daughter and *heiress* of Edward IV'.[22] Rous's use of the key word 'heiress' to characterise Elizabeth makes crystal clear Henry's motivation for doing everything in his power to ensure that Eleanor Talbot and her marriage with Edward IV were 'forgot'. Obviously, if Eleanor Talbot was Edward IV's true wife, then Henry VII's *own* wife, and the mother of his dynasty, Elizabeth of York (the eldest daughter of Edward IV and Elizabeth Woodville) could not have been the Yorkist heiress. She was merely a royal bastard. This was very accurately perceived by Henry VII's well-known twentieth-century historian, Professor S. B. Chrimes.

> The subject-matter of the act of Richard III's parliament had now [autumn 1485] become so scandalous that to think of that all the justices in the Exchequer chamber advised that it would be best to avoid rehearsing the actual words in the act of Henry's parliament designed to nullify it. Nullified, however, it was, without being too specific about its contents, and until this was done, the legitimacy of Elizabeth remained questionable.[23]

Interestingly, Henry VII's immediate actions after his accession included, not only the repeal (unquoted) of the 1484 Act, but also the execution of Richard III's supporter, William Catesby (who had family connections with Eleanor Talbot), and also the persecution and imprisonment of Bishop Stillington.[24] As we have seen, Henry VII's historians also assisted the airbrushing of Eleanor Talbot out of history by substituting for her name that of Edward IV's mistress Elizabeth Wayte (Lucy). This was lest a situation ever arose in which mention of the case brought forward in 1483, which stated that Edward IV had committed bigamy, could not be avoided.

They pretended that Richard III had claimed that Edward IV had contracted a prior marriage with Elizabeth Wayte, but that she had categorically denied this. This, of course, was a deliberate lie.

As for Henry VII, obviously his wisest and best procedure (had it been possible) would have been to present clear evidence to his first Parliament to disprove the Edward IV bigamy allegation. But instead of doing so, Henry chose merely to suppress the 1484 Act (forbidding any copy of it to be kept, and prohibiting any discussion of it). In fact, Henry VII's actions very strongly indicate that Edward IV really had made a complete muddle of his royal marriage policy; that he had contracted a secret marriage with Eleanor Talbot, and that in September 1485 this claim could not be disproved. The logical conclusion seems to be that the case set out in Richard's *titulus regius* was unassailable. However, even those who are not inclined to accept that Edward IV had married Eleanor have to acknowledge that Richard III was offered the crown in a legal manner. Richard III was therefore never a usurper.

7

Richard, the Tyrant

The viii. day of Maie [1525], the Cardinall [Wolsey] again sent for the Maior and his brethren, ... Then it was answered to the Cardinall, by a counsailer of the cite, that by the lawe there might no such benevole[n]ce be asked, nor men so examined, for it was contrary to the statute made the first yere of kyng Richarde the thirde, ... The Cardinall hard this saiyng verie paciently, and answered: 'Sir I marvell that you speak of Richard the third, which was a usurper and a murtherer of his awne nephews, then of so evill a man, how can the actes be good, make no suche allegacions, his actes be not honourable'. 'And it please your grace' said the cou[n]sailer, 'although he did evill, yet in his tyme wer many good actes made not by hym onely, but by the consent of the body of the whole realme, which is the parliament'.

E. Hall, *Chronicle*, 1542 (reprinted London 1809), p. 698

Cardinal Wolsey appears to have thought that, in the case of an evil man, none of his actions could possibly have been good. And, of course, he considered Richard III an evil man. Some of Richard's contemporaries (such as the Bishop of St David's and also John Rous – while Richard was still upon the throne) had characterised him as a good king. It is also well known that the city of York noted in its records its deep regret at his death.[1] Nevertheless, thanks to the propaganda of the new government, by the sixteenth century most people would probably have accepted the cardinal's assumption in respect of Richard III's character. But, like the Lord Mayor of London, they would not necessarily have agreed with the cardinal's other conclusion.

Later historians have suffered to some extent from precisely the same confusion as Cardinal Wolsey. For example, in the nineteenth century, Gairdner wrote that by November 1483 'the kingdom was now at rest and his [Richard's] authority undisputed. Nor can it be doubted that one so competent to rule might have reigned for a long time if he had not already lost the confidence of his people by acts of treachery and violence'.[2] This is a curious sentence. On the one hand Gairdner states that by the end of 1483 Richard III held undisputed control of a kingdom at peace. Yet on the other hand he also claims that Richard had committed acts of treachery, and had forfeited popular support.

Presumably Gairdner's perceived acts (plural) of treachery comprised Richard's acceptance of the decision reached by the three estates of the realm that, based upon the evidence of Edward IV's bigamy, Edward V was illegitimate and could not be crowned king. The other implication in Gairdner's strange sentence is that Richard III was predestined to lose the battle of Bosworth in 1485 because the country would not support him. Given that Richard III's army at Bosworth was considerably larger than that of Henry VII, and that Henry VII's army was primarily a French invasion force, that appears to be a very strange conclusion.

Gairdner continued his assessment of Richard's rule in the odd, and partisan way in which, as we have just seen, he began it. Thus he went on to note that very full documentation of Richard's actions in terms of government survived, and 'some who have sought to call in question the evidence of Richard's crimes, have certainly not shown themselves over-critical in accepting evidence as to his better qualities'.[3] Apparently when clear evidence of good government exists, as it does in this case, Gairdner felt that it should be received very dubiously (because, of course, Richard III was a criminal). Indeed, he appears to be adopting exactly the same stance as that of Cardinal Wolsey in 1525.

His nit-picking continues. Thus, although the 'Docket Book of [Richard III's] grants does indeed confirm the character given him even by Sir Thomas More for profuse liberality, ... there is every appearance that this bounty was stimulated by the necessity of gaining friends'.[4] Moreover, doubt is expressed as to whether 'expressions of a religious purpose'[5] should really be naïvely accepted as evidence of genuine religious motives. Indeed, Gairdner describes such acceptance as evidence of 'an extreme degree of simplicity'.[6]

Thus, when Richard III stated that we should respect 'possessions or other things of right belonging to God and His said Church'[7] and that failure to do so could risk placing our souls in peril (a sentence which the king's great-nephew, Henry VIII, should perhaps have studied), Gairdner reaches the astonishing conclusion that

Even if words like these were to be taken as perfectly sincere, as one of Richard's biographers seems to consider them, they certainly by no means indicate that the king was not at this very time suffering inward pangs of remorse for the great crime by which he had attempted to secure himself more firmly on his usurped throne.[8]

At this point we need to remind ourselves that

a) the evidence of Richard III's declaration regarding respect for the rights of the Church is incontestable.
b) genuine evidence for his 'great crime' (the alleged murder of his nephews) is non-existent.
c) the claim that Richard III had usurped the throne is outrageous.

It may then be possible to reach a logical conclusion as to how to evaluate Gairdner's extraordinary claims about the value of the very large amount of evidence which survives, all of which appears to show that Richard III was a kindly, devout and well-motivated monarch, a prince who, as Gairdner himself had earlier described him, was 'so competent to rule' (see above).

Indeed, despite those very curious statements of his which we have already reviewed, even Gairdner appeared, in the end, to find himself forced to admit that Richard III had genuinely been responsible for 'charitable and praiseworthy acts'.[9] He cites several such cases from Harleian MS 433, and concludes that 'however necessary Richard may have found it himself to endeavour to secure men's loyalty by large gifts, he saw clearly the importance of checking corruption, and promoting economy in the service of the state'.[10]

Further evidence of the strength of mythology and legend in respect of allegations that Richard III was a tyrant has been published by Annette Carson.[11] Carson cites versions by Desmond Seward, Christopher Skidmore and Rosemary Horrox of the legend of the 'Black Knight', Sir Ralph Ashton, who was appointed Richard III's Vice-Constable of England to deal with Buckingham's Rebellion. In fact, the reality is probably that Ashton became known as 'the Black Knight' simply because he chose to wear black armour. Indeed, Seward acknowledges this point. However, he also offers what he himself specifically categorises as a *legend* associated with Ashton, suggesting that his conduct 'earned him much hatred. The King gave him power to try treason cases "without formalities or appeal" ... The "Black Knight", as he was popularly known on account of his armour, is credited – in legend – with rolling prisoners downhill in barrels filled with spikes.'[12]

Skidmore goes much further than Seward, asserting, as though it were a known *fact*, that Ashton's nickname was given to him

> not only on account of his black armour, but for his ruthless punishments meted out after Buckingham's rebellion, when Richard had given him the power to try treason cases 'without formalities or appeal'. Tradition records that he sentenced his victims to being rolled downhill in barrels filled with spikes.[13]

But, like Seward, Skidmore gives no source for his allegations, merely citing 'tradition'.

Horrox states that Ashton 'died at some time after 1486, leaving behind an unsavoury local reputation'.[14] In her footnotes she adds that 'Ashton's harshness has passed into folklore'. Unlike Seward and Skidmore, Horrox does actually offer two sources for her statement. However, they are not very impressive. One is a publication of 1870, and the other, a collection of folk tales.[15] By contrast, Carson consults eight sources. One of these is Wedgwood's *History of Parliament* which offers a brief entry referring to 'the black knight of Assheton', created Vice-Constable on 24 October 1483 to deal with 'Buckingham's rising' to try treason cases 'without formalities or appeal' (a standard legal formula since the reign of Edward IV). But actually, in this instance, 'few were executed,' says Wedgwood, who has nothing to say regarding Ashton's alleged nefarious reputation.[16]

Carson also examines further 'evidence' presented by Skidmore in support of the traditional view of Richard III as a potential tyrant.

> As instances of rebellion began to increase, Richard was determined to make an example of those who crossed his authority. This time there were to be no further pardons. Sir Roger Clifford, captured near Southampton, was tried and condemned to death at Westminster, to be executed on Tower Hill. Passing the sanctuary of St Martin's le Grand on his journey to meet his death, he nearly succeeded in escaping when his confessor and crowds nearby almost dragged him to safety, but the king's officers shouted for help; brought under restraint he was taken to the block. To those watching, it merely confirmed the growing suspicions that Richard was a tyrant, leading a merciless regime.[17]

Having noted and commented upon the vagueness of Skidmore's

terminology – what evidence does he offer for the increase of rebellions, and what is the meaning of 'this time'? – Carson then points out that 'he fails to mention that all this happened in 1485, when Clifford had been a wanted criminal on the run since being attainted for his part in the rebellion of October 1483. Nor does he mention the blood feud between the Cliffords and the house of York which had encompassed the killing of Richard's brother Edmund, Earl of Rutland. Admittedly Richard sought reconciliation with many who attempted his downfall, but one wonders why this fugitive, of all people, should have merited a pardon'.[18] Carson also identifies the original surviving account of Clifford's attempted escape as written by Robert Fabyan, which shows very clearly that Skidmore's claim that the crowd tried to assist him is merely another example of modern myth-making.

> But whenne he [Clifford] came fore agayne Seint Martynes the Graunt, by the helpe of a fryer whiche was his confessour, and one of theym that was nexte aboute hym, his cordes were so lowsyd or cut that he put hym in deuoyr to haue entred the seyntwary. And likely it had beene that he shuld haue so done, hadde nat been the quycke helpe and rescous of the sheryffes & theyr officers, the whiche constrained hym to lye downe ypon the hardyll, and ... so haryed hym to the sayd place of execucion.[19]

In the final analysis, there appears to be no evidence whatever that Richard III was a bad king in terms of his laws and his day-to-day government of the country. It is therefore hard to see why he should be characterised as a 'tyrant'. Indeed, although they struggled against it, both Cardinal Wolsey, in the sixteenth century, and James Gairdner, in the nineteenth century, appear, in the end, to have found themselves forced to acknowledge that, in terms of its legislation, the reign of Richard III had to be accepted as a good and positive period in the history of England.

8

Marriage Mythology

Was ever woman in this humour woo'd?
Was ever woman in this humour won?
Shakespeare, *Richard III*, act 1, scene 2

According to the text of a letter dated 12 October 1469, written by the eighteen-year-old Infanta Isabel of Castile (later Queen Isabel the Catholic) to her half brother, Henry IV (then king of Castile), the future Spanish queen at that point had one of her English cousins – a brother of King Edward IV – as her suitor and prospective husband.[1] I have translated into English the relevant portion of the text of Isabel's (rather long) letter, which runs as follows:

And then to remedy the danger and harm which could grow again if the said kingdoms and lordships did not have someone who could later legitimately succeed to them, it was agreed by your Excellency and by the Grandees and Lords Spiritual and gentlemen of his court and by the high council that, according to the laws and regulations regarding such things, they would diligently explore which of four possible marriages – to the Prince of Aragon (King of Sicily),[2] to the King of Portugal, to the Duke of Berri, or to the brother of the King of England – seemed more honourable to your Royal crown, and to offer a better chance of peace and growth in size to your said kingdoms.[3]

Isabel was referring to the fact that her half brother had no legitimate heir, so that she herself, together with whoever married her, would ultimately inherit his crown.

She does not name of any of her suitors, but refers only to their ranks and titles. Thus she does not specify which brother of Edward

IV was seeking her hand in marriage. However, the date of the letter makes it virtually certain that the brother in question must have been Richard, Duke of Gloucester. George, Duke of Clarence, had married Isabel of Warwick three months previously, and at the time of their marriage he must have been committed to her – apparently with the support of his brother, the king – for at least a year. The papal dispensation permitting George to marry his cousin dates from 14 March 1468/9. It was obtained thanks to Edward IV's proctor at the papal curia, Dr James Goldwell, who probably received the royal authorisation to request the dispensation before Christmas 1468.[4]

If Richard had gone on to marry Isabel the Catholic, both his subsequent life and hers would have been very different. Perhaps, instead of dying on the battlefield at Bosworth, Richard would have shared Isabel's conquest of Granada. Maybe England would never have experienced the trauma of the Reformation (together with its catastrophic loss of religious art treasures and medieval records). However, all such imaginary history is merely another kind of mythology. Isabel's proposed English marriage never did take place. Instead, shortly after the writing of the letter she married her cousin Ferdinand, heir to the throne of Aragon, thereby ultimately creating the Spanish state.

The relationship of Richard III and Isabel la Católica

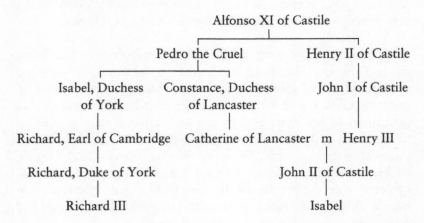

As for Richard, Duke of Gloucester, he went on to marry his cousin Anne of Warwick. According to Shakespeare's play *Richard III*, Richard married Anne very much against her will and better judgment. There is a famous scene (*Richard III*, act 1, scene 2) in which, in London, shortly after the arrest of his brother George, Duke of Clarence (an event which, in reality, occurred in 1476, at least five years after Richard and Anne had married), Richard, Duke of Gloucester, encounters Anne. In the play, this appears possibly to be their first meeting, despite the fact that the real Richard and Anne had shared part of their youth in the household of Anne's father, the Earl of Warwick, covering approximately the years from 1464 until 1469.[5]

According to Shakespeare, when Richard met Anne she was accompanying the body of her father-in-law, King Henry VI, to his burial (which took place at Chertsey Abbey in 1471) and she was lamenting the recent death of her husband, Edward of Westminster (who had also died in 1471). Although Shakespeare derived some of his material for his English 'historical' plays from the *Chronicle* of Raphael Holinshed (published in 1577), this story of Richard's meeting with Anne appears to be the playwright's own invention. Holinshed describes the transportation of Henry VI's dead body from the Tower of London to St Paul's Cathedral (where it lay exposed for one day) and thence to Blackfriars, before finally being transported by river to Chertsey Abbey. But he makes no mention of Anne's presence. Despite the fact that Shakespeare's Anne holds Richard guilty of the deaths of both Henry VI and Edward of Westminster – and indeed, Shakespeare's Richard actually admits the killing of Henry – she emerges as an obviously naïve character who, in the final analysis, is easily persuaded to accept Richard's invitation to his London home at 'Crosby-place' (Crosby's Place, in Bishopsgate).

Apart from any other consideration it is evident immediately that both the chronology and the geography of Shakespeare's account bears little relationship to the truth. It is possible that Richard, Duke of Gloucester, encountered Anne of Warwick somewhere in the county from which he derived his ducal title, at some stage in the aftermath of the battle of Tewkesbury (1471) – the event at which Anne's Lancastrian husband had been killed. However, this would hardly have been their first meeting. Richard and Anne almost certainly already knew each other well, and the possibility of their marriage had probably been explored much earlier, in the 1460s, before Anne's father changed sides and married her to Edward of Westminster for political reasons.[6] More will be said about this presently, when considering the question of a papal dispensation for Richard's marriage to Anne (see below). There is also no evidence that Anne attended the funeral ceremonies of Henry VI, either in London, or at Chertsey Abbey. Indeed, although Henry was technically her father-in-law, Anne may never have met the last Lancastrian King.

It is true, however, that, following the death of Edward of Westminster, Richard, Duke of Gloucester, seems to have made up his mind to marry his widow. According to the account of the Crowland chronicler, written probably about the end of April 1486,[7]

> after King Henry's son (to whom the earl of Warwick's younger daughter, the lady Anne, was married) had fallen at the battle of Tewkesbury ... Richard, duke of Gloucester sought to make the same Anne his wife; this desire did not suit the plans of his brother, the duke of Clarence ... who therefore had the girl hidden away so that his brother would not know where she was, since he feared a division of the inheritance. ... The Duke of Gloucester, however, was so much the more astute, that having discovered the girl dressed as a kitchen-maid in London, he had her moved into sanctuary at St Martin's.[8]

According to James Gairdner, writing in the nineteenth century, 'the hand of Warwick's co-heiress was a prize sure to be eagerly sought for; and, monstrous as the thing must appear, it was sought for by the very man who, as we have seen, was considered, in the next generation at least, to have been Prince Edward's murderer'.[9] Once again, Gairdner's position is equivocal. He was a serious scholar. He sought – and discovered – original source material, and at times he questioned the received wisdom. Nevertheless, he is clearly very strongly influenced by almost four preceding centuries' mythology regarding Richard III. Thus he quotes the legend which made Richard the murderer of Edward of Westminster (see above, chapter 4), even while explicitly stating that the sources for this dated from a generation after the event (in other words from the Tudor period). Likewise Gairdner quotes the tradition which saw Richard's desire for marriage with Anne as due, not to his affection for her, but to his ambition to gain half of the Warwick inheritance.

Despite this, there is some evidence that Richard and Anne shared common interests once they were married. 'Their grief at their son's death was almost bordering on madness, and they did share common religious interests in the north during the 1470s'.[10] For example, 'in 1477 Richard and Anne marked their special bond with the city [of York] by joining the Corpus Christi Guild'.[11] Thus, Richard's motives for marrying Anne – and Anne's motives for agreeing to marry Richard – may, in the end, have been mixed. This is probably not unusual. Indeed, we should also note that, even if the motives could be proved to have been purely commercial, there would be nothing very remarkable about that. Many royal and aristocratic marriages at that period and later were based on financial considerations. The apparently very successful marriage of Richard III's parents, Richard, Duke of York and Cecily Neville, had undoubtedly been arranged for them when they were very young, by Cecily's parents, chiefly because the Duke of York was a royal prince and a very significant landowner.

In order to marry Anne legally, Richard would have required a papal dispensation. When his brother George, Duke of Clarence, had married Anne's elder sister, Isabel, their close blood relationship (consanguinity) meant that a papal dispensation was required. A similar dispensation would have been needed for the marriage of Richard and Anne, since they were related by blood in precisely the same degrees as George and Isabel. Indeed, one element of Ricardian mythology has been the debate as to whether or not such a dispensation was ever issued – and therefore whether or not the marriage of Richard and Anne was valid. 'Central to this question is the claim by generations of historians that Richard married his cousin Anne Neville without a papal dispensation. For many years little enough was made of this accusation, and the attendant consequences were let lie. More recently, however, it has provided the springboard for a new attack on Richard's character and legitimacy as king'.[12]

In 2006 Peter Clarke discovered and published the fact that at least one papal dispensation for the marriage of Richard and Anne had in fact been granted. The record of this is preserved in the following format:

Richard, Duke of Gloucester, a layman of the Diocese of Lincoln, and Anne Neville, a woman of the diocese of York, desire to contract marriage with each other, but because they are related to one another in the third and fourth degrees of *affinity*, they request a dispensation. Item, with a declaratory letter in respect of the third and the fourth degrees.[13]

One might have thought that this important discovery by Peter Clarke would finally have resolved any question of the validity of Richard's marriage to Anne. But of course, in Ricardian affairs things are never so simple. The key point about the dispensation discovered by Clarke is that it addressed the issue of *affinity* (relationship by marriage), not the issue of *consanguinity* (relationship by blood).

If we compare Richard's and Anne's dispensation with the dispensation, granted in March 1468/9 for the marriage between

Richard's brother, George, and Anne's sister, Isabel, the difference between the two dispensations is clearly revealed. The earlier dispensation was worded as follows:

> A dispensation of Pope Paul III [*sic* for II] for contracting a marriage between the noble man George, Duke of Clarence and Isabel the daughter of the noble man Richard Nevill, Earl of Warwick, even though George and Isabel are joined in the second and the third and the third and fourth degrees of *consanguinity*, and in spite of the fact that George's own mother is the godmother of the same Isabel [literally 'raised the same Isabel from the sacred font']. Given at Rome, at St. Peter's the day before the Ides of March in the year 1468, the 7th year of the reign of Edward IV.[14]

Following Clarke's discovery, aspersions were cast upon the Richard and Anne dispensation by Michael Hicks,[15] who argued that their real affinity (relationship by marriage) was in the *first* degree, owing to George's marriage to Isabel. Hicks was mistaken. According to the rules of the Church the marriage of George to Isabel did not, in fact, create any affinity between Richard and Anne.[16] However, by 1471, a genuine affinity did indeed exist between Richard and Anne – though it had not existed prior to 1470. This genuine affinity (overlooked by Hicks) was caused by Anne's marriage to Edward of Lancaster. And it was this affinity which the dispensation discovered by Clarke addressed. As the following table shows, the earlier marriage of Anne created an affinity between her and Richard in the third and fourth degrees – precisely as stated in the dispensation – owing to the common descent both of Richard (3 generations) and of Edward of Westminster (4 generations) from John of Gaunt.

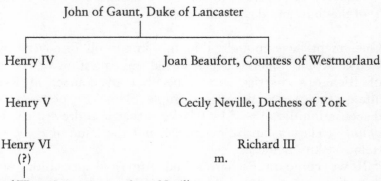

The normal way of calculating a relationship of consanguinity requiring a papal dispensation was, and is, to count the number of generations between the couple planning to marry and their closest common ancestor. Affinity is calculated on the same basis, by assessing either the man or the woman's relationship to his or her intended partner's previous spouse.

In the case of the consanguinity of George and Isabel, their closest common ancestors were Ralph Neville, Earl of Westmorland, and his wife, Joan Beaufort. These were George's grandparents, and Isabel's great-grandparents. Thus they were related in the second and third degree, as this table shows:

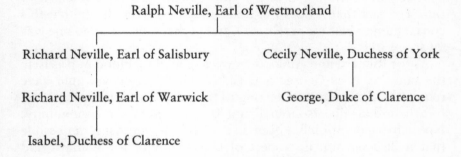

George and Isabel were also related in another line of descent in the third and fourth degree, thus:

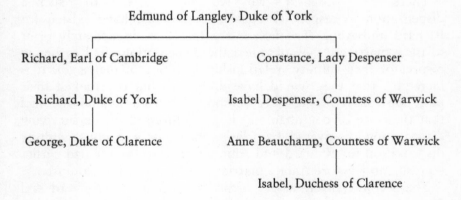

The papal dispensation for the marriage of George and Isabel takes account of both of these facts, describing the couple as related in the second and third degree, and also in the third and fourth degree.

In point of fact they were also related in another line of descent in the fourth and fourth degree, thus:

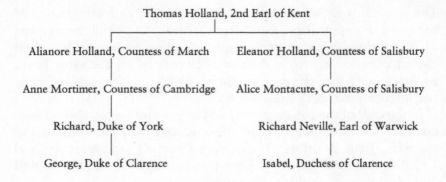

Therefore, their papal dispensation could also have referred to this. The fact that it does not do so may perhaps indicate that this consanguinity was more remote – and perhaps also that no one was aware of it!

As for Richard and Anne, they were related by blood in precisely the same ways as George and Isabel. Therefore they would have required a dispensation referring to the second and third, third and fourth, and ideally also fourth and fourth degrees of consanguinity. No such dispensation has been discovered. However, it is impossible that a dispensation in respect of consanguinity for Richard and Anne did not exist. Indeed, the document may well have been obtained by Anne's father at the same time as George's and Isabel's dispensation for consanguinity.

There are two reasons why we can be certain that such a dispensation in respect of consanguinity must have existed for Richard and Anne. The first is the fact that, immediately prior to their marriage, they obtained the dispensation cited earlier in respect of their affinity (relationship in terms of marriage). It is incredible that they would have done this, but overlooked their more obvious consanguinity (blood relationship). And the fact that the issue of consanguinity is not addressed in the surviving dispensation discovered by Clarke means that a consanguinity dispensation for Richard and Anne must have been issued earlier – presumably before Anne's marriage to Edward of Westminster.

The second reason why we can be certain that Richard and Anne must have had a consanguinity dispensation is the fact that Richard's brother George was strongly opposed to Richard's union with Anne, because he wished to ensure that all the property of Isabel and Anne's dead father descended to him by right of his marriage to Isabel. It is therefore absolutely certain that, if George had been able to contest Richard's marriage to Anne on the grounds that a papal dispensation covering their consanguinity had never been granted, he would have done so. The fact that George never raised this issue proves beyond any shadow of doubt that a consanguinity dispensation must have been granted to Richard and Anne, even if no copy of it now survives, or has been discovered.

Richard and Anne did marry – it is thought at some time in 1472, though the precise date is not on record. Their marriage appears to have been happy, but not noticeably productive. Only one living child was born: a son known as Edward of Middleham. However, he died at the end of March 1484, to the great grief of his parents. In the aftermath of their son's demise, Anne also began to sicken.

Later in his play *Richard III*, Shakespeare tackles the death of Queen Anne. In act 4, scene 2, Richard summons his servant, Catesby, and commands him

> rumour it abroad
> That Anne my wife is very grievous sick;
> I will take order for her keeping close.

When Catesby has departed to carry out his instructions, Richard soliloquises,

> I must be married to my brother's daughter,
> Or else my kingdom stands on brittle glass.
> Murder her brothers and then marry her!

Although previously, Shakespeare's Richard had spoken of the daughter of the Duke of Clarence, it is clear, from the mention of her brothers' murder, that the 'brother's daughter' referred to in this instance is Elizabeth of York, eldest daughter of Edward IV and Elizabeth Woodville, and the future queen of Henry VII. We shall assess the allegation that Richard planned to marry Elizabeth shortly.

First, however, according to the much earlier account of the Crowland Chronicle (1486), Elizabeth of York had been a prominent figure at her uncle's court during the Christmas celebrations in 1484. Possible reasons for this will be explored presently. The rather miserable Crowland chronicler considered that the court's Christmas celebrations had been too light-hearted, stating that

> it should not be overlooked that during this Christmas feast too much attention was paid to singing and dancing and to vain changes of dress – similar in colour and design – of Queen Anne and of the Lady Elizabeth, eldest daughter of the late king. People spoke against this, and the nobility and the upper ranks of the clergy

were very surprised. Many people say that the king was applying his mind in every way to a marriage with the said Elizabeth, either by awaiting the queen's death, or by means of a divorce[17] – for which he considered that he had sufficient grounds.[18]

Incidentally, a Channel 4 documentary on Richard III, broadcast in August 2014, entitled *Richard III: The New Evidence*, introduced a piece of new Ricardian mythology, linked to the Crowland chronicler's suggestion that the Christmas feast of 1484 was too luxurious. It invented a story that Richard was a glutton and 'dissolute'. Worryingly, the documentary also described Richard as 'disabled'. Television, of course, often seeks to attract more viewers by offering slightly scandalous suggestions. In this case it would therefore be wiser not to focus on the new mythology produced by the documentary itself (which is probably best ignored), but to look rather at the precise evidence published in the scientific report upon which the documentary was based.[19]

In its Abstract, this report states that

> In terms of his [Richard's] diet, there is a significant shift in the nitrogen, but not carbon isotope values, towards the end of his life, which we suggest could be explained by an increase in consumption of luxury items such as game birds and freshwater fish. His oxygen isotope values also rise towards the end of his life and as we know he did not relocate during this time [*sic* – see 'Richard III's Royal Progress' below], we suggest the changes could be brought about by increased wine consumption.[20]

The report itself cites historical evidence as follows:

> The Late Medieval diet of an aristocrat consisted of bread, ale, meat, fish, wine and spices with a strong correlation between wealth and the relative proportions of these, with more wine and spices and proportionally less ale and cereals with increasing wealth (Dyer, 1989). The wealthier you were the more variety of meat and fish you consumed.[21]

Moreover, it concludes that

> The isotope changes evident between Richard's femur and rib bones, when assessed against historical documentations, suggest a significant increase in feasting and wine consumption in his later years.[22]

However, unlike the television documentary, the scientific report itself invented no new mythology, but simply set its scientific results and their analyses in their correct historical context.

> Should we expect to see a significant change in diet when Richard was crowned King? Evidence remaining from coronation banquets throughout the Medieval period suggests that during the 15th Century, the coronation banquet was on average 25% larger in size than previous centuries and Richard III's banquet was noted for being particularly long and elaborate (Sutton and Hammond, 1983). As Richard's reign was short, such excesses are likely to have persisted and following his coronation in 1483, Richard went on Royal progress, during which he is likely to have been treated to elaborate banquets at each accommodating household. Thus it is not unexpected that his consumption of wine and rich foods increased over the last few years of his life.[23]

It is unfortunate, though, that the phrase 'as Richard's reign was short' appears to imply (as historians have often done) that Richard III *knew* his reign would be short! This is another part of the traditional mythology, which is based purely on the application of hindsight.

In addition, Fellow of the Society of Antiquaries of London Chris Dyer has also commented very wisely upon references to the allegation that, as king, Richard III drank 'a bottle of wine a day'.

> Many dubious things have been written about Richard III, but it is news to me that he drank wine out of bottles, as they were not in use in his time. If the word 'bottle' is being used as a measure of quantity – 75 cl – there is much documentary evidence for aristocratic wine consumption to suggest that bishops, earls, dukes and their companions regularly drank this amount and more, so the analysis of the isotopes is not really telling us anything new![24]

Perhaps the best summary of this 'new evidence' and its meaning is a recent article by Christopher Catling. He condemns the fact that 'the qualified and tentative statements on Richard III's diet were turned into certainties by every reporter, including the BBC, whose website now states as a matter of established fact that Richard III regularly ate swan, crane, heron and egret'. Catling then goes on to castigate 'the authors [of the scientific report] – no doubt being very abstemious people themselves – [for having] used the word "excess" to describe such a diet'. As Catling observes, 'this judgement was taken up by the media, who accused [Richard of] hitting the bottle and snacking on endangered birds'. Catling very appropriately concludes, 'thus are new myths created'![25]

Incidentally, although this point has not been picked up by the media, the evidence that Richard III consumed a considerable amount of seafood protein may offer scientific evidence in strong support of his religious faith. In the fifteenth century all Catholics were required to abstain from meat during Lent, on the vigils of great feasts, and on every Friday. The surviving household accounts for Richard III's distant cousin and key supporter John Howard, Duke of Norfolk, prove conclusively that he and his entourage conformed to these basic rules in terms of their food consumption.[26] However, the most pious went far beyond this basic abstinence, and included Wednesdays, and in some cases also Tuesdays and Saturdays, as days on which to avoid consumption of meat. The fifteenth-century Bryene household in Suffolk observed such rigorous traditions, proving that their religious scruples were very strict. The Bryene household abstained from meat on Wednesdays, Fridays and Saturdays throughout the year. They also sometimes avoided meat on Tuesdays, particularly during Advent.[27] The Howard household did not go that far. But maybe Richard III did – making him one of the truly pious in terms of his diet.

As for Richard's niece Elizabeth, she had had a varied life. Brought up as a significant princess at her father's court, from 1475, she had been betrothed to the Dauphin Charles of France (later King Charles VIII). But in 1482 the Dauphin's father, Louis XI, contracted the treaty of Arras with the Duchy of Burgundy. As a result Charles was betrothed to a new *fiancée*, the three-year-old Margaret of Austria, daughter of Marie, Duchess of Burgundy, and the step granddaughter of Elizabeth's aunt, Margaret of York. Thus Elizabeth had suddenly found herself bereft of the glorious prospect of one day becoming queen of France.[28] In the opinion of Philippe de Commynes this diplomatic setback was one of the possible causes of Edward IV's death – though in reality, Edward survived the news of the treaty of Arras by at least three months, and showed every sign of believing that he could cope with what had happened.

Following her father's death, and the failure of her mother's attempted Woodville coup, Elizabeth had joined her mother and sisters in sanctuary at Westminster Abbey. But after her uncle Richard had been offered the throne by the unofficial Parliament of 1483 (the three estates of the realm), on the grounds that the marriage of Edward IV and Elizabeth Woodville had been bigamous and that its children were illegitimate, Elizabeth found herself in a very odd new situation. Nevertheless, her uncle promised to look after her and her sisters, and arrange suitable marriages for them.

Memorandum that I Richard by the grace of God king of England and of Fraunce and lord of Irland in the presens of you my lords spirituelle & temporelle and you Maire and Aldermen of my Cite of London promitte & swere *verbo Regio* & upon these holy evangelies of god by me personally touched that if the doghters of dam Elizabeth Gray late calling her self Quene of England that is to wit Elizabeth Cecille Anne Kateryn and Briggitte wolle come unto me out of Saintwarie of Westminstre and be guyded Ruled & demeaned after me than I shalle see that they shalbe in suertie of their lyffes and also not suffer any maner hurt by any maner persone or persones to theim or any of theim in their bodies and persones to be done by wey of Ravisshement or defouling contrarie to their willes not theim or any of theim emprisone within the Toure of London or other prisone but that I shalle put theim in honest places of good name & fame and theim honestly & curtesly shalle see to be(e) foundene & entreated and to have alle thinges requisite & necessarye(te) for their exibicione and findings as my kynneswomen And that I shalle do marie sucche of theim as now bene mariable to gentilmen borne and everiche of theim geve in mariage lands & tenementes to the yerely valewe of CC marc for terme of their lyves and in like wise to the other doghters when they come to lawfulle Age of mariage if they lyff and suche gentilmen as shalle happe to marie with theim I shalle straitly charge from tyme to tyme loyngly to love & entreat theim as their wiffes & my kynneswomen As they wolle advoid and eschue my displeasure ... In witnesse wherof to this writing of my othe & promise aforsaid in your said presences made I have set my signemanuelle the first day of Marche the first yere of my Reigne [1 March 1483/4].[29]

Indeed, Richard is known to have acted on this promise. On Sunday 29 February 1483/4 he arranged a suitable marriage for his own illegitimate daughter, Catherine, the marriage to be celebrated 'before the fast [feast?] of St Michael next commyng [Wednesday 29 September 1484] by God's grace'.[30] The husband chosen for Catherine was one of Richard's noble supporters, William Herbert, 2nd Earl of Pembroke and Earl of Huntingdon. It was probably at about the same time that a marriage was also arranged for one of the daughters of Edward IV and Elizabeth Woodville. This was not their eldest daughter, Elizabeth, but their second surviving daughter, Cecily. Her marriage was to another of Richard III's supporters, Ralph Scrope, younger brother of Thomas, 6th Baron Scrope.[31]

Of course, Cecily's marriage to Ralph Scrope was a less prestigious union than the one arranged by Richard III for his own illegitimate daughter. Cecily was merely a younger illegitimate daughter of a deceased king. Nevertheless, by 1485 Richard was thinking in somewhat higher terms in respect of Cecily's elder sister Elizabeth. The marriage he planned for Elizabeth after the Christmas celebrations of 1484 would undoubtedly have taken place had Richard not subsequently been defeated at the battle of Bosworth. And had the marriage gone through, it would eventually have made Elizabeth a queen. Thus it might appear that Richard was echoing her late father's plans for Elizabeth during the period from 1475 to 1482. However, this would be an overstatement. For Richard III, Elizabeth was a royal bastard, and the marriage he planned for her was to a cadet member of the Portuguese royal family. When the marriage was planned in 1484–85, it would only have given Elizabeth the rank of a princess and a royal duchess. No one could have foreseen, at that time, that her projected husband would one day ascend the Portuguese throne.

Nevertheless, Elizabeth was delighted at the prospect of a foreign royal marriage which would restore her officially to royal status. It seems that she was so eager for the planned marriage to go ahead that she wrote to her uncle's leading supporter John Howard, Duke of Norfolk, beseeching him to do everything in his power to encourage Richard III to ensure that the planned marriage did take place.[32]

Elizabeth of York's letter to Norfolk appears to have been written in mid February 1484/5. It was preserved among the Howard family papers until at least the early seventeenth century, but the manuscript cannot now be found. We are therefore reliant on a single report of it written in the first half of the seventeenth century by George Buck. He had seen the document, but unfortunately he did not quote it precisely, but merely produced a paraphrase. Moreover, his interpretation of the document was influenced by the story we encountered earlier, in Shakespeare's play, to the effect that Richard III planned to marry Elizabeth himself. As a result, Buck misunderstood which planned royal marriage Elizabeth was seeking to push forward. One version of Buck's account reads as follows:

When the midst and last of February [1484/5] was past, the

Lady Elizabeth being more impatient and jealous of the successe then everyone knew or conceived, writes a Letter to the Duke of Norfolk, intimating first, that he was the man in whom she most assied, in respect of that love her father had ever bore him &c. Then she congratulates his many courtesies, in continuance of which, she desires him to be a mediator for her to the King, in the behalf of the Marriage propounded between them [*sic*], who, as she wrote, was her onely joy and maker in this world, and that she was in his heart and thought: withal insinuating, that the better part of February was past, and she feared the Queen would never die. All these be her own words, written with her own hand; and this is the sum of her Letter, which remains in the Autograph, or Original Draft, under her own hand, in the magnificent Cabinet of Thomas Earl of Arundel and Surrey.[33]

Rumours of a planned marriage between Richard III himself and his bastard niece Elizabeth were certainly current in London, and possibly also in York, in the spring of 1485. Indeed, Richard III was very annoyed about this and took firm steps to deal with the situation. What is not certain is how the rumours began to circulate. Possibly Elizabeth herself made some indiscreet remark about the Portuguese royal marriage plans, at a time when these were still under negotiation, and therefore not a matter of public knowledge. It is apparent from the surviving *résumé* of her letter on the subject of the marriage plans for her that Elizabeth was perhaps a rather thoughtless and insensitive girl, for she reportedly wrote that 'she feared the queen would never die'.[34] Obviously she was aware that the king's possible marriage to the Infanta Joana – and hence her own possible marriage to Joana's cousin the Duke of Beja – could not proceed while the ailing Queen Anne survived. Nevertheless, the remark sounds tactless. It was excusable, perhaps, on the grounds of her youth and her eagerness to have her royal rank re-established as a result of such an arranged marriage. However, perhaps it was because of careless and tactless remarks by Elizabeth that Richard's true plans were both noised abroad, and at the same time misunderstood as a project for a single royal marriage, uniting the king to his niece.

In effect of course this would have been a completely ludicrous plan. Richard III's claim to the throne in 1483 was based solely on the cause of legitimacy. Both the three estates of the realm in 1483, and a formal Parliament, in 1484, had declared that Edward IV's marriage with Elizabeth Woodville was bigamous and therefore invalid. In consequence of this it was also publicly stated that the children of the Woodville marriage were all bastards. Nothing had been done since Richard's accession, and the passing of the Act of Parliament, to reverse this legislation. It is therefore completely illogical to suggest that Richard III would ever have considered marrying one of his elder brother's illegitimate daughters.[35] Nevertheless, this story clearly circulated in 1485 – and still circulates today. Possibly it was circulated deliberately and maliciously in 1485, by enemies who wished to use it to undermine the king. Certainly it was vigorously denied. Nevertheless, it has continued to circulate. In fact it is one more example of how difficult it is to clear the picture regarding the mythology of Richard III.

In this particular case, it was the king himself who made the first effort to rectify the myth. On Wednesday 30 March (the day before Maundy Thursday) at the Priory of the Knights of St John at Clerkenwell, with both the mayor and significant London citizens in attendance, Richard explicitly denied any plans for a marriage between himself and his niece. Moreover, he then went on to order the mayor to arrest and punish anyone who was caught spreading this tale.[36] A couple of weeks later, after Easter, on 19 April, the king sent similar instructions to the city of York.

Incidentally, the letter from Richard's niece Elizabeth to the Duke of Norfolk also reveals to what extent John Howard enjoyed the king's confidence regarding the sad case of Queen Anne's decline and death. Of course, given Richard's position as king, although his wife's sickness and death may have a deeply personal matter for him (because he had known Anne since their youth) it was also an affair of state. Indeed, it was a vital matter in terms of the future royal succession in England, given that in 1485 Richard had no surviving legitimate child. Thus, all the evidence clearly indicates that the royal council was aware that Anne was dying before she actually passed away, and that the members had already begun to advise the king to negotiate a second, and royal marriage as a matter of urgency – and indeed, to seek for a suitable royal bride.

In the end, Anne lingered on until Wednesday 16 March 1484/5. Almost immediately after her death, however, in addition to arranging for her royal burial, Richard also hastily sent ambassadors to Portugal and to Spain to seek a replacement consort. Significantly, both the Portuguese and the Spanish infantas were direct descendants of Henry IV's sisters. Thus Richard III was attempting to do what Henry VII would later claim to have done. He obviously hoped that his second marriage would finally reconcile the long divided branches of the Plantagenet family – the rival houses of York and Lancaster.

For Richard III, and for his royal council, Joana of Portugal was the preferred infanta. This was firstly because her family were the senior living line of descendants from John of Gaunt and his first wife, Blanche of Lancaster – and therefore the most legitimate Lancastrian claimants to the English throne. But the second reason was that Portugal also offered the opportunity of a really excellent royal marriage for Richard's bastard niece Elizabeth. By arranging such a marriage for her, Richard III would be keeping, in quite a spectacular way, the promise which he had made to the girl's mother.

PART 5

Legends of Richard's Last Days

Up with my tent! Here will I lie tonight;
But where tomorrow?
Shakespeare, *Richard III*, act 5, scene 3

9

The Inn and the Bed

Listen to the spooky sounds recorded by ghoul hunters beside the
bed where legend says king spent his last night alive.

Emily Kent Smith, *The Daily Mail*[1]

Many writers have implied that Richard III spent the last months of
his life utterly preoccupied with thoughts of his forthcoming defeat
at the battle of Bosworth. Of course this is ludicrous. Richard
III never heard of the battle of Bosworth. It is true that he knew
that his second cousin Henry, self-styled 'Earl of Richmond', over
in France, was plotting against him, but the evidence shows that
Richard's prime concern during the final months of his life was to
arrange a suitable second marriage for himself, in order to beget
an heir and to secure the future of his own dynasty. And although,
when news came that a French invasion force was on its way,
Richard summoned his army to support him, he was also feeling
relaxed enough to go off for a hunting holiday in Sherwood Forest.
This does not suggest that he had been utterly depressed by the
news of the invasion. Indeed, as his strong and numerous forces
assembled, Richard III probably had every hope of victory in the
coming fight.[2]

When he ended his Sherwood Forest hunting holiday, King
Richard returned to Nottingham Castle. From there, in due course,
he moved south to Leicester, where he may have arrived on Friday
19 August.[3] As we saw above in chapter 1, during his lifetime,
Richard had not been a frequent visitor to Leicester. He is not
known ever to have gone there prior to his accession, and in the
course of his short reign as king he appears to have slept there
for a maximum total of six nights (out of the 12,011 nights of his
lifetime). This comprised four nights in 1483 (17–20 August and

22 October), and two nights in 1485 (from 19–21 August). In 1484 he called briefly at Leicester Abbey, but on that occasion there is no evidence to show that he stayed at the abbey – or anywhere else in Leicester – overnight.

Records relating to the visit of 1483 indicate that during the day the king was conducting his business at the royal castle in Leicester. It is therefore probable that he spent his nights there. A royal castle was a perfectly normal place for a visiting monarch to spend his time when touring his country. We know, for instance, that both Edward IV and Richard III stayed regularly at Nottingham Castle. It would therefore be logical to suppose that the king spent the nights of 19 and 20 August 1485 at Leicester Castle, particularly since in August 1485 he was embarking on a military campaign and was in the process of assembling his army. In fact, however, no contemporary records tell us precisely where Richard stayed in August 1485, and his Leicester venue on that occasion is, in fact, unknown.

Astonishingly, however, a myth began to emerge around the end of the sixteenth century (over one hundred years after the event) which claimed that Richard III spent the nights of 19 and 20 August 1485 at a Leicester Inn called 'The White Boar' – an inn sign which, had it existed, might have been a deliberate reflection of the king's own personal livery badge. Today this myth is frequently assumed to comprise absolutely accurate information, despite the fact that not one shred of evidence exists to substantiate it.

There is no doubt that, at the time when the story began to circulate (a century after the death of Richard III), there was an inn in Leicester called 'The *Blue* Boar'. This inn was a fine timbered building in Northgate Street, in the town centre. One day in the 1580s a woman called Agnes Clarke (*née* Davy), whose husband was at that time the innkeeper at the Blue Boar, was making beds in the inn's bedchambers. In one of the rooms she was surprised to find a late medieval gold coin under the bed. Reportedly, when Agnes investigated further, she found that the bed in question had a false bottom, within which a small hoard of medieval gold coins was concealed.

According to the story this gold then became the source of new wealth for the Clarkes. They went on to become prosperous citizens of Leicester. Indeed, in due course, Agnes' husband, Thomas, found himself elected mayor of Leicester. However, it would be wise to take account of the fact that in actuality Thomas Clarke had been actively involved in the civic affairs of Leicester since his late twenties. This had been years before he became landlord of the Blue Boar, and years before Agnes reportedly found some late medieval gold coins in the false bottom of one of the inn's beds.[4] Nevertheless, when the story of Agnes' discovery of treasure began to circulate, it apparently inspired speculation. First, who had hidden medieval gold coins in the bed? Apparently the coins dated from the Yorkist period, and the one Yorkist leader who had some kind of link with Leicester was Richard III, who was known to have stayed somewhere in Leicester in August 1485, while mustering his royal army. Gradually it therefore came to be assumed that the coins were part of Richard III's treasury, and that the king himself had concealed them in the false bottom of the bed.

The legend which then gradually emerged was that the bed at the inn had been Richard III's own bed. He had brought it with him to Leicester, and had spent the nights of 19 and 20 August 1485 at the Blue Boar Inn. He had left the money in the bed intending to collect both the bed and the treasure after his victory at the battle of Bosworth. But in fact he was defeated and only returned to Leicester as a corpse, so his money had remained hidden in the bed for a century, until it was accidentally discovered by Agnes Clarke. Would Richard III really have stayed at the Blue Boar Inn in Leicester? It is true that some medieval inns did have established connections with aristocratic patrons, being either owned by them and run by a tenant 'landlord' on their behalf, or enjoying the patronage of a particular nobleman on a regular basis.[5] The claim was therefore made that Leicester's Blue Boar Inn had only been given that name after Henry VII's victory at the battle of Bosworth. The blue boar was a heraldic badge of John de Vere, Earl of Oxford, one of Henry's chief supporters. It was claimed that before the battle of Bosworth the Leicester inn had not been called 'The Blue Boar' but 'The White Boar'. In other words the inn was named originally in honour of Richard III's heraldic emblem. Thus the story evolved that the inn had some kind of link with the king – which would explain why he chose to sleep there in August 1485.

Significantly, however, not one shred of contemporary evidence survives to substantiate the existence of a Leicester inn called either 'The White Boar' or 'The Blue Boar' in the fifteenth century. The earliest surviving mention of the inn dates only from the 1570s, at which time it was certainly called 'The Blue Boar'. In other words, there is nothing to indicate that a 'Boar' inn (either blue or white) existed in Leicester in August 1485, or that Richard III had any connection with it – let alone that he slept there. Nor is there anything to substantiate the story that the colour of the inn sign was rapidly repainted from white to blue in order to make the inn more politically acceptable to the new regime of Henry VII, in the aftermath of the battle of Bosworth.

Nevertheless, an inn called 'The Blue Boar' had certainly been created in Leicester by the second half of the sixteenth century, and reportedly some gold coins were found in one of the bedrooms by the innkeeper's wife about 100 years after the battle of Bosworth. The story of the treasure – and its supposed link with Richard III – and his imagined nights at the inn are all traceable only to the early years of the seventeenth century, and to a writer called John Speede.[6] This is an interesting point, because we shall meet Speede again later in connection with another very famous – and completely false – Leicester legend concerning Richard III.

Thanks to John Speede, a detailed story grew up, and was disseminated, to the effect that Richard III slept at the 'Boar' inn 'in a large gloomy chamber, whose beams bore conventional representations of vine-tendrils executed in vermilion, which could still be seen when the old building was pulled down' in 1836.[7] Here the king was said to have had his own bed set up, having brought it with him from Nottingham Castle in his baggage train. After two nights, when Richard departed in the direction of his fatal battlefield, the story reports that Richard left his bed at the inn, intending to have it picked up after the battle.

According to the legend, the royal bed, never reclaimed or sent for, subsequently remained at the inn. This reputed royal bed supposedly still exists, and is now on show at Donington-le-Heath Manor House, Leicestershire. Sadly, however, the Donington bed appears, for the most part, to be a seventeenth-century construction. The bed as it is today also differs in certain details from a surviving engraving of Richard III's supposed bed published by John Throsby in 1777. The differences between the eighteenth-century engraving and the surviving bed appear to be greater than can be accounted for by Throsby's report that the bed had been lowered by the removal of its feet.[8] It is therefore highly questionable whether any part of the Donington bed has a genuine connection with Richard III.

But if anyone doubted the story of Richard's stay at 'The Blue (White) Boar Inn', and his ownership of the bed at Donington-le-Heath, an attempt has recently been made to undermine such doubts by the production of a new piece of Leicester mythology as part of the aftermath of the 2012 discovery of Richard III's bones. This latest addition to the myth comprised a night watch beside the Donington bed by a group of local ghost hunters. To reassure anyone who might ever have doubted the king's connection with the bed and the inn, these ghost hunters claimed that they were able to record the voice of Richard III, whose spirit still inhabits the bed in question.

Unfortunately, however, the reporting by the media of this latest addition to the 'Blue Boar Inn' myth was inaccurate – like a great deal of other media reporting of the story of the discovery of Richard III and its follow-up. For example, Emily Kent Smith, writing for the *Daily Mail*, said,

> Is this the 'voice of Richard III's ghost'?: Listen to the spooky sounds recorded by ghoul hunters beside the bed where legend says *king spent his last night alive*.
>
> Amateur ghost hunters from Leicestershire have recorded the voice.
>
> Said sound was heard by the bed at *Donington le Heath Manor House*.
>
> *It is believed King spent final night there* before Battle of Bosworth in 1485.[9]

Emily's *Daily Mail* report added two new fallacies to the traditional myth. First, she alleges that Richard III 'spent his last night alive' in the bed in question. This is obviously impossible. The traditional story – even if it could be authenticated – only ever claimed that Richard III slept in the bed in question on the nights of 19 and 20 August 1485. But the last night of his life was the night of 21 August, which he spent, not in Leicester, but in his camp near Sutton Cheney. There is another alleged bed in which he spent that last night of his life, and we shall explore that story shortly.

The *Daily Mail* also reports that Richard not only spent the last night of his life in the *bed* which is now displayed at Donington-le-Heath Manor House, but also that he (and the bed) had been at the Donington Manor House itself in August 1485. The report states specifically that 'it is believed that King Richard III spent the night at the house before riding out to the Battle of Bosworth in 1485 and dying on the battlefield'.[10] Of course, this is not what was claimed by the traditional mythology. However, it shows very clearly just how dangerous the thoughtless and slovenly recycling of such mythology can be.

Sadly, another rather regrettable move to reinforce the mythology of the 'Blue Boar Inn' story was undertaken recently by the University of Leicester, which presented a picture showing Richard III at the Blue Boar Inn to the new Richard III Visitors' Centre in Leicester.[11] This, of course, will almost certainly reinforce public perception of the Blue Boar Inn myth as historical fact. Indeed, on its website, the university already states as a fact that,

> While the church of the Greyfriars was the last resting place of Richard III, the last place where he actually rested was the Blue Boar Inn, a large, modern (for the time) establishment on Leicester's old High Street. After riding from Nottingham, Richard stayed at the Blue Boar on the night of 20 August 1485, reputedly in his own bed which he had brought with him. ... The Blue Boar itself was constructed in the mid–15th century and was a large coaching inn, providing food, drink and accommodation for wealthy travellers. On his previous visits to Leicester, Richard had stayed in the Castle but by 1485 that was starting to fall into disrepair.[12]

However, although the building may have been constructed in the mid fifteenth century, as has already been shown, there is absolutely no proof that it was functioning as an inn in 1485, or that Richard III stayed there, or that it had a name including the word 'Boar'. It also sounds rather extraordinary to acknowledge that Richard stayed at Leicester Castle in the summer of 1483, while claiming that two years later he was unable to do so because it was in a state of disrepair.

In the final analysis, it is impossible to ascertain whether any part of the Blue (White) Boar Inn and bed story is based upon fact. It is therefore a matter for serious concern that an academic institution should write as though a traditional myth had now been proved to be a historical fact. But since 2012 the University of Leicester has been manipulating the reporting of Richard III's story in various ways (see chapter 16 and appendices). The motivation of the university could perhaps be a wish to reinforce King Richard's perceived connection with Leicester.

The bed at Donington-le-Heath is not the only bed which claims that Richard III slept in it. There are other contenders for this role. A few years ago rumours began to surface that there was a 'Richard III bed' at a farmhouse in Sheepy Magna.[13] But an indication of the ease with which 'Richard III beds' may be invented, is provided by the fact that the present writer was also told at one point that a wooden bedstead at the Guildhall in Leicester had belonged to Richard III. Subsequent enquiries revealed that the bed in question is seventeenth-century, was purchased for the Guildhall as part of a room display in the 1950s, and has absolutely no historic connection either with Leicester or with King Richard.[14]

Possibly a little more credible is the story of a piece of furniture preserved today at Coughton Court in Warwickshire. Whether or

not Richard left one of his beds behind in Leicester on the morning
of 21 August 1485, it is very probable that he passed the last night of
his life in a small camp bed. Indeed, this may possibly explain why
the king is said to have experienced a somewhat uncomfortable and
sleepless night (see below). Parts of the royal camp bed said to have
been used by Richard on the night of 21–22 August are reputed
to survive today. Some of the wood was reportedly reused later
to make a chair which is now at Coughton Court. The tradition
relating to this chair seems to be an old one. But like all Ricardian
mythology, the story lacks documentary proof.

10

The White Horse and the Sleepless Night

Saddle white Surrey [Syrie] for the field tomorrow.
Shakespeare, *Richard III*, act 5, scene 3

Hall's sixteenth-century chronicle reports that in August 1485, when Richard III arrived in Leicester, he was 'mounted on a great white courser'. Such a white horse is depicted as bearing the king in the painting showing Richard in front of the Blue Boar Inn, recently presented by the University of Leicester to the Richard III Visitor Centre, and mentioned in the previous chapter. Unfortunately, however, as with the story of the inn – and indeed, with many of the stories relating to Richard III, particularly those which relate to his final days – no source dating from earlier than the sixteenth century appears to survive to support Hall's account of the white horse.

Nevertheless, Shakespeare later picked up the white horse story. The playwright assumed that Richard III took the same steed with him when he departed from Leicester, for in Shakespeare's play *Richard III* it figures as the king's steed on 22 August, at the battle of Bosworth. Indeed, Shakespeare also recorded a name for the horse, either 'White Surrey' or 'White Syrie'.[1] Syria was at that period a significant source for high quality horses of what would nowadays be referred to as 'arab stock'.

Among modern horse experts there is some reservation regarding the use of the term 'white' to describe a horse. Most horses which look white have an outer coat of white hair, but their underlying skin is dark in colour, as are their eyes. Nowadays such horses are therefore normally described as 'grey'. However, there are a few true 'white' horses. These have not only the white coat of hair, but also a pink skin underneath. They also usually have blue eyes. Naturally there is now no way of knowing whether 'White Surrey' or 'White Syrie' really existed. Nor is it possible to guess whether such a steed would have been described by modern experts as 'white' or 'grey'.

At one time it was believed that a horse called 'White Syrie' was actually listed among King Richard's horses in a surviving fifteenth-century manuscript.[2] However, this ultimately proved to be due to a misreading of the manuscript in question. There is therefore no surviving fifteenth-century evidence of the name of the horse that Richard rode into his last battle. There is also no real evidence for Shakespeare's belief that Richard used in the battle the same white (or grey) horse which he had reportedly ridden into and out of Leicester on the preceding days.

On the other hand, evidence does exist that some late fifteenth-century horses bore names which referred to their colour. Such horses are recorded both in the stable of Richard III and in the stable of his distant cousin John Howard, Duke of Norfolk.[3] The surviving list of Richard III's horses includes twenty named mounts which were either grey (*liard*, *lyard* or *gray*) or white (*whit*). These included a 'gret gray ... being at Harmet at Nottingham'. Given the fact that he was apparently stabled in Nottingham, Richard III could possibly have ridden his 'gret gray' from Nottingham to Leicester in August 1485. Thus, although there is no surviving contemporary evidence to support the story, it is possible that Richard III did indeed ride to Leicester on a grey (or white) horse from the royal stable, just as Hall later reported. It is also conceivable that Richard owned a horse named 'White Syrie', as Shakespeare later claimed. But in the final analysis the existence of a royal horse of that name remains unsubstantiated.

Whichever horse Richard rode on Sunday 21 August, on that day he definitely left Leicester, heading westwards. On his way out of Leicester the king is said to have crossed the little river Soar by means of Bow Bridge. This is almost certainly correct, because at that period Bow Bridge would have been the only way of crossing the River Soar in a westerly direction. In those days the bridge was not the Victorian cast iron construction which today bears the name of 'Bow Bridge', but a small, stone-built structure with a humped back, supported on four low arches (see plate 22). This stone bridge was quite narrow, with a low stone parapet on either side.

According to folklore, as Richard crossed the narrow bridge on horseback his heel struck the stone parapet, whereupon an elderly pauper woman, whose cries for alms the king had ignored, prophesied that 'where his spurre strucke, his head should be broken'.[4] Medieval fortune tellers certainly did exist.[5] However, this particular 'prophecy' which appears to foretell Richard's defeat and death might well be a later invention, made with the benefit of hindsight. Although Richard III's skull is now broken, this is not due to damage caused by striking the stonework of old Bow Bridge in August 1485, but rather to a blow from Dr Jo Appleby's mattock in September 2012.

Richard's journey on 21 August 1485 took him in the direction of the village of Sutton Cheney, near which he and his army camped that night. It is often reported that Richard III's tent the night before the battle of Bosworth was a very unquiet place as the king tossed and turned in a troubled sleep, the prey of visions and nightmares. There are two early sources for this story: the Crowland Chronicle continuation (1486) and Polydore Vergil (early sixteenth century). The continuator of the Crowland Chronicle reports that 'the king … had seen that night, in a terrible dream, a multitude of demons apparently surrounding him, just as he attested in the morning when he presented a countenance which was always drawn, but was then even more pale and deathly'.[6] We should note that this version of the story is not identical to Shakespeare's later version. In Shakespeare's *Richard III* play, of course, we find the king beset, during the last night of his life on earth, by the ghosts of his alleged murder victims (see above, chapter 4).

As for Polydore Vergil, his version of the 'sleepless night' tale agrees, on the whole, with that of the Crowland Chronicle continuator. However, Vergil explains things at greater length. He states that

yt ys reported that king Rycherd had that night a terrible dreame; for he thowght in his slepe that he saw horrible ymages as yt wer of evell spyrytes haunting evidently abowt him, as yt wer before his eyes, and that they wold not let him rest; which vision trewly dyd not so muche stryke into his brest a suddane feare, as replenyshe the same with heavy cares: for forthwith after, being troublyd in mynde, his hart gave him theruppon that thevent of the battale folowing wold be grievous, and he dyd not buckle himself to the conflict with such lyvelyness of corage and countenance as before, which hevynes that yt showld not be sayd he shewyd as appallyd with feare of his enemyes, he reportyd his dreame to many in the morning.[7]

In both cases we are dealing with second-hand accounts. Neither the continuator of the Crowland chronicle nor Polydore Vergil had personally spent the night of 21–22 August 1485 at Richard III's bedside. Therefore in both cases the evidence presented is hearsay. The ultimate source for both Crowland and Vergil is unknown, but could possibly have been the royal servants. Unlike the king himself, some of these members of the royal household survived the battle of Bosworth.

However, both the Crowland chronicler and Vergil claim that the king himself was the ultimate source of their information. They report that on the morning of 22 August Richard looked drawn. Since he reputedly wished to make it clear that this was not on account of any fear of the enemy, the king is then said to have explained to his entourage that his sleep had been disturbed by nightmares. Richard's reported solution to the problem of his sleepless night is a strange one, since, in a way, it turned out worse than the problem itself. One is left wondering why the king didn't simply pretend to his companions that he had toothache. But of course, if he was suffering from some kind of illness, Richard III might have felt reluctant to reveal his state of health. After all, public knowledge of the fact that their leader was ill might potentially have given rise to anxiety in the royal army.

Nevertheless, the picture of a reluctant and lacklustre Richard on the morning of the battle, which emerges from the 'sleepless night' stories of Crowland and Vergil, clearly conflicts with reports of the king's courage during the preceding days. It also conflicts with the reports of Richard's courageous and determined conduct on the battlefield itself. But in the end, as with so much of the traditional Ricardian mythology, we simply have no way of knowing whether Richard III slept well or badly on the night of 21–22 August.

The Crowland chronicler states that Richard III 'presented a countenance which was always drawn'.[8] This gives the impression of being a report made by someone who had personally seen King Richard on a fairly regular basis, and it may therefore be accurate.[9] There are a number of possible reasons why Richard may have looked drawn in the summer of 1485. In the recent past he had suffered intimate bereavements. He had also been forced into the unexpected role of king. And, following his coronation, he had learnt the hard way that oaths of friendship and support are not always sincere. It is extremely doubtful whether Richard III found the English throne to be a bed of roses.

Of course, it is just possible that the story of Richard III's sleepless last night was merely a deliberate invention on the part of early Tudor propagandists. But although such people may have invented some of the traditional stories about Richard III, it seems rather unlikely that the tale of the sleepless night fits into this category. It would therefore seem reasonable to conclude that a fairly early tradition existed which genuinely suggested that Richard III did not sleep well on the night before his last battle. And in this context it is interesting to note that the stories relating to the king's bed imply that for some reason it might have been quite important for Richard to spend the night in his usual sleeping place. Possibly, therefore, he was one of those people who find it difficult to sleep really comfortably other than in their own familiar beds. Of course, on the final night before the battle the story has it that he slept in a camp bed – portions of the woodwork of which are now said to comprise a chair preserved at Coughton Court in Warwickshire (see above). This unfamiliar piece of rather makeshift army furniture may have made it hard for the king to sleep.

As we have seen, one other possible explanation for his reported sleepless night could be that he was not feeling well. It is reported that in August 1485 the sweating sickness struck England. 'The malady was remarkably rapid in its course, being sometimes fatal even in two or three hours, and some patients died in less than that time. More commonly it was protracted to a period of twelve to twenty-four hours, beyond which it rarely lasted. Those who survived for twenty-four hours were considered safe. It is said to have particularly attacked the rich and the idle'.[10] Lord Stanley claimed to have been suffering from this disease in August 1485. Indeed, this was his reason (or excuse) for not obeying the king's summons to the royal muster. Therefore if Richard also happened to fall victim to this unpleasant – but not necessarily fatal – complaint, that could perhaps explain his restless night.

Since the sweating sickness was a fever, its most obvious symptoms were high temperature and perspiration. Moreover, the illness usually lasted for about twenty-four hours. Therefore such an illness could also possibly explain the fact that, on the battlefield the following morning, Richard III is reported to have been thirsty, and to have stopped to drink from a local well. Obviously there would have been no opportunity for him to do this once he had initiated his final and fatal charge. Therefore if he did indeed experience a demanding thirst, this must have been in the early stages of the battle. But apart from wearing full armour on a possibly warm morning, at that stage of the fighting Richard would not yet have undertaken any strenuous activity which could have accounted for his thirst.

11

The Last Mass and the Last Battle

On Sunday, the Commemoration in St James' Church, Sutton Cheney was very well attended, and as always, very poignant. A memorial sermon by the Revd Alison Adams, from Leicester Cathedral, is printed elsewhere by the Society, and called for reconciliation once Richard is reburied. The Dean was delighted that there was such a full church and I found the music and song [*sic* which?] filled that small, holy place *where Richard had once bowed his head before battle*, very poignant.

Cris Reay Connor, 'Bosworth 2014', *The Ricardian Recorder*, August 2014 (my emphasis)

Whether or not he slept badly, on the last day of his life, Richard III apparently woke up early. Reports tell us that he got up at dawn, which, in August, would have occurred at about 6 o'clock in the morning in terms of the modern British Summer Time. This might possibly have been because he had not slept well, though by itself it does not prove it. We have no way of knowing for certain whether this was unusually early rising time for Richard, or whether it was a more or less normal part of his daily routine. In any case, on the morning of a battle, early rising was common practice.

Unfortunately at this stage a piece of twentieth-century Ricardian mythology makes its presence felt in the story of the king's last day. This particular piece of mythology was invented by the 'Fellowship of the White Boar' in the 1920s, and regrettably it is endorsed annually by the Fellowship's successor, the Richard III Society, to this day. Given its stated aim of seeking the truth about Richard, the society which bears his name should really be ashamed of itself for its backing of this particular myth.

The story asserts that early on the morning of 22 August Richard III made his way from his camp to Sutton Cheney Church in order to attend morning mass there. No source prior to the 1920s exists for this unlikely tale, which appears to have been invented in order to provide an ecclesiastical focus for modern commemorations of Richard III. Indeed, it is still used in that way today, to endorse an annual service held at Sutton Cheney Church which usually figures as part of the Bosworth commemorations of the Richard III Society. Fifteen years ago, as a member of the society's executive committee, the present writer tried to change this, by moving the focus of the service to Leicester Cathedral. In August 2005 the commemoration of Richard III and others who died at the battle of Bosworth was celebrated in the cathedral, in the form of the modern Catholic rite of Vespers for the Dead. The service was led by the Precentor, Canon Dr Stephen Foster, and included a wreath-laying on the stone in the cathedral choir which then commemorated Richard III. But subsequently the Richard III Society reverted to its established practice of holding its August commemoration service at Sutton Cheney Church.

The Sutton Cheney 'Last Mass' story is misleading for two reasons. First, although morning masses in those days were the norm (see below), it seems unlikely that a medieval parish church would have celebrated its daily mass at dawn. Second, we have clear contemporary evidence from the continuator of the Crowland Chronicle that Richard III was accompanied by his own household chaplains in his military camp on the night of 21–22 August 1485. Obviously these royal chaplains would have celebrated their daily mass in the king's camp, using a portable altar and other equipment belonging to the chapel royal. One item of the equipment belonging to Richard III's chapel royal appears to have survived in the form of the Bosworth Crucifix, found on the battlefield site in the late eighteenth century and now preserved at the Society of Antiquaries in London.[1]

Under normal circumstances, one or more of the royal chaplains would have celebrated mass for the king in his own tent, soon after he arose on the morning of Monday 22 August – and of course, before he had breakfast (because according to Catholic practice taking communion had – and has – to be preceded by a period of fasting). Curiously, the Crowland chronicler tells us that 'at dawn on Monday morning the chaplains were not ready to celebrate mass for King Richard'.[2] However, this by no means suggests that Richard had to go elsewhere for his last mass, it merely means that there may have been some slight delay, perhaps because the king had arisen somewhat earlier than expected.

Of course, as we have already noted, the continuator of the

Crowland Chronicle is unlikely to have been present in the royal camp on the morning of 22 August. His account of what took place is therefore, once again, hearsay, presumably derived ultimately from one or more of Richard III's servants. Even so, the information he offers may, in this instance, be correct, because evidence exists from another – and slightly later – source which supports the notion that preparations for the royal mass on the morning of 22 August were surrounded by some degree of confusion.

The second source is the *Account of Miracles Performed by the Holy Eucharist*, which Henry Parker, Lord Morley produced for Queen Mary I in 1554. Lord Morley was the son of a Yorkist who fought on Richard III's behalf at Bosworth. And Morley states that his information came from a servant of King Richard, whose name he cites as 'Bygoff'. This servant is now usually identified as Sir Ralph Bigod. According to Bygoff/Bigod, 'Kyng Richard callyd in the morning for to have had mass sayd before hym, but when his chapeleyne had one thing ready, evermore & they wanted another, when they had wyne they lacked breade, And ever one thing was myssing'.[3]

Lord Morley was elderly in 1554, while Sir Ralph Bigod (if he was indeed the source) had died in 1515. Also Morley was writing for a granddaughter of Henry VII, the enemy of Richard III. It appears therefore that Lord Morley was producing or endorsing a story which at that time was taken to imply that maybe the wicked tyrant King Richard had died without receiving the comfort of the Blessed Sacrament. Similar stories exist in the cases of other leaders defeated in battles, including the losers at Agincourt and Coutrai.[4]

In reality, however, some confusion and a slight delay in getting things ready to celebrate mass in the tent of a king who had, perhaps, arisen slightly earlier than expected, would not have prevented mass from being celebrated. All priests would know the required preparations so well that they could get things ready very quickly, once they were summoned to do so. Moreover, since, like all Catholic priests, Richard III's royal chaplains would have been required and obliged to celebrate mass on a daily basis, it is impossible that the necessary items were not available somewhere in the royal camp, even if they were not immediately to hand early on the morning of 22 August. It cannot have taken more than a maximum of about thirty minutes to have got everything ready absolutely from scratch. Since the celebration of a said mass would also have taken only about thirty minutes, the service must have been completed, and the king would have been free to have his breakfast, within an hour of his getting up.

The continuator of the Crowland Chronicle also reports that

breakfast was not ready when the king first rose from his bed. This tends to confirm the notion that on the morning of 22 August Richard III was perhaps up and about somewhat earlier than his servants had anticipated. But a medieval royal breakfast bore no relationship to what is popularly known as an 'English Breakfast' today. That rich meal was a much later invention! Medieval breakfast would have been a very simple meal. Probably a royal medieval breakfast comprised bread and wine. This could have been got ready very quickly, while the king was attending his mass.

There is therefore no reason to suppose that Richard did not hear mass on the morning of 22 August, or that it was celebrated anywhere other than in the royal tent. There is also no reason to suppose that the king had no breakfast. However, the evidence of the continuator of the Crowland Chronicle does appear to imply that Richard III got up earlier than expected on the last morning of his life – possibly because he had not slept well – and perhaps because he was suffering from an illness of some kind. But of course, the writer of the Crowland Chronicle continuation seems not to have been Richard III's committed friend. Therefore it may be that, for motives of his own, he wished to create an impression that Richard III had died without the support of either divine or human nourishment.

As for the invented 1920s story that Richard III attended his last mass at the church of Sutton Cheney, that is still being promoted by parts of the Richard III Society (as the quote at the head of this chapter shows). The legend also received a kind of confusing reinforcement recently from Leicester Cathedral. On 14 October 2014, in an announcement of the plans for Richard's re-interment, the Cathedral issued the following statement:

> The cortege will visit Dadlington as some of the battle-dead are buried in the churchyard of St James' the Greater. *Sutton Cheney has been chosen because it is believed that King Richard took his final Mass at St James' church on the eve of the battle.*[5]

Curiously, this announcement appeared to offer an updated version of the original 'Last Mass' myth invented by the Fellowship of the White Boar. This new version implies that the king attended mass at Sutton Cheney Church *on the evening before the battle*. But in medieval churches a regular mass on Sunday evenings would have been highly unusual. In the thirteenth century, action had been taken by the Catholic Church to limit the daily celebrations of mass by a priest to a single mass (except on special feast days).[6] Moreover, at that period there was an obligation on anyone receiving Holy

Communion to have fasted from the previous midnight. Therefore the celebrant priest (who, of course, *had* to take Holy Communion as part of his celebration of mass) would have needed to fast for eighteen hours if, for example, he celebrated mass at 6 o'clock in the evening. No priest is likely to have done this except on very special occasions. (Of course, when celebrating vigil masses on the eve of major feast days like Easter and Christmas, he would, in any case, have been required to fast; therefore, an evening mass on specific liturgical occasions such as those would have presented no problem.) Similarly, if Richard III had attended an evening mass at Sutton Cheney on Sunday 21 August, and himself wished to receive Holy Communion, he too would have needed to fast all day that Sunday.

Fortunately, in this instance, when I contacted the Cathedral's communication officer she proved willing to listen to the mythology evidence which I presented to her, and said she would correct the cathedral's material on this point – though as far as I am aware no corrected version of the original and erroneous public announcement was formally circulated.

As for Richard III's experience at the battle of Bosworth itself, we certainly cannot assume that his defeat was predestined. The truth appears to be that the king was well supported. Even Tudor sources (for their own motives) all admit that Richard was backed by a much larger army than his opponent, the self-styled Earl of Richmond. For Tudor writers, this made Richmond's defeat of Richard III sound wonderful and almost miraculous! Moreover, a significant part of Henry's army comprised foreign invasion forces (French mercenaries), who are unlikely to have been well regarded by the native population. It is therefore arguable that, logically, Richard III should have won the battle at which he was killed.

Another noteworthy point is the fact that, despite receiving an appeal from the rebel invader (and future King Henry VII) – who also seems to have spent a sleepless night – the army of Lord Stanley refused to commit itself to Henry's side, but initially simply sat on the fence at Bosworth. Obviously, therefore, the leader of the Stanley contingent was by no means convinced, when the fighting started, that King Richard would lose the conflict. Indeed, he must have considered that there was a real possibility that Richard would win the battle. Presumably whichever of the Stanley brothers was in command of the Stanley contingent at Bosworth would therefore have brought his army in on the king's side if and when Richard's forces appeared to be winning. The Stanley commander only finally entered the battle on the side of the rebel invader when Richard III made his big mistake of embarking upon a fatal cavalry charge.

PART 6

Richard III's Dead Body

ἰὼ ἰὼ βασιλεῦ βασιλεῦ, πῶς σε δακρύσω;
φρενὸς ἐκ φιλίας τῖ ποτ᾽ εἴπω;
κεῖσαι δ᾽ἀράχνης ἐν ὑφάσματι τῷδ᾽
ἀσεβεῖ θαανάτῳ βίον ἐκπνεύων.

Alas king, alas king, how shall I mourn you?
What can I say to show that I care?
Thus you lie in a spider's web
Sacrilegiously slaughtered, your life breathed forth.
                    Aiskhylos, *Agamemnon* (trans. J. A-H.)

12

Burial Myths

Burton had spoken disrespectfully of King Richard ... saying that he was buried in a ditch like a dog.

James Gairdner[1]

For whatever reason Richard III decided to leave his commanding position on higher ground and personally lead a cavalry charge down into the marshy area where his opponent and second cousin was based; once he had made this decision the reigning king had condemned himself to defeat and death. He lost his horse and helmet, was hit on the top of his bare head by an enemy soldier – a blow which stunned him and possibly brought him to his knees – and was then dispatched by a violent cut to the back of his skull.

But his death did not end the battle. The greater part of the royal army was still in its commanding position on the higher ground, and many of his troops – including those led by the Earl of Northumberland – had not yet been engaged in the fighting at all. The rebel invasion forces therefore left Richard's body lying where it had fallen, and continued the fighting, moving in the direction of Dadlington.

Some time later, when the rebels had won, and the self-styled Earl of Richmond had transformed himself into the self-styled King Henry VII, he sent some of his soldiers to find the royal body. The new king needed this in order to assert his own claim to the throne. When Richard's body was found it was naked, presumably having been stripped of its valuable clothing and royal armour by battlefield looters. The body was placed over the back of a horse. Some of Henry's soldiers – as victorious soldiers still do today – wanted to inflict wounds on the dead body, but Henry VII quickly put a stop to that. For him it was vital that the identity of Richard III's corpse should not be compromised by post-mortem injuries.

1. Richard III's Spanish great-great-grandfather, Pedro I, King of Castile (from a gold *gran dobla* of 1360, by courtesy of Luis Garcia, under GNU free documentation licence). Should this king be remembered as 'Pedro the Cruel' or 'Pedro the Just'? Was he the wicked ancestor from whom Richard inherited his evil character, or were the reputations of both kings ruined by usurpers who overthrew them?

2. Images of Richard as Duke of Gloucester, in about 1475. *Left:* the Barnard Castle Church image, courtesy of Margaret Watson. *Right:* the Wavrin image, a nineteenth-century engraving, after a miniature from the copy of his *Chronicle* which Wavrin presented to Edward IV.

Above: 3. The 'Paston' Portraits of Edward IV and Richard III, *c.* 1520, courtesy of the Society of Antiquaries of London.

Left: 4. The 'Broken Sword' Portrait of Richard III, *c.* 1530, courtesy of the Society of Antiquaries of London.

Left: 5. Mohammed Reza Shah Pahlavi of Iran, from an Iranian 20 Rials banknote of 1969.

Right: 6. Eva María Duarte de Perón.

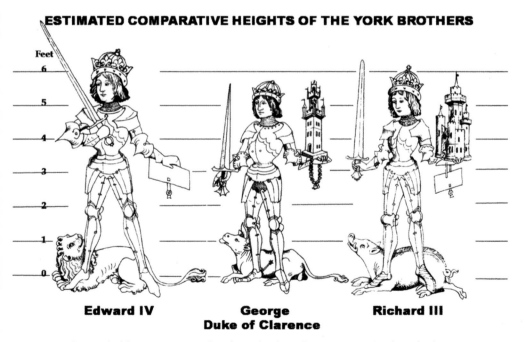

7. The probable comparative heights of Edward IV, George, Duke of Clarence, and Richard III.

Above: 8. Richard III seems to have resembled his father in terms of his features, as is shown by this comparison of his modern facial reconstruction (*left*, courtesy of the Richard III Society) with a portrait of his father, Richard, Duke of York (*right*, redrawn by the author after BL MS Royal 15 E VI, fol. 3).

Below left: 9. Anthony Woodville, 2nd Earl Rivers (nineteenth-century engraving after BL MS. 265, fo. 6).

Below right: 10. A caricature of William, Lord Hastings, in the guise of a pig, redrawn from a contemporary marginal illustration accompanying an account of his 1483 execution in the register of the Abbot of St Albans, © M. Hanif.

ANTONY WIDVILLE EARL RIVERS.

Above left: 11. The Infanta Isabel of Castile (later Queen Isabel la Católica): in 1469 she was mentioned as a prospective bride of Richard, Duke of Gloucester.

Above right: 12. The other women in the picture: Top left: Anne of Warwick (from the Rous Roll); top right: Elizabeth of York (nineteenth-century engraving); bottom left: Isabel of Aragon; bottom right: Joana of Portugal (both redrawn by Geoffrey Wheeler, © G. Wheeler).

Below: 13. A nineteenth-century imaginary engraving showing 'Edward (*sic*) Duke of York parting from his mother'.

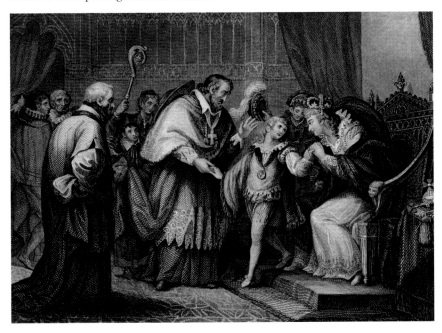

WESTERN CATHOLIC ROME POPE | **EASTERN ORTHODOX CONSTANTINOPLE PATRIARCHS**

Above right: 14. A nineteenth-century imaginary engraving of the alleged murder of the 'Princes in the Tower'.

Above left: 15. The Great Schism of 1054 had divided the Church into two parts. Richard III unquestionably belonged to the western, Catholic Church. He was in communion with Rome and faithful to the Pope.

Below: 16. The Talbots: Eleanor (centre – based on a facial reconstruction of the skull found at the Norwich Carmel), her sister, Elizabeth, Duchess of Norfolk (left – from Long Melford Church, Suffolk), and their father, the Earl of Shrewsbury (right – from his tomb effigy).

Bottom: 17. Facsimile of an autograph letter of King Richard III, reading 'My lorde Chaunceler we pray you in all hast to send to us a pardon under our Gret Seale to Sir Harry Wode preste &c & this shalbe yor warrant Ricardus Rex'. A note at the bottom right reads 'M[aster] Skypton sped this forth with ex[pediti]on Jo Omcots'.

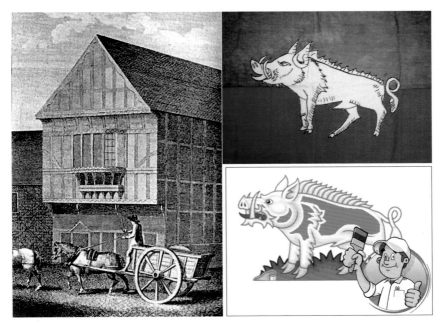

18. Elements of the Boar Inn mythology of Richard III. Left: a nineteenth-century engraving of the sixteenth-century Blue Boar Inn, Leicester; upper right: the alleged original inn sign – Richard III's White Boar emblem (from a modern banner made by Mary Talbot of the former Richard III Society Essex Group); lower right: allegedly the White Boar Inn sign was repainted as a blue boar, following Richard III's defeat at Bosworth.

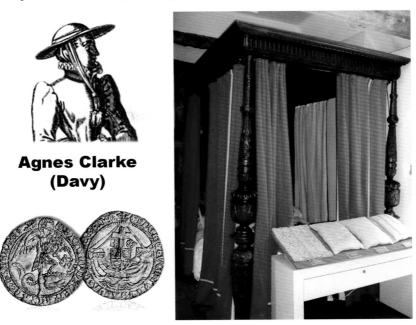

Agnes Clarke (Davy)

19. Elements of the story of how fifteenth-century gold coins – assumed to be 'Richard III's royal treasure' – were found hidden in a bed at the Blue Boar Inn by the innkeeper's wife about a century after the battle of Bosworth. This was taken as 'proof' that Richard III had slept there.

20. Part of the ruins of Leicester Castle, where King Richard III is known to have stayed when he visited Leicester in 1483.

RICHARD Y WHITE SURREY

21. Richard III and White Surrey, a modern image, © Frances Quinn.

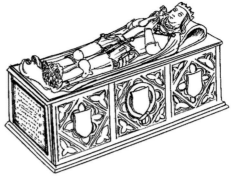

Left: 22. A nineteenth-century engraving of Sutton Cheney Church. The only connection between this church and Richard III stems from the 'Last Mass' myth invented by the Fellowship of the White Boar in the 1920s.

Right: 23. A tentative reconstruction of Richard III's royal tomb of 1495, commissioned by the author in 2007, © Geoffrey Wheeler.

24. The author's suggested appearance of the Leicester Greyfriars Church, first published in 2010, before the excavation of the site. The yellow pit now added beneath the last bay of the choir marks the site where Richard III's grave was discovered.

Left: 25. What the choir of the Leicester Greyfriars Church might have looked like today, if it had survived. A reconstruction based upon a photograph of the choir of the Norwich Blackfriars Church.

Right: 26. John Speede, a leading (if unintentional) Richard III mythologist.

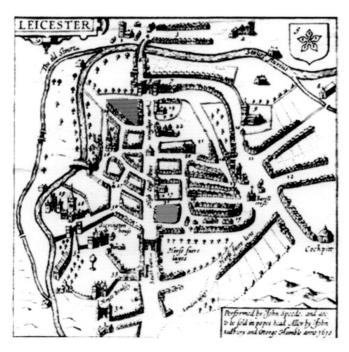

27. John Speede's map of Leicester, *c.* 1610. The red triangle marks the Dominican Priory (Blackfriars) site, where Speede mistakenly sought (and failed to find) Richard III's gravesite – leading to his story that the body had been exhumed at the Dissolution. The green area is the real Greyfriars site, which Speede did not mark or visit, but where Richard III's gravesite was still marked by an inscribed column in the first quarter of the seventeenth century.

This plaque, originally erected by Mr. B. Broadbent in 1856 on the nearby site of the Austin Friars, records the 17th century tradition, now generally discredited, that at the dissolution of the monasteries the body of King Richard III was disinterred from his tomb at the Greyfriars in Leicester and thrown into the River Soar.

Richard III Society 2005

28. The 'Body in the River' legend. Centre: a nineteenth-century engraving of the original Bow Bridge; right: the Victorian Bow Bridge Plaque erected by Mr B. Broadbent in 1856 (the arrow and circle show its original position); upper left: the author's new Bow Bridge plaque of 2005, erected through the Richard III Society and with the permission of Leicester City Council.

Right: 29. The author's discovery of Richard III's mtDNA as reported by the *East Anglian Daily Times* and the University of Essex *Wyvern* Magazine in 2005, © *East Anglian Daily Times* / Archant Suffolk.

Below: 30. Dr Turi King taking a DNA sample from Michael Ibsen on 24 August 2012, © M. Hanif.

31. Joy Ibsen's first DNA letter to the author.

32. Richard III as depicted on the Coventry Tapestry, *circa* 1500, courtesy of St Mary's Guildhall/ Coventry City Council.

Above: 33. The 'Paston Portrait' (left, courtesy of the Society of Antiquaries of London) and the 'Leicester Portrait' (right).

Right: 34. Left: Richard III Sunglasses. Right: A bar of Richard III Chocolate. © M. Hanif.

Bottom: 35. The Bosworth Battlefield Centre Stone Coffin.

36. The Richard III 'Death Stone'.

37. Philippa Langley standing on the exact site of the alleged Richard III grave (actually a Saxon grave) at 70, George Street, Leicester, August 2012. © Philippa Langley.

38. Clearing the tarmac from the spot which proved to be Richard III's gravesite on 25 August 2012, © M. Hanif.

Left: 39. Recording the discovery of Richard III's grave and his remains, © M. Hanif.

Right: 40. A fifteenth-century brass, showing two corpses laid out with their hands crossed in roughly the same position as the hands of Richard III's remains.

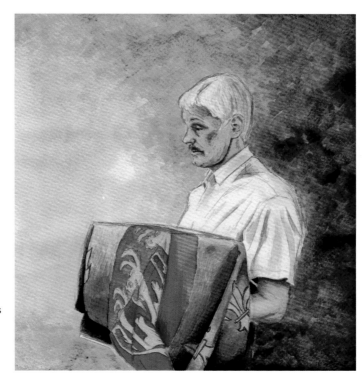

41. The author carrying the remains of Richard III from the Greyfriars site in September 2012, © Riikka Nikko.

42. Richard III's gravesite after his bones had been removed. The yellow peg marks the position of his head, © M. Hanif.

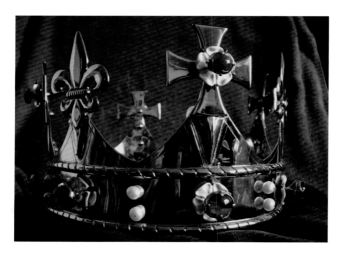

43. The funeral crown commissioned for Richard III by the author and made by George Easton. The crown is set with rubies, sapphires, emeralds and turquoises upon enamelled white roses, and also with pearls.

44. The rosary made donated by the author for burial with Richard III. The crucifix is a copy by George Easton of the 'Clare Cross', which may once have belonged to Richard III's mother.

Henry VII's army, with Richard III's corpse in its wake, made its way to Leicester, probably arriving in the early evening. On the new king's orders the dead king's remains were then put on display at a church in the Newarke, near Leicester Castle (where Henry himself was probably staying, in the very rooms in which his predecessor had slept before him). Although the present situation was somewhat unusual, it was by no means atypical for the dead body of a monarch to be displayed in this way. We know that, when Richard III's brother Edward IV had died, in April 1483, his naked corpse (with the genital region covered by a cloth) had been shown to the public for twelve hours in the Palace of Westminster, before it was prepared for burial.[2]

However, stories soon began to circulate that Richard III's body had been treated with a great deal of disrespect. Once again, the prime sources are the Crowland Chronicle continuator, and Polydore Vergil. The former reports that

> King Richard's body having been discovered among the dead
> ... many other insults were offered and after the body had been
> carried to Leicester with insufficient humanity (a rope being
> placed around the neck).[3]

Vergil later wrote,

> Meanwhile they took Richard's body to the Franciscan Priory in
> Leicester, stripped of all clothing and placed on a horse's back
> with the head, arms and legs hanging down on either side; a sorry
> sight by Hercules, but one worthy of the man's life; and there,
> after two days, he was buried in the ground without any funerary
> honours.[4]

Vergil's account is definitely slightly inaccurate, since it seems that Richard III's body was not taken directly to the Franciscan Priory, but to a church in the Newarke (see above). It would have been difficult to put the royal body on public display in a Franciscan Priory Church, only the nave of which would normally have been accessible to the laity.

The public display of Richard III's remains must have been arranged on the personal instructions of Henry VII. Since it was very important for the new king that the corpse should be easily recognisable, the remains may have been washed and the small facial cuts may have been pressed shut rather than being left as open wounds. It is unlikely, though, that the body was embalmed in any way, since in April 1483 Edward IV's corpse was only embalmed *after* its public display. In the case of Richard III his unembalmed body was probably displayed for two days and then buried without ever undergoing any process of preservation.

Subsequently, various fifteenth- and early sixteenth-century written accounts were produced, citing five different burial locations. One account (William Burton, York Records, 1491) stated that Richard was buried in a ditch, like a dog. Another (Jean Molinet, *c.* 1500) said that he was buried in an unidentified village church. A third (Diego de Valera, 1486) claimed that he was buried at an unnamed hermitage. A fourth account (Frowyk Chronicle, 1485) implied that he was buried in the church in Leicester's Newarke where his body had been publicly displayed. The fifth account named his burial site as the Franciscan Priory (Greyfriars) in Leicester.

There was always a slight weight of evidence in favour of the Leicester Greyfriars, since this was named as Richard's burial place by two independent sources: Polydore Vergil's slightly inaccurate account (see above), and an account written by John Rous, who moreover specified that Richard's remains had been interred in the choir (eastern end) of the Greyfriars Church. Nevertheless, controversy over the burial place continued well into the present century,[5] and was only finally resolved when the present writer first published a key sentence from a document in The National Archives which specified that a Nottingham alabaster man, Walter Hylton, should erect a tomb for the dead king 'in the Church of Friers in the town of leycestr where the bonys of Kyng Richard the iij[de] reste'.[6] I first published this sentence in the first (2010) edition of my book *The Last Days of Richard III*,[7] where I also argued for the first time that the priory church may have been dedicated to St Mary Magdalene.[8] However, my new evidence confirming that Richard was buried at the Franciscan Priory Church in Leicester was known to my colleague Philippa Langley (founder and leader of the Looking For Richard Project) some years before I published it in my book. Indeed, it comprised a key part of the argument used by her to persuade Leicester City Council to agree to the excavation of their Social Services Department car park in August 2012.

Of course there has been a great deal of controversy as to where Richard III himself hoped to be buried. There is absolutely no possibility that he would ever have contemplated Leicester as a potential site for his interment. Indeed, as we have seen, he hardly ever went there during his lifetime. Thus, the fact that his remains have spent some 500 years in the ground in Leicester, and now look set to spend the rest of time there, would probably have struck the king himself as a very ironic outcome. This end result is obviously based upon motives which had nothing whatever to do with seeking to ascertain and respect Richard III's own wishes.

However, there is also no evidence to suggest that Richard III ever intended to be buried at Westminster Abbey, beside his first wife, Anne of Warwick. The position he chose for Anne's grave allowed for no large royal tomb to be erected above it, and Anne was simply given a matrix with a representation of her as a 'brass'.

It is certainly possible that, during the years he spent in the north of England as Edward IV's lieutenant, Richard, then Duke of Gloucester, considered having his remains interred in York Minster. But of course no King of England was buried there, so in 1483, when he succeeded to the throne, Richard probably thought again. In a previous publication I backed a suggestion that, as king, he probably planned to be buried – together with his intended second wife – in the first bay on the south side of the altar at St George's Chapel, Windsor.[9] And I still feel that in 1483–85 this was probably Richard III's intention. Once he had ascended the throne 'Richard may have shared Edward [IV]'s concept of the new foundation [of St George's Chapel at Windsor Castle] as the mausoleum of the Yorkist dynasty. ... The suggestion has been made that he had Henry [VI] interred in the second bay of the south choir aisle because he had reserved the first bay as his own place of burial'.[10] Probably his plans were for a double royal tomb in this location, which would ultimately house both the remains of Richard himself, and those of his second queen, Joana – the intended mother of his successor.

It was only Richard III's death at the battle of Bosworth which prevented his plans for a second marriage from coming to fulfilment. One result of this was that his intended bride, Joana, never married. Instead, she became a religious. Many years after her death she was then beatified. Thus, instead of sharing Richard III's royal tomb at Windsor, Joana was given a splendid tomb/shrine in Portugal. It can still be seen today, at the Dominican convent of Aveiro. This raises the intriguing question of whether Joana's intended husband, King Richard III, should perhaps have been reinterred in 2015 beside his chosen and intended bride in Portugal, instead of in Leicester Cathedral!

In the event, reburial of Richard III at Aveiro was never proposed. But a number of alternatives to Leicester Cathedral were put forward during the period from 2012 to 2014 as possible reburial sites. Places mentioned included York Minster, Westminster Abbey,

St George's Chapel, Windsor, Fotheringhay Church, and Wingfield Church in Suffolk (all now Anglican Churches), and also the Dominican Priory of the Holy Cross in Leicester, Westminster Cathedral, and Clare Priory in Suffolk (Catholic).

If Richard ever expressed plans for his interment in writing, the most likely way to have done this would have been in his will. Unfortunately there is no surviving source that reports that on the eve of the battle of Bosworth Richard III made a will, and no text of any Ricardian will has survived. However, making a will before fighting a battle was common practice, at that period. It is therefore possible that the king did so. Of course, such a will would have addressed wider issues than that of the king's ultimate interment. Since Richard was the king, and was about to embark upon an important battle, with no direct heir in prospect, he may have felt the need to detail who should succeed to the throne.[11] It would be extremely interesting to be able to read Richard III's will, but no such document has come down to us. Surviving medieval wills are normally the official copies which were made when the wills were proved in the appropriate church court. But of course, even if he drafted one, no will of Richard III ever went through such a legal process.

The precise manner of Richard III's burial at the Franciscan Priory in Leicester has been clarified in some respects by the rediscovery of his remains. In other respects, however, new mythology has once again threatened to surface. Vergil suggests that the Franciscan friars themselves asked to bury the dead king's remains, and while this is certainly possible, given the order's relationship with the house of York, the truth in this respect remains uncertain.

What is clear from the burial as discovered in 2012 is that fact that the grave had evidently been dug (presumably by the friars themselves) before Richard's body arrived at the church – and therefore without the body having been measured. Presumably an average-sized grave was dug, but when Richard III's corpse arrived it proved to be of somewhat above average height. Thus the body had to be inserted in the grave with the head somewhat raised. Partly as a result of this, Dr Jo Appleby broke the king's skull with her mattock when extracting the remains in September 2012. The skull was lying higher in the ground than she had expected. In fact, the bones of Richard III should have been excavated and examined by Harriet Jacklyn of ULAS. Unfortunately she was ill at the time, so the work had to be passed to Dr Appleby of the University of Leicester.

Incidentally, we should, perhaps, note at this point that ULAS

(University of Leicester Archaeological Services) and the University of Leicester itself are – or were – distinct and separate bodies. ULAS is based at premises belonging to the University of Leicester's Centre for Excellence, and works closely with the university, but it is an independent business, and not a department of the university. The salaries of the archaeologists are not paid by the University of Leicester, and ULAS pays rent to the university for the premises occupied by the archaeological team.[12]

When found, Richard III's body lay with its hands crossed in the pelvic region. There has been some subsequent speculation that this may indicate that the dead king was buried with his hands tied together. In fact, there is no evidence to substantiate this theory. As can be very clearly seen from plate 39, the position of Richard's hands was one of the normal positions for hands in a fifteenth-century Christian burial. Even if the hands were indeed *tied* in this position, it is possible that this would have been simply to allow them to 'hold' a small and simple wooden cross, placed there by the friars, as the corpses depicted on the illustrated fifteenth-century brass are doing. That this position for the hands was a common one during the medieval period in general – and specifically in Leicester – is further proved by an illustration in the book *Visions of Ancient Leicester*.[13]

Earlier speculation sometimes suggested that the body was interred without any Christian burial rites. This was based upon a misinterpretation of the wording employed by Polydore Vergil. But, as the present writer argued in 2010, Vergil's wording merely meant that there was no solemn or royal funeral.[14] The idea of burial in a religious house but without religious rites, at this period, would have been incomprehensible and impossible. Fortunately, this point now appears to have been generally accepted.

About nine years after Richard's death, possibly for political reasons, Henry VII decided to create a royal tomb above his predecessor's interred remains.[15] We have no way of knowing whether the burial site had previously been marked in any formal way, but since the choir of the Franciscan Priory Church was paved with small encaustic tiles, and since it would have been very hard to replace all of these tiles in their original positions after Richard's interment, it is possible that the king's grave had always been marked in some way, even if only with an uninscribed slab of stone.

There has always been much debate regarding the precise appearance of the tomb installed in 1495. I have previously suggested that it may have resembled the surviving tomb of Richard III's brother-in-law, John de la Pole, Duke of Suffolk, at

Wingfield Church in Suffolk. I asked Geoffrey Wheeler to produce a reconstruction of the tomb's probable appearance (as I saw it) in 2007 (see plate 25).[16] After the discovery of Richard III's remains the University of Leicester commissioned artist Jill Atherton to produce an image of a less impressive tomb.[17] Given the surviving evidence of the cost, this version is probably less likely to be accurate. More recently the De Montfort University in Leicester produced an image of a very credible tomb design. Unfortunately, however, this latest reconstruction shows the tomb surmounted with a flat brass image of the dead king.[18] Since we know from surviving fifteenth-century sources that the tomb was topped by 'a picture of the king' in alabaster, that part of De Montfort University's otherwise very credible reconstruction appears to be inaccurate.

Whatever it really looked like, following its erection and inauguration, Richard III's royal tomb, together with its epitaph, then remained in place in the Franciscan Priory Church for forty-three years.

13

The Body in the River

Richard III ... may subsequently have been exhumed and thrown into the nearby River Soar after the Dissolution in 1538.
Richard Buckley, ULAS Exhumation Licence Request,
September 2012[1]

The next chapter in the history of Richard III's burial began in the 1530s, with Henry VIII's dissolution of the religious houses of England and Wales. In most cases the many burials contained in the churches and graveyards of the dissolved religious houses were left undisturbed. The number of burials recorded as having been moved by living relatives to other churches is very small indeed.

In Richard III's case, there were few close relatives around to rescue his remains when the Franciscan friars were expelled from the Leicester house in 1538. One of his closest living relatives was his niece Margaret of Clarence, Countess of Salisbury. But she probably had other things to think about in 1538, and if she had started trying to rescue remains of deceased relatives from religious houses her list would have been a very long and costly one. And of course, like all members of the royal house of York, normally she would have been far from Leicester in geographical terms.

Once the friars had left Leicester, and the lead and woodwork had been removed from their former church roof for sale, the superstructure of Richard's royal tomb probably remained for some time in the roofless ruin of the former choir. However, the Nottingham alabaster of which the tomb was made was a soft stone which does not cope well with exposure to the elements. Bit by bit the tomb would have been destroyed by rain and frost.

Beneath the decaying alabaster of its royal tomb, the body of the dead king remained underground where it had been buried on 25

August 1485. Even before the excavation of 2012 took place, the available evidence strongly suggested that this was so. Towards the end of the sixteenth century the Greyfriars' site was acquired by the Herrick family. Robert Herrick, a former mayor of Leicester, constructed a house and laid out a garden on the eastern part of the site, where once the choir of the priory church had stood. Here in 1612 Christopher Wren (future dean of Windsor and father of the architect of St Paul's Cathedral), who was then tutor to Robert Herrick's nephew, saw and recorded 'a handsome stone pillar, three foot high', bearing the inscription 'Here lies the body of Richard III, some time King of England'.[2] This pillar had been erected by Robert Herrick when he redeveloped the site, in order to preserve the location of Richard's grave.

The subsequent fate of this 'handsome stone pillar' is unknown. 'It may not have survived the taking of Leicester by the Royalists [during the English Civil War], when desperate fighting took place near St Martin's Church [Cathedral] which was immediately north of the Grey Friars' grounds'.[3] However, Robert Herrick's former garden now comprises three Leicester car parks. In one of them, surviving traces of Herrick's garden design were discovered beneath the tarmac in 2012.

But in spite of the fact that King Richard III's gravesite was known and recorded at the beginning of the seventeenth century, that same century also saw the development of one of the most extraordinary Ricardian legends. The earliest version of this myth was published in 1611 by the mapmaker John Speede.

The slaine body of the usurping Tyrant, all tugged and torne, naked, and not so much as a clout left to cover his shame, was trussed behind *Blanch Seint-Leger* [*sic*] (or *White Bore*, a Pursevant at Armes,) like a hogge or Calfe, his head and Armes hanging on the one side of the horse, and his legges on the other, and all besprinckled with mire and bloud, was so brought into *Leicester*, and there for a miserable spectacle the space of two days lay naked and unburied, his remembrance being as odious to all, as his person deformed and loathsome to be looked upon: for whose further despite, the white Bore his cognizance was torne downe from every Signe, that his monument might perish, as did the monies of *Caligula*, which were all melted by the decree of the Senate:[4] Lastly his body without all funeral solemnity was buried in the Gray-Friers Church of that city. But King Henry his Successor, of a princely disposition, caused afterward his Tombe to bee made with a picture of Alablaster [*sic*], representing his person, and to be set up in the same church, which at the suppression of that Monastery [*sic*] was pulled downe, and utterly defaced; since when his grave overgrown with nettles and weedes, is very obscure and not to be found. Only the stone chest wherin his corpse lay is now made a drinking trough for horses at a common Inne, and retaineth the onely memory of this Monarches greatnesse. His body also (as tradition hath delivered) was borne out of the City and contemptuously bestowed under the end of *Bow-Bridge*.[5]

It is noteworthy that Speede does not say that Richard III's body was thrown into the river, but rather that it was reburied under one end of Bow Bridge. Subsequently, however, his story gradually developed into the lurid and popular myth of 'the body in the river'. This proclaimed that at the time of the Dissolution, Richard's body was dug up and dragged through the streets of Leicester by a jeering mob, before finally being cast into the River Soar.

The development of 'the body in the river' myth was a slow process. As I have shown previously, in the 1620s, Leicester inhabitants and their tourist visitors were apparently unaware of this myth.[6] Nevertheless, the story gradually developed and spread. It probably sounded consistent with the accounts of Richard III's evil reputation propagated by the Tudor propaganda machine. Moreover, in seventeenth- and eighteenth-century Leicester it also supported the display of an old – and empty – stone coffin in which Richard was then reputed to have been interred at the Greyfriars'. This coffin, dug up, perhaps, from the site of a religious house (maybe Leicester's former abbey), was chiefly employed by its new owner as a horse trough. But despite the obvious fact that the object actually dated from many centuries prior to the time of King Richard, the Leicester innkeeper – with his eyes on possible profit – not only used it for watering horses, but also displayed it to eighteenth-century tourists as 'Richard III's coffin'.

The existence of the (empty) coffin, combined with the fact that an existing tradition linked Richard III with Bow Bridge (see above, chapter 10), gradually made the 'body in the river' myth sound credible, and it became very well known. By the eighteenth century, both coffin and legend were widely reported. Then in the nineteenth century a local businessman, Mr B. Broadbent, who, with the best possible motives, wished to commemorate Richard III and his association with Leicester, unfortunately erected a large stone plaque by Bow Bridge which recorded in a very prominent way the notion that Richard III's remains now lay in the river. Thus the tale of 'the body in the river' became so widely accepted that a skull of unknown age, dredged up from the Soar, and exhibiting damage which was thought to be attributable to sword cuts, could not fail to be hailed, on its appearance, as 'King Richard's skull'. Although Carbon–14 dating subsequently showed that the skull dated from before the Norman Conquest, this did not kill off the 'body in the river' myth.[7]

Meanwhile, the king's authentic grave site, once well known and clearly marked, had quietly become lost. What exactly happened at the Leicester Greyfriars is unknown. As we have already seen, John Speede (widely followed by incautious later writers) stated that Richard's tomb 'was pulled downe and utterly defaced'.[8] But, sadly, Speede's account was completely unreliable. His map of Leicester shows clearly that, when he searched for Richard III's Greyfriars gravesite, he went to the wrong place. Instead of the Franciscan Priory he visited the site of the former Dominican Priory (Blackfriars). It is therefore not surprising that he could find no trace of King Richard's grave. The fact that Speede wrongly labelled the Greyfriars site on his map of Leicester had been noted by earlier historians, but none of them made any connection between this important error and Speede's story of the exhumation of Richard III's remains. Not until the present writer made this connection was the plausibility of Leicester's 'body in the river myth' effectively discounted.

My research into this myth started in 2004, when I was commissioned by the BBC to write an article on the story for their 'Local Legends' website. Following my research, and the conclusions I reached, I asked Leicester City Council whether the misleading Broadbent plaque by Bow Bridge could be taken down. They said that it could not, but that a small new plaque could be erected beside it, stating that the nineteenth-century plaque was in error. Through the Richard III Society (of whose executive committee I was then a member) I had the small new plaque erected in 2005. But that by no means quashed the myth. Sir Peter Soulsby, then Mayor of Leicester, told me in 2012 that he was familiar with the large Broadbent plaque, but had never noticed my adjacent small one!

Nevertheless, in public lectures from 2007 onwards, and in print in 2010, I continued to seek to show that the 'body in the river' story was nothing but a myth, and that the logical conclusion was that the remains of King Richard III still lay on the Greyfriars site, where he was buried in 1485. Philippa Langley was convinced – and delighted by – my evidence. But it had very little impact in

Leicester. There, on the morning when the Greyfriars dig started (25 August 2012) I was told by local inhabitants that 'you won't find him – he's in the river!' Even in September 2012 – when the bones that proved to be Richard III's had already been found – Richard Buckley, leader of the ULAS archaeologists (who had finally, and after much effort, been persuaded by Philippa Langley to exhume these bones) phrased the official application as follows:

A research excavation is underway to investigate the remains of Leicester's Franciscan Friary and also potentially locate the burial place of Richard III whose remains were interred here in 1485, *although those may subsequently have been exhumed and thrown into the nearby River Soar after the Dissolution in 1538.*[9]

14

The Mythology of Rediscovery

The discovery of Richard's remains was due to the meticulous research by the historian, Dr. John Ashdown-Hill, in his book *The Last Days of King Richard III*.
Judgement of Lady Justice Hallett and Mr Justices Ouseley and Haddon-Cave, High Court of Justice, Queen's Bench Division, 23 May 2014[1]

In his well-known study of Richard III, Charles Ross wrote,

During Henry VIII's reign, the Franciscan convent was dissolved, the bones were thrown out, and the coffin became a horse-trough outside the white horse inn. ... With the problematic exception of Edward V, Richard III is the only English king since 1066 whose remains are not now enshrined in a suitably splendid and accredited royal tomb.[2]

As the judgement of a supposedly academic historian, Ross' statement is really quite amazing. Apparently he simply accepted the mythology of the 'body in the river' without submitting it to any investigation. He also unquestioningly accepted the unlikely story that a stone coffin from the wrong period had been used to inter Richard III's remains prior to becoming a horse trough. Possibly this raises serious questions about some of his other conclusions!

Certainly Ross' claim that Richard III was possibly the only post-Conquest English king 'whose remains are not now enshrined in a suitably splendid tomb' is absolute nonsense. Indeed his claim was very effectively refuted by Bill White, of the Museum of London, in 2007.[3] As White points out, Henry II and Richard I may have surviving tombs at Fontevrault Abbey in France, but their bodies do not lie in these tombs, or beneath them. In fact their remains are lost – dug up during the French Revolution. William II's remains are thought to have been scattered during the English Civil War, and the tomb of his brother, Henry I, at Reading Abbey, was lost at the Dissolution, just like that of Richard III. White gives other examples (though even he omits from his list the later case of James II). Overall, therefore, White's very convincing argument is that the Richard III exhumation myth simply grew and spread as yet another sign that this king was so reviled that his grave was 'singled out for special destruction'.

During the twenty years or so before their rediscovery, there were also various (and conflicting) reports in the *Leicester Mercury* about the likely fate of Richard III's remains. On 6 October 1993, Adrian Berry reported that Leicester historian David Baldwin thought the remains probably still lay somewhere under the city centre. However, Baldwin also considered that if a body was ever found it would be virtually impossible to identify it.

About eighteen months later, the traditional story of the 'body in the river' resurfaced, when the *Leicester Mercury* contradicted its earlier version and published the following report:

> Richard was buried in a stone coffin in the chapel of the Grey Friars Fransiscan (*sic*) Abbey (*sic*), which was sited near the present cathedral. The defeated king was not allowed to rest in peace though. The story goes that Richard's body was later dug up and hurled unceremoniously into the River Soar from Bow Bridge. But the story does not end there. Almost 400 years later in 1830, when foundations were being excavated for a new Bow Bridge, two skulls were found. One had a gash across the cranium. Later carbon dating proved the owner would have lived about 1500. Was this the skull of Richard III, the last King of England to lead his troops into battle? We will never know for sure.[4]

In 2002, Adam Wakelin published both versions of the story. First he gave an extensive account of no fewer than three sets of remains which had been found in the River Soar and which had been thought to be possible bones of Richard III. However, he then went on to reiterate the alternative version.

> Historian David Baldwin has grave doubts whether Richard III is even in the Soar. The University of Leicester expert argues it is far more likely his remains lie somewhere *close to the former NatWest Bank in Greyfriars Lane*, the site of his original tomb.

... 'It is my opinion that he is still there, *somewhere under those well trodden streets towards St Martins*,' said Mr Baldwin. 'We will never be certain, of course, unless we excavate the whole area. I don't think there is much prospect of finding him, but you never know. Stranger things have happened'.[5]

David Baldwin was clearly focussing attention on Greyfriars Lane and the vicinity of the former NatWest Bank. But subsequent excavation in the vicinity of the former bank building found absolutely nothing.

In 2005, the version of the story current in Leicester was definitely that Richard III had been thrown into the river. In May of that year, the *Leicester Mercury* published a report in which Ben Farmer wrote,

> Legend has it that the king's body was dug up from his tomb in Greyfriars, and flung in the Soar by an angry mob, fifty years after his death in 1485 on Bosworth Field. At least two skulls or sets of bones are said to belong to the king. One set was taken from a Leicester Museum in the 19th century and another is thought to be in the hands of a private collector.[6]

Ben Farmer's 11 May 2005 *Leicester Mercury* report was inspired by, and focussed upon, the announcement of the recent discovery of Richard III's mtDNA sequence by the present writer. Farmer was speculating that the mtDNA sequence which I had revealed might now be able to prove that the remains found in the River Soar were not those of Richard III. But despite my discovery of the king's mtDNA, there was still no thought in Leicester, in 2005, of excavating for Richard III's remains on his original burial site.

Outside of Leicester, however, such a project was already being promoted. Philippa Langley and I had not actually met at that time, but we were already in touch through our mutual membership of the Richard III Society. And in 2005, as a result of my discoveries in respect of 'the body in the river' myth, and of the king's mtDNA, Philippa urged me to propose to the television programme *Time Team* a project for the excavation of the Social Services Department car park in Leicester. Although nothing had as yet been published on our work in this area, both Philippa and I had already decided by 2005, for different reasons, that the northern area of the Social Services car park was the right place to look.

My motivation for this belief was based upon my knowledge of medieval English priories of the mendicant orders (including the Franciscans), which were very standard in their layout, and which typically chose to build their churches as close as possible to a major highway because of their obligation to preach to the laity.[7] However, even six years later, my arguments were contested by ULAS. During my discussions with Richard Buckley, I found it hard to persuade him that the church would have stood on the northern side of the site. This was during the summer of 2011, while Philippa Langley and I were in Leicester for the ground penetrating radar survey of the Social Services Department car park which the Looking For Richard Project had commissioned.

Richard Buckley kept referring to the tentative reconstruction of the Greyfriars site which he and his colleagues had then recently published in *Visions of Ancient Leicester*. This showed the priory church on the *south* side of the site. But the image published by Buckley and his colleagues was worrying in several respects. Not only was the priory church on the wrong side of the site, in my opinion; it was also a very abnormal and improbable reconstruction of a medieval English priory church building belonging to a mendicant order. The published image showed no choir and no *ambulacrum* (or slype).[8]

Several years earlier, in 2005, as Philippa Langley suggested, I had contacted *Time Team*, sending them a full written outline of the proposed project, together with a photograph of the Social Services Department car park showing the area in which I was suggesting that we would find the remains of the priory church. This 2005 photograph was subsequently published in the first edition of my book *The Last Days of Richard III* (plate 29), with the caption,

> The Social Services Department car park which occupies part of the Leicester Greyfriars' site today. Richard III's remains probably still lie somewhere beneath this tarmac.

Unfortunately the *Time Team* television project was based upon a standard format of using of only three days for an excavation. Although they were very interested in the idea which I had put to them, *Time Team* quite correctly considered that three days would probably be insufficient to carry out a proper search for Richard III's remains.

Subsequently, in 2009, Philippa Langley invited me to lead a study day on the fate of Richard III's remains in Edinburgh for the Scottish Branch of the Richard III Society, of which she was the secretary. As a result of this, at our lunch at the Cramond Inn, she formally founded the Looking For Richard Project (which was the body ultimately responsible for the discovery of the remains of King Richard III in August 2012). Shortly after this, at Philippa's suggestion I wrote to the University of Leicester Archaeological Services (ULAS) to try to interest them in the project. My letter received no reply.

Philippa then took over the task of trying to interest Leicester in the search for Richard III. This proved a very difficult and uphill struggle, but eventually, as the world now knows, she succeeded. The actual excavation was carried out by ULAS (the University of Leicester Archaeological Services) who, as we have seen, were not formally part of the university itself, but a commercial enterprise, housed in university premises. ULAS was paid for this work by Philippa Langley (on behalf of the Looking For Richard Project). Philippa had a written agreement with ULAS which is published in full in *Finding Richard III, the Official Account*.[9] This agreement was put together over four separate amended versions by Buckley and Langley. Unfortunately, however, in the end many aspects of the written agreement were not honoured by ULAS.

The official lead archaeologist on the actual dig was Richard Buckley, who, however, had little faith in the idea that the remains of Richard III would be found – as shown by his famous remark about eating his hat if the quest for Richard proved successful. Although he was an experienced archaeologist, Buckley was not a specialist in the medieval period, and apparently had little precise knowledge of the layout of medieval friaries, as his published reconstruction of the Greyfriars had already shown (see above). Prior to the start of the excavation, it had been hard to convince him that the church was likely to have stood on the northern side of the site. It also required some effort to persuade him to apply for the exhumation of the remains of Richard III, when what ultimately proved to be the king's lower leg bones were found in Trench 1 on the very first day of the dig.

Indeed, the practical leader of the excavation was generally Matthew Morris. Buckley was not always on site in person, because he was then reconstructing his own kitchen, having allocated the three week period of the dig in August–September 2012 to undertake this domestic task. Thus he was not present when the leg bones which later proved to belong to Richard III were first uncovered. Nor was he there when the rest of the royal remains were exposed, a week later.

Curiously, when the 2012 dig, commissioned and funded by the Looking For Richard Project, finally got under way, yet another intriguing Leicester myth about Richard III's burial surfaced. The following account of this new story was recorded as follows by Philippa Langley:

The king had been exhumed in the Social Services car park on 4–5

September. On Sunday 9 September 2012, with the Greyfriars dig closed for a day, and the DSP television team finally able to go home and take their first break from filming, I was taken to the site of the burial of another fallen warrior.

Two retired builders had approached me on the second day of the dig, Sunday 26 August, when the Looking For Richard Project team was in Castle Gardens doing interviews for the Dave Andrews' History Show on Radio Leicester. 'K' and 'A' knew I was looking for Richard, and believed they might know the whereabouts of the king's grave. I was intrigued. They were concerned that they might be prosecuted for what they were about to tell me so I agreed not to know their names.

In 1999, whilst excavating the foundations of a new block of flats in the north of the city, a burial had been uncovered. It was, they said, at the same time as the total eclipse. Approximately ten feet (3m) down they found a heavy slate coffin with the skeletal remains of a horse. The excavator had taken away most of the horse's remains, but left the head. On opening the coffin the builders found the skeletal remains of what they presumed was a man. He had a sword, and his right arm was crossed up to his left shoulder where he was still holding his wooden shield. The shield had an acorn design in the centre.

K and A believed that relatives of King Richard had come to Leicester, dug up his body in the church of the Grey Friars, and reburied him, with his horse, in this new place. It was a great local legend that I had never heard before, but it didn't sound like a fifteenth century burial and, I reasoned, why would relatives dig up Richard only to rebury him a few miles away. It sounded more like John Speede's River Soar story from 1611. I asked if the discovery site was a former church. Yes, they said, it had been a chapel.

'I checked with Richard Buckley the following day. He confirmed it sounded like a Saxon burial. So K and A picked me up from the Belmont Hotel on Sunday 9, and took me to 70 George Street, Leicester. It was a small, modern development of two storey red brick town flats. In the centre of the yard, on the south side of the property by the front door, is the exact site of the burial. The shield was taken by one of the builders, but the sword and horse's head were left in situ. The builders had also filmed the burial before placing a large concrete slab on top of the slate coffin to protect it. Sadly it seems the videotape is now lost. Photographs of the location were taken and passed to Richard Buckley for the burial to be placed on the archaeological register. Perhaps one day, this left-handed Saxon warrior may also be recovered.

15

The DNA Link

The academic life has ceased to be about learning. It's now all about raising funds and doing deals.

Simon Brett, *Blood at the Bookies*, 2008, p. 131

My discovery of Richard III's mtDNA sequence took place in 2004. My genealogical research was originally not directly connected with King Richard himself, but was related to possible remains of his sister Margaret of York, Duchess of Burgundy, which had been found in Belgium. At the request of colleagues in Belgium, and with the aim of attempting to establish whether any one of three sets of female remains which had been found in the general vicinity of the tomb of Richard III's sister Margaret, Duchess of Burgundy, really were the remains of the duchess:

a) I performed the difficult task of tracing a line of female descent from Richard III's eldest sister, Anne, to the present day
b) I persuaded the living female line descendant I had traced to give a DNA sample
c) in 2007, with her permission, I published a clear mtDNA sequence for Richard III and his siblings

Naturally, given that it relied upon one single line of living descent which I had traced, I stated very clearly in my own publication of this discovery that the mtDNA sequence which I had revealed still required confirmation from other sources if and when possible.[1] Indeed, with the kind help of the Ashmolean Museum in Oxford, and of the Catholic University of Leuven, I then attempted to confirm the mtDNA sequence using strands of Edward IV's hair. However, that attempt proved unsuccessful, owing to contamination of the hair sample as a result of excessive handling in the past. I was therefore still seeking a second source to confirm the mtDNA sequence in 2012, when the Greyfriars dig took place.

Nevertheless, the Royal Archaeological Circle of the Belgian town of Mechelen,[2] the Archaeological Department of Mechelen and the Department of Human Genetics of the Catholic University of Leuven all had no difficulty in accepting my discovery – and its status – as and when I presented it to them. Thus they used the DNA sequence which my research had produced in an attempt to identify possible remains of Richard III's sister Margaret of York, Duchess of Burgundy, found in the remains of the Franciscan Priory (*de minderbroeders*) in Mechelen.[3] Subsequently, another British archaeologist – at Tewkesbury Abbey – also welcomed my discovery, and contacted me in 2006, seeking to use the DNA sequence I had revealed to clarify the truth as to whether the bones preserved in Tewkesbury's Clarence Vault really were those of Richard III's brother George, Duke of Clarence.[4]

Ultimately a second living source for the mtDNA sequence of Richard III and his siblings was found by the University of Leicester. This confirmed the mtDNA sequence which I had originally discovered. Both living sources were then used by Dr Turi King, geneticist of the University of Leicester, whose admirable hard work then succeeded in extracting mtDNA from the bones found in the Greyfriars' car park, and in proving that the mtDNA of the bones matched that of the two independent living lines of female descent from Richard III's eldest sister.

Of course, use of mtDNA in this way in a historical context is never the same as the forensic use of DNA. While the latter can absolutely prove or disprove the identity of a criminal – or of a victim – the use of DNA over a five-century time gap (as in the case of Richard III) can only *disprove* identity (if it reveals a mismatch). Matching mtDNA does not, by itself, prove the identity of the individual whose remains have been found. It merely shows that the person belonged to a certain family line. However, in the case of the remains found on the Greyfriars site in Leicester the mtDNA match (together with the rarity of the group to which it belonged) coupled with the mass of supporting circumstantial evidence, combined to offer very convincing proof of the identity of the remains found.

Unfortunately some historians and others have nevertheless questioned the identification of the Leicester bones – thereby risking inaugurating yet another new piece of Ricardian mythology.

However, when I originally did my research on the mtDNA living link in 2004–05, I also investigated the possibility that another member of the same female line of descent as Richard III might possibly have been buried in Leicester and that the remains of such a relative, if found, could then be mistaken for the remains of the king. The results of my research in this area are rather complex, but they are published here for the first time in full (see appendix 1, below). This evidence shows convincingly that most of Richard III's known female-line relatives could not possibly be identified with the remains found in Leicester in August 2012. My previously unpublished evidence in this respect therefore fully supports the identification of the Leicester bones as the remains of King Richard III.

Another point which is not, perhaps, widely known is the fact that my work on Richard III's DNA did not focus exclusively on the female line and mtDNA. I also highlighted the Somerset family as potential living bearers of the Plantagenet Y-chromosome. I did this for the first time in 2006, at my talk on the discovery of Richard III's mtDNA sequence, given before HRH the Duke of Gloucester, and also in conversation with His Royal Highness afterwards. I published the same point in 2010, in my book *The Last Days of Richard III*.[5] And in 2012 I drew the attention of Dr Turi King to this connection (see appendix 2). Unlike my work on Richard III's mtDNA (which revealed the hitherto unknown royal descent of Joy Ibsen and her children in 2004) I do not claim, and have never claimed, to have *discovered* a potential living Plantagenet Y-chromosome link. The theoretical line of descent of the Somerset family was, and has always been, very well known to genealogists (unlike the female-line descent of Joy Ibsen from Anne of York, Duchess of Exeter, which was unknown – even by Joy Ibsen and her family – until I revealed it). But from the well-documented putative male-line royal descent of the Somerset family, I extrapolated the fact that living male members of that family might potentially be able to reveal the Plantagenet Y-chromosome, and I publicised this fact from 2006 onwards.

The fact that I was the first person to highlight the possibility that male members of the Somerset family could potentially reveal details of the Plantagenet Y-chromosome is significant. It reinforces the wider fact that I introduced science into the search for Richard III, and it demonstrates that I did this in more than one way. Subsequent claims of discovery of the Y-chromosome genealogical link by staff of the University of Leicester have to be assessed and evaluated in the light of my earlier publication of this point.

An example of the claim now advanced on this front by the

University of Leicester can be found in the following statement published by Morris and Buckley.

> There are no direct all-male lines of descent from Richard III or his brothers. The last direct male descendant of the House of York was Richard III's nephew Edward, Earl of Warwick who was executed for treason in 1499.[6] However, by tracing Richard III's family back four generations to Edward III (1312–77) an alternative all-male line of descent can be traced down through the Lancastrian side of the Plantagenet family, through John of Gaunt (1340–99) and his descendants, the Beauforts and the Somersets. Research of this line by Professor Kevin Schürer has identified a number of living male descendants of Henry Somerset, fifth Duke of Beaufort (1744–1803), whose Y-chromsome DNA should be consistent with Richard III's.[7]

Although the University of Leicester has now published its Y-chromosome results,[8] the precise human sources from which the necessary samples were obtained remain anonymous – merely defined in the paper as SOM 1 – SOM 5. This makes it impossible to determine precisely how the list of names and addresses of members of the Somerset family living in the UK, in Australia and in South Africa, which I supplied to Dr King in September 2012 (see appendix 2), relates to the actual sources used by the university for its Y-chromosome analysis. Nevertheless, the occurrence of the name Fitzroy among certain Somerset family members listed both in the university's family tree and among some of the individuals named in my list is potentially significant. It may well imply that the sources used by the university were closely related to those members of the Somerset family whom I had brought to their attention in September 2012.

The revelation that the Y-chromosome of living Somersets does not match that found in the bones of Richard III – and indeed, does not always match that of other supposed living Somersets! – is intriguing. It confirms that documented males lines of descent do not always correspond with biological male lines of descent. It also suggests that the Duke of Beaufort was perhaps well-advised to decline my invitation to give a DNA sample in 2006. Of course, the supposed Plantagenet descent of the Somersets was always known to pass through two illegitimacies. It now seems that there may have been more than two. Alternatively, one of the two may have been misrepresented. In fact, John of Gaunt's paternity of John Beaufort has long been disputed by some historians and genealogists.

However, it is sad – and rather worrying – that a dispute over issues relating to DNA discoveries associated with the finding of Richard III's remains now comprises a significant element of a new and rather depressing modern addition to the traditional Ricardian mythology. This new element is the apparent need, in some quarters, to claim total 'ownership' of Richard III in every possible way. This need appears to spring from the desperate requirement of modern academic institutions to acquire kudos, and credit (in both senses of that word).

PART 7

Kudos, Fantasies and Profit

I'll eat my hat if we find Richard III in a car park!
Richard Buckley, 2012[1]

16

The post-2012 Leicester Edition
of Richard III

> Cool, impersonal, take it or leave it
> Vestal virgins open the shrine.
> Shuffling pilgrims, hot and sweaty
> Pass through the portals at five quid a time.
>   Margaret Cornish, 'Conducted Tour'

Post 2012 actions in Leicester relating to publicity about Richard III and the rediscovery of his remains represent rather worrying developments in the ongoing saga of the mythology of Richard III. In 2013 the University of Leicester arranged a press conference to confirm officially that the remains of Richard III had been found. Although this press conference included employees of the university who had played no role whatsoever in the finding of the remains, members of the Looking For Richard Project, without whom the discovery would never have been made, were excluded.

Subsequently, Leicester City Council opened a temporary exhibition at the Leicester Guildhall. This exhibition also excluded all mention of the role of the Looking For Richard Project. Following complaints from members of the public – who knew better, having seen the Channel 4 television documentary *The King in the Car Park* – Sarah Levitt, Leicester City Council's Head of Arts and Museums, told the present writer that this lack of mention 'in no way reflects our view, which is that we hold both yourself and Philippa in the highest regard, and we fully acknowledge the all work [*sic*] that you have done over so many years in this area ... sadly ... you were in the last panel but in all squeeze [*sic*] to get the news conference information in we had to sacrifice you! ... when we redo that panel soon we can put you back and also Philippa as "originators of the quest". This will be for late May but we will keep you posted.'[2] In fact, however, nothing was done that summer. Indeed, it was not until October – ironically, shortly before the temporary Guildhall exhibition was closed – that the corrections to the display were made.

The permanent Leicester Richard III Visitor Centre which replaced the temporary Guildhall exhibition was supposed to include material prepared by members of the Looking For Richard Project. But at the last minute, shortly before opening, this material was significantly edited by the University of Leicester, post deadline and without our knowledge or consent. A return to the original account has subsequently been formally agreed with Leicester City Council but once again, these corrections are still awaited.

Apart from the issue that the Richard III Visitor Centre does not accurately reflect the role of the Looking For Richard Project team in the rediscovery of Richard III's remains, there is also the much more worrying fact that the exhibition does not reflect the project's research on the real Richard III. For example, one visitor has reported that 'the overriding impression I came out with was that Richard was a usurper. ... the rehabilitation of his reputation there, and the good he did, was "blanked out" by the shadow of the princes – even though, as we all know, any implication in their deaths is circumstantial and not proven beyond doubt'.[3]

We have already noted that the visitor centre does not tell the highly significant story of Eleanor Talbot, and of the bigamy of Edward IV which was officially recognised by Parliament in 1484 (see above, Introduction). Presumably this was because it was assumed that most visitors would be unfamiliar with Eleanor, and that they would be much more eager to see something about the story of 'the murder of the "Princes in the Tower"'. After all, one of the chief aims of the Richard III Visitor Centre is clearly to attract and interest visitors. The organisers may therefore have decided that this would be better achieved by presenting well-known aspects of the story of 'Richard the murderer' – whether or not that story is true.

In March 2013, following confirmation of the identity of Richard III's remains, Leicester Cathedral also apparently decided that the king had not been a very honourable man. In their own words as quoted by *The Guardian*, 'it should not be forgotten that Richard demonstrated both the honourable and dishonourable characteristics of human beings. Opportunities for prayer and reflection should focus on themes of sin and redemption'.[4]

The final words of the cathedral's rather condemnatory

pronouncement are oddly reminiscent of the epitaph that Henry VII commissioned for Richard III's tomb in Leicester's Franciscan Priory in 1494 or thereabouts.

> *At mea, quisquis eris, propter commissa precare,*
> *Sit minor ut precibus poena levata tuis.*

> [Whoever you are, pray for my offences,
> That my punishment may be lessened by your prayers.]

Of course, Henry VII was Richard's enemy. It is perhaps not surprising, therefore, that, in the opinion of many readers of the *Guardian* article, the judgement of Richard III which they had published implied that the same was true of Leicester Cathedral.

As the present writer pointed out to the Bishop of Leicester at the time, on one level it could probably be said of all of us that we have both honourable and dishonourable characteristics. In Christian terms, all human beings are seen as being born in a state of sin. This is one of the consequences of the 'Fall of Adam'. But I asked the bishop to consider whether it might not sound inappropriate for Leicester Cathedral to specifically judge Richard III in this way, even if clear evidence existed to justify such a statement (which in fact it does not). I therefore requested that such judgemental statements should, in future, be avoided.

The cathedral's reponse to this request was that 'to paraphrase Leicester's Professor of Medieval History – "the most I can say is that he was a Medieval king with a mix of honourable and dishonourable human characteristics".'[5] But unfortunately, as we have already seen, Leicester's Professor of Medieval History cannot really be regarded as an expert on the subject of Richard III.

The Bishop of Leicester also told me that 'the Cathedral has made no claim to the right to re-inter the remains of Richard III. It has responded to a request from the University which is the institution licensed to disinter the remains by the Ministry of Justice'.[6] This statement includes another piece of mythology, since actually ULAS was meant to apply for the exhumation licence on behalf of the landowner, Leicester City Council.[7] As we have seen, the bishop also argued that 'the choice of Leicester Cathedral conforms to usual practice in the discovery of human remains, namely that they are re-interred in the nearest consecrated ground which in this case is Leicester Cathedral'.[8] But in fact Leicester Cathedral does not represent the closest consecrated ground to Richard III's grave site, as was shown earlier (see chapter 5).

In March 2013, the then acting Dean of Leicester, Canon Naylor, assured me,

> we will work in close collaboration with the local Roman Catholic Church to ensure that Richard III is given fitting and appropriate rites surrounding his reinterment and being laid to rest, in dignity, accompanied by the prayers of the Church. It would be good if, as part of those prayers, there was a Roman Requiem offered at Holy Cross, or elsewhere, for his soul.
>
> I was sorry to hear about your experiences with Leicester University – this was the first I knew of that. I appreciate that you must be feeling wounded and hurt after what you related.
>
> I will ask my PA to contact you to arrange a meeting with myself, my colleague, Canon David Monteith, who is leading on issues relating to Richard III for us, and others, when we can discuss further some of these issues.[9]

Subsequently the proposed meeting did take place. Later I had further contact with the cathedral, via Mandy Ford and later Pete Hobson, particularly in respect of the use of the funeral crown which I had commissioned for Richard III, and also the donation of a rosary for interment with the king's remains (see illustrations).

The actions taken by the University of Leicester to which Canon Naylor referred included my exclusion from the revelation of the mtDNA results (see above). Subsequently, however, the university apparently engaged in other, very clearly focussed activity, aimed at attempting to boost public perception of its role in the discovery of Richard III's remains at my expense. This was brought to my attention by a correspondent from across the Atlantic. On 9 August 2013, this correspondent informed me that

> Your works and credits are being completely and misleadingly airbrushed from the Wikipedia Page: 'Exhumation of Richard III of England'
> http://en.wikipedia.org/wiki/Exhumation_of_Richard_III_of_England
> This airbrushing is the direct work of the University of Leicester PR Department and their employee Victoria Russell their Online Communications Officer. ... I would assume her bosses had her make the changes on Wikipedia. Her Wikipedia user / editing name is 'Victoria Russell' as noted with all the changes she has made below to mainly erase your name. Here's a prime example where she removed a reference to you and substituted:

'The Greyfriars car park in Leicester had been identified as the likely burial site by David Baldwin in a 1986 paper for the Leicestershire Archaeological and Historical Society'. I think this is one more 'provable incident' where the University of Leicester PR Department is deliberately taking steps to minimize your works and airbrush you out of this story. My opinion is that they are doing [*sic* this] to raise their commercial brand and diminish your commercial brand and scholarly credentials in respect to the King Richard III research narrative.

In reference to your name and research, here are some of the items they airbrushed out between today and yesterday:

'The University of Leicester Archaeology Department had in 2010 rejected Ashdown-Hill's written overtures to dig at this site'.
'The King Richard III burial site had been accurately located in 2005 by Dr. John Ashdown-Hill'.
'The dig was carried out by University of Leicester archaeologists, who uncovered a human skeleton on the first day of work *at the exact location which Ashdown-Hill had pinpointed back in 2005*'.
'In an apparent effort to have 100% of the credit given to the University of Leicester Richard III Team Members, Dr. Ashdown-Hill was deliberately not invited to this Press Conference by the University PR Team'.[10]

Following action on my behalf taken in response to this information by my MP, Bernard Jenkin, the university did subsequently modify its conduct. However, the university still claims to have played the key role in the discovery of the bones of Richard III. Since this is untrue, it obviously constitutes a potentially dangerous addition to the Richard III mythology of the future. Two pieces of recent evidence may reveal the ongoing development of this new mythology.

The first of these is a message, addressed to Philippa Langley by Colin Tregear, Complaints Director of the BBC. This message was in response to a complaint from Philippa Langley about an entry on the BBC website which described the discovery of the remains of King Richard III as having been made 'by archaeologists'. Philippa had made a very small and reasonable request, to the effect that the two simple words 'and researchers' should be added after 'archaeologists' on the website entry.

Her complaint – and her request – had been submitted to the Editorial Complaints Unit, and it was what he described as the *provisional* findings of that unit which Colin Tregear wished to communicate to Langley.

Basically the answer was that Tregear did not accept that there were any grounds to uphold Langley's complaint. Although he could see why Langley was unhappy with the wording – and the fact that she hoped for and expected due recognition on the web page to the work of the Looking For Richard Project – Tregear argued that the omission of recognition of the vital work of the research team could not be regarded as materially inaccurate or misleading. He cited the BBC's Editorial Guidelines on Accuracy. These refer to the concept of 'due accuracy', where the term 'due' is interpreted as meaning that the accuracy of the content 'must be adequate and appropriate to the output, taking account of the subject and nature of the content, the likely audience expectation and any signposting that may influence that expectation'. Tregear stated that this wording recognises that the degree of accuracy required in any specific instance will depend on a number of factors and that the accuracy required of, for example, a comedy or entertainment programme would not usually be regarded as the same as that required in an article which reported factual material.

Tregear then argued that, in this particular case, the BBC website article merely offered a very brief profile of Richard III and only included cursory details of the king's life. That being the case, he stated that he could not agree that the omission of any reference to the researchers who were involved in the discovery of his body could be considered to give a seriously misleading impression. He also acknowledged that, if the article had focused exclusively upon the project to discover Richard III's remains, arguably the degree of accuracy in the reporting of how that discovery was made might well increase. But given the focus of the reporting in this instance, his provisional conclusion remained that there were no grounds to uphold Langley's complaint.

A second piece of evidence showing the ongoing process of mythologising the story of the discovery comprises an email received by the author from the editorial staff of *Current Archaeology* on 13 August 2014, regarding instructions they had received from the University of Leicester Press Office:

> Unfortunately we were unable to mention you as a co-founder of the project; that is because The University of Leicester specifically asked us to use the following wording: 'The Dig for Richard III was led by University of Leicester, working with Leicester

City Council and in association with the Richard III Society. The originator of the Search project was Philippa Langley of the Richard III Society.', which is the wording that appears on all their press materials. We suggest that you may consider contacting the university press office so they can make sure that you are included in future press coverage, as I imagine that's the wording they're giving out to all journalists!

The wording specified by the University of Leicester is misleading in a number of respects; most specifically in terms of the nomenclature employed. Thus:

The Dig for Richard III did not directly involve *the University of Leicester*.

The originator of the Search project was Philippa Langley, leader of *the Looking For Richard Project Team*.

The project was led by Philippa Langley on behalf of the Looking For Richard Project.

Philippa, as the client, *employed ULAS* (the University of Leicester Archaeological Services – not formally part of the university) to carry out the excavation of the Social Services car park site, and paid for it upfront.

The Richard III Society was not directly involved in the project, though it did provide support in a number of ways. (For example, the Richard III Society awarded Philippa Langley a bursary towards the Archaeological Desk-Based Assessment (DBA) and agreed to authorise a last-minute international appeal to its branches and groups to save the search for the king when other funding had failed. Members of the Richard III Society contributed the majority of the overall funding required for the original three-week dig project during which the king was found. Further funding for the dig from the council and university was only authorised post discovery.)

17

Images

Additional Dialogue by William Shakespeare.

The Black Adder

In the summer of 2011, the author presented to Leicester Cathedral an oil-on-canvas copy of the Society of Antiquaries 'Paston Portrait' of Richard III, which he had commissioned (see plate 33). The main aim behind this gift was to ensure that, if no remains of Richard III were found in Leicester in the Looking For Richard Project's archaeological excavation of 2012, the cathedral would still have an additional focus on Richard III for its visitors to see.

The gift was acknowledged by the then Dean of Leicester on 4 November 2011. She expressed her regret at the fact that she had not acknowledged the donation earlier, describing it as my 'precious copy of the Richard III portrait'.[1] She explained that she had originally hoped that it would be possible to formally present it to the meeting of the Fabric Advisory Committee meeting scheduled for September. However, that meeting had subsequently been postponed until December, causing some delay. Nevertheless, she hoped that the cathedral Chapter would be delighted with the gift and would want to display it safely on suitable occasions when the cathedral was highlighting the story of Richard III – something which she considered would happen with increasing frequency in the future.

Later, when the remains which proved to be the bones of Richard III had been found, this portrait of Richard III was indeed used very extensively in various publicity by the university and others. As the then Dean of Leicester wrote on 9 October 2012,

As you know, John Ashdown-Hill kindly presented his copy of the image of Richard III to Leicester Cathedral. I am glad you are well ahead in developing publicity material, and wondered if we might have a conversation about how the University, Leicester City Council, and the Cathedral might work on this together to ensure maximum impact and mutual benefit.[2]

Unfortunately, although the cathedral authorities were aware of the origin of the painting, apparently the media were not. Thus my modern Leicester image of Richard III sometimes appeared on the internet and elsewhere labelled as 'the earliest surviving portrait of Richard III'. For that reason it is very important that the source of this portrait should be clearly on record, in order to prevent the growth of yet another piece of Ricardian mythology.

As for early portraits of Richard, no fifteenth-century paintings survive, though there are representations of Richard, both in stone and in manuscript miniatures, which date from 1475–85 (see plate 2). As we have seen, however, it is probable that the 'Paston Portrait' (plate 3) and the portraits in the royal collection at Windsor Castle, and at the National Portrait Gallery are copied from a contemporary image of Richard, the original of which does not now survive. However, the image in the royal collection was later altered to create a hunched back, and other early sixteenth-century images of Richard, such as the 'Broken Sword' portrait owned by the Society of Antiquaries (plate 4), appear to reflect the hostile Tudor propaganda.

More recent 'portraits' of the king include the statue presented to Leicester by the Richard III Society, and the statue commissioned for Middleham Castle, both of which have been received in various ways by different observers. There is also the 'two-faced' portrait of Sir Laurence Olivier as Richard III by the celebrated Spanish artist Salvador Dalí. A recent copy of this painting, commissioned by the author, but with one of Olivier's faces substituted with a copy of the 'Paston portrait' head of Richard III, is featured on the back cover of this book.

Theatrical images of Richard III first appeared in the sixteenth century, and Shakespeare's famous (but in many ways inaccurate) depiction of him has been popular ever since. Much more recently BBC television's *Blackadder* stories presented an alternative history over a range of period from the late middle ages to the First World War. The introduction to the first series, which was set towards the end of the fifteenth century, proclaimed,

History has known great liars. Copernicus. Goebbels. St Ralph the Liar. But there have been none quite so vile as the Tudor King Henry VII. It was he who rewrote history to portray his predecessor Richard III as a deformed maniac who killed his nephews in the Tower. But the truth is that Richard was a kind and thoughtful man who cherished his young wards, in particular Richard, Duke of York, who grew into a big strong boy. Henry also claimed he won the battle of Bosworth Field, and killed Richard III. Again, the truth is different. For it was Richard, Duke of York, who became king after Bosworth Field and reigned for thirteen glorious years. As for who really killed Richard III and how the defeated Henry Tudor escaped with his life, all is revealed in this, the first chapter of a history never before told: the History of ... the Black Adder'.[3]

This first series of *The Black Adder* was written by Richard Curtis and Rowan Atkinson and first broadcast in the summer of 1983. Set in 1485 it offered an alternative history. In this version of the story Richard III won the battle of Bosworth, but was then mistaken for someone else and murdered. His successor on the English throne was the younger son of Edward IV, Richard, Duke of York, who became King Richard IV. The role was played by Brian Blessed. But the series focussed chiefly on the adventures of Richard IV's younger son, Edmund, Duke of Edinburgh (alias 'The Black Adder').

The series dealt comically with a number of medieval issues in Britain: witchcraft, Royal succession, European relations, the Crusades, and the conflict between the Church and the Crown. Along with the secret history, many historical events portrayed in the series were anachronistic (for example, the last Crusade to the Holy Land ended in 1291) ... The series also featured Shakespearean dialogue, often adapted for comic effect; the end credits featured the words 'Additional Dialogue by William Shakespeare.'[4]

Twenty years after 'Black Adder' first appeared, Heather Hacking's *Historical Cats* offered us 'Richard the Furred', who was described as a much maligned king. According to Hacking's assessment, 'the real villain was probably that arch-propagandist, Henry VII'.[5] However, Hacking's illustration depicts Richard as a slim, dark (black) cat with his left shoulder slightly higher than his right. Interestingly, 'Richard the Furred' is the only English medieval reigning cat included in this book. It therefore seems that from Hacking's perspective, Richard must be seen as the only really significant English historical figure between 1066 and 1509.

There are, of course, many other pictorial and literary references to Richard – too many to deal with all of them here. However, two significant new additions to the mythology of Richard III have arisen from the king's facial reconstruction (see plate 8). The first of these concerns Richard III's hair. The hair (wig) placed on the facial reconstruction depicts straight hair, whereas the surviving portraits of Richard III all show slightly wavy hair. The second issue relates to the hat commissioned for the facial reconstruction by the Richard III Society. This large and rather angular piece of headgear does not resemble the rather small, rounded hat, shown in the earliest surviving portraits of Richard III (see, for example, plate 3). Nor does it appear to accurately reflect the style of male headwear of the 1480s. However, both the straight hair and the large, angular hat now seem to have been picked up and copied by various artists. In plate 21, for example, Frances Quinn has copied the new (mythological) hat – though she has avoided the straight hair. Nevertheless, it seems that there is now a risk of both of these erroneous features becoming accepted as normal for Richard III.

18

The Tourist Trade

We felt that we were in the presence of the dead King and must
do him reverence.

H. Carter & A. C. Mace, *The Discovery of the Tomb of
Tutankhamen*[1]

Since the discovery of his remains in August 2012, Richard III,
whose alleged stone coffin had been on show to tourists in Leicester
in the seventeenth and eighteenth centuries, has become a new
source of income for Leicester in various ways. For example,
Richard III Freetrade Chocolate is now on sale in Leicester –
though sadly the mysterious fifteenth-century source of the recipe
is not revealed on the product's label! The Richard III Society has
endorsed the use of its boar emblem on 'Richard III Ale'. It also
appears to have become possible to buy Richard III Sunglasses in
Leicester. Could this be a new attempt at an explanation as to why
Richard III lost the battle of Bosworth? Of course the battle was
fought in the month of August, and it was a sunny day. Perhaps
the king had left his sunglasses in his tent, and was dazzled by the
morning sun – causing him to make an error in his manoeuvring.

According to press reports, 'Curators hope that the museum [*sic*
for the new Richard III Visitors Centre] will attract up to 100,000
visitors in its first year.'[2] Although Jonathan O'Callaghan's *Daily
Mail* article, from which this published news is taken, was certainly
inaccurate in some of its statements, this particular assertion may
be correct.

On Tuesday 2 September 2014, another national paper – *The
Independent* – accused Leicester Cathedral of also cashing in on the
remains of the king. The article by Jonathan Brown was entitled
'Leicester Cathedral denies it is "cashing in" on Richard III's

reinternment [*sic*]'. However, it bore a subtitle reading 'Cathedral is offering benefactors seats at the service for £2,500'. The full article read as follows:

Leicester Cathedral has been accused of cashing in on the reinternment [*sic*] of Richard III next year after it emerged that it was offering benefactors the right to attend the historic service marking the arrival of his remains in return for a £2,500 donation.

In a letter to supporters, the cathedral said the money would go towards funding a new £100,000 ambulatory around the last of the Plantagenet's tomb which is expected to attract tens of thousands of visitors a year.

Mary McKenzie of the For Richard Society [*sic*], which is campaigning to rehabilitate the reputation of the late monarch, accused the cathedral of repeatedly reneging on its commitment to treat Richard's body with respect.

'It is an elitist method of raising cash that draws a line between rich and poor, discriminating against those who cannot afford to pay £2,500,' she said. It is believed £100,000 had already been raised by the offer.

In a letter to supporters the cathedral said the coffin's return flanked by descendants of nobles that fought at Bosworth would be a 'very powerful moment'.

'The medieval rites and wonderful music will be a service that would have been familiar to Richard,' it added.

Benefactors would also have their names included in a Book of Recognition and invited to attend a special reception after sharing in the 'joy and emotion of this most unique occasion'.

A Cathedral spokeswoman denied it was seeking to profit from hosting the tomb. 'We are not a wealthy cathedral, there is no public funding and we will rely on the support of trusts and individuals to make this happen.

'As a thank you to the benefactors who have contributed directly to the creation of ambulatory in which the tomb will lie, the cathedral will be inviting them to a service to witness the unveiling of the place of quiet reflection and beauty which they directly funded,' she said.

The remains of the notorious [*sic*] king were discovered in a car park in Leicester in 2012.

A judicial review concluded that his body should be buried in the city following objections by the descendants of distant relatives [*sic*] [3] and rival claims that he should be returned to York in accordance with his own wishes.

Last month the cathedral authorities announced a week-long series of events to mark the reinternment [*sic*] which will see his coffin travel from the battlefield where he met his death in 1485 eventually reaching his final resting place at St Martin's.

The public will be given three days to visit the coffin ahead of its reinternment [*sic*]. Attendance at special services will be at the invitation of the Very Revd David Monteith, Dean of Leicester Cathedral.[4]

The Cathedral responded to this attack thus:

In light of the current publication of misinformation concerning seating at the events in March, Leicester Cathedral issues the following statement:

The reinterment of the last Plantagenet King of England is an event of national and international importance, funded from private donations. This is entirely in line with large-scale heritage projects which rely on the philanthropic support of individuals, trusts and foundations.

The cost of reordering the cathedral fabric and of building the tomb is £1.54million. The cost of the reinterment events, interpretation and learning, liturgy and the gardens is £500k. The central costs, contingency and the preparatory works are covered by a £500,000 grant from the Diocese. Every pound raised is therefore going directly into the project itself.

A particular element of our fundraising programme was designed to raise £100,000 from existing supporters and advocates to fund the ambulatory around Richard's tomb. We are delighted that the people of Leicester and Leicestershire donated the full costs in under three weeks. We are very proud of them for their support. As a thank you to these benefactors, they will be invited to the first service so they can witness the unveiling of the place of quiet reflection and beauty which they directly funded.

It is the philanthropy and good will of so very many people which will ensure the success of this momentous event and we look forward to reinterring King Richard III in March 2015 with dignity and with honour.

There will be no tickets but invitations will be sent to a wide cross section of the community in due course. Anyone will be able and is welcome to come and pay respects during the days when the King's remains will lie in the Cathedral awaiting reinterment. We are also planning that the main service will be broadcast on television. Thus everyone who wishes will be able to share in laying Richard III to rest.[5]

Whether or not Leicester Cathedral is benefitting from its newly invented connection with Richard III, the parish church at Sutton Cheney has, as we have already seen, been benefitting from a similar invented connection with the king for nearly a century – and is still doing so today. The recent report from Cris Reay Connor of the Richard III Society repeated once again the groundless myth that Richard III attended mass at the church before fighting his final battle.

Conclusions

Richard III 'worth £45m to Leicester economy'
The discovery of the last Plantagenent king, Richard III, has boosted Leicester's economy by about £45m, BBC News reports.[1]

In all men and women, religious or secular, normal reason becomes evil when it makes them proud of their worldly attainments; when they covet position, possessions, pomps, and popularity in this present world.
The Cloud of Unknowing (written by an anonymous English priest, possibly from the East Midlands, *c.* 1390)[2]

For five hundred years there has been a great deal of mythology about Richard III. This has had several distinct lines of development: the ill-checked writings of supposedly serious historians; inaccurate drivel circulated by the media; and local inventions. Examples of all three have been cited in this case study, raising serious questions as to whether supposedly academic writings, media reports, or local traditions are ever to be trusted without careful checking of the evidence.

Many supposedly serious historians still circulate aspects of Ricardian mythology. This has been made clear by a number of examples cited in this book. These include statements about Richard III made by Gairdner in the nineteenth century, by Ross in the twentieth century, and by Skidmore in the present century.

There is also the very important story of Eleanor Talbot. For five hundred years, most historians ignored Eleanor and her real role in the story of Richard III. Some wrote rubbish about her (echoing Tudor propaganda). But until the present writer began work on her in the 1990s, virtually no one had ever sought genuine source material in an attempt to discover the real Eleanor. Moreover, as we have seen, even when the truth about Eleanor's birth, life and character was revealed, not all historians rushed to correct their earlier miswriting about her. Thus, for example, at least one worrying article survives on the ODNB which, disgracefully, still questions the very basic fact of whether Eleanor was the Earl of Shrewsbury's daughter.

As for Leicester's new Richard III Visitor Centre, sadly its account leaves Eleanor out of Richard III's story. Its display tends to follow the official government line laid down by Henry VII in 1485 – thereby potentially backing the 'usurper' myth. Nor is it unique in this. The official website of the British Monarchy still employs the term 'usurper' to describe Richard III. It is very hard to understand how a king who was offered the crown by the three estates of the realm can be described in this way, particularly when other fifteenth-century kings who seized the throne by force in battle are not condemned by the application of the same pejorative term.

But the story of Richard III is full of nonsense which is backed by no evidence. There is no proof that Richard ever murdered anyone. He certainly had a very small number of people who opposed him executed. But what this shows is that Richard was not really a strong-handed ruler or a harsh person. If he had been, he would have executed many *more* people – all those opponents who, in reality, survived to oppose him and his reputation!

There is also no evidence that Richard was an ambitious plotter who spent his life trying to force his way to the throne. If he had been, instead of remaining loyal to his eldest brother, Edward IV, he would have followed a similar path to his middle brother, George, Duke of Clarence, and sought powerful allies to help him oppose Edward.

Apart from the serious allegations against him, there are also many little stories about Richard III – often of local origin – which are widely believed, despite a total lack of evidence. Thus there is nothing to show that he stayed at an inn called the Blue (or White) Boar, in Leicester, in the run-up to the battle of Bosworth; there is nothing to prove that he was riding a horse called White Syrie (Surrey); there is nothing to show that he attended a mass at Sutton Cheney Church before the battle of Bosworth – or indeed that he ever set foot inside that building. Once again, it is very worrying that organisations such as the new Richard III Visitor Centre in Leicester, Leicester Cathedral, and the Richard III Society, all seem inclined to back such myths and keep them going.

It is also worrying that, with the help of the media, academic writers and institutions still seem to find it all too easy to create new myths about Richard III. Such recent additions to the mythology include the false stories that Richard's long lost remains were rediscovered by Leicester, or by the University of Leicester, or by the Richard III Society; that he really was a hunch-back; that his remains prove that he was indeed a corrupt man who drank too much; and that he may not really have been a sincere (and possibly rather conservative) Catholic.

Sadly, of course, it is not uncommon, nowadays, for British academic institutions to behave as the University of Leicester appears to have done in this instance. This is because of the recent government policies, as a result of which, in practical terms, universities have been privatised.[3] Thus they have been transformed into commercial, money-seeking, competitive bodies. They feel the need to promote their own 'brand', and they seek to maximise investment and their share of the market. As a result, academic integrity may now figure quite low on their list of priorities. At the same time, science-based subjects have come to be much more highly valued than subjects such as history. This made the recent opportunity to link the history of Richard III and Leicester with scientific work to establish the identity of the king's remains (not to mention the colour of his hair, and his diet) seem incredibly valuable from the university's point of view, and far too good to be missed.

On the other hand, some of the conduct of Leicester Cathedral seems harder to understand in this day and age. Nowadays, ecumenical relationships are normally quite strongly advocated. Indeed, Christianity seems to be so much on the ebb in the western world that different denominations usually appear to feel the need to work together whenever possible.

Despite the fact that evidence has been assembled here to show how misleading are many of the traditional stories about Richard III, and that even in the modern world, for profit-making motives, lies are still sometimes told deliberately about his story, there is absolutely no guarantee that the lies and legends about him will now cease. Indeed, visitors to the city of Leicester, or to the Bosworth Battlefield Centre are sometimes confronted today with very confusing information. Apart from problems which have already been mentioned concerning the material in its new Visitor Centre, Leicester also still has, close to the River Soar, the nineteenth-century Broadbent plaque (see plate 28), which proclaims that Richard III's remains lie nearby! Also, a large stone which misleadingly states that 'Richard died here' (plate 36) stands today just outside the Bosworth Battlefield Centre – which is certainly not where Richard III died. Moreover, it is positioned close to a medieval stone coffin (plate 35) which is not the one which was on show in Leicester in the eighteenth century, and which has absolutely nothing to do with Richard III.

So it seems that the problem of the mythology of Richard III is ongoing. The task of trying to deal with it must now pass into the hands of you, the readers. When you encounter the myths, please refer to the evidence presented here – or go in quest of new evidence – and do your best to bust them!

APPENDIX 1: POTENTIAL CANDIDATES FOR IDENTITY WITH THE LEICESTER GREYFRIARS BONES[1]

Michael Hicks and others have suggested that the mtDNA match between the Leicester bones and two all-female lines of descent from Richard III's eldest sister, Anne, Duchess of Exeter, does not, by itself, prove the identity of the Leicester remains. But both the Looking For Richard Project and the University of Leicester archaeologists and geneticists were always aware of this point. Therefore the identity of the bones as Richard III has always been based upon the mtDNA match *together with the mass of other circumstantial evidence which indicates that the bones are those of Richard III.*

As part of my original mtDNA research I began investigating all possible female-line relatives of Richard III who would have shared his mtDNA sequence, and who would have died in approximately the right time period. My research has been largely based on published and online resources, because it is quite wide ranging. Ideally, in the long run, more detailed research, checking original source material, is desirable. However, the work done so far indicates that almost all the known mtDNA-identical uncles, cousins and second cousins, nephews and great nephews of Richard III can be excluded from possible identity with the Leicester bones for one or more of the following reasons:

✠ died/buried at the wrong place
♦ died at the wrong age (outside the range 30–33 years)
✪ died in the wrong manner
✿ died at the wrong period in terms of carbon dating (outside the period 1475–1530)

The following list comprises the female-line male descendants of Catherine de Roët and her sister Philippa, who died in approximately the right time period (as revealed by the carbon dating of the Leicester bones), and indicates why these descendants cannot possibly be identified as the Leicester bones (if a reason is known). Apart from Richard III himself, this evidence shows that there are only seven known relatives of the king who are not thereby demonstrably excluded from possible identification with the Leicester Greyfriars bones. These seven relatives, together with Richard III himself, are marked in uppercase letters and in bold. Of the total of eight individuals, however, Richard III is the only one specifically reported to have been buried at the Leicester Greyfriars, and reported to have suffered from a twisted spine. He is also the only aristocrat of the period known to have been buried in this relatively high-status location (the priory church choir) but in an unusually low-status manner (no coffin or embalming).

It is also worth observing that it is quite likely that Richard III's seven relatives for whom we have no record of their age, place and manner of death died in childhood (like some of Richard III's own brothers), and that this is the reason why no further records of them survive, and why they apparently produced no descendants. In addition, both the Greystoke and the Manners candidates are likely to have died in the wrong place (both families were based in Yorkshire). Also, if Richard III's Manners great nephews did not die in childhood, like their two brothers of whom more detailed records survive, they may well have died at the wrong period in terms of carbon dating (ie outside the period 1475–1530).

The earliest known female-line ancestor of Richard III is the Dame de Roët, wife of Sir Giles ('Paon') de Roët. She may well have come from the Low Countries. Her first name and maiden name are unknown. She had three daughters and one son.

Children of Dame de Roët
1 Philippa de Roët – two sons and two daughters
2 Elizabeth (Isabelle) de Roët, nun – no children
3 Catherine de Roët – four sons and two daughters
4 Walter de Roët ✿

Children of Philippa de Roët
1 a Elizabeth Chaucer, nun – no children
1 b Thomas Chaucer *c.* 1367–1434 ◆ ✠ ✿
1 c Lewis Chaucer 1381–1403 ◆ ✿
1 d Agnes Chaucer *c.* 1385–99 – no children

Children of Catherine de Roët
3 a Sir Thomas Swynford, 1367–1432 ♦ ❁
3 b John Beaufort, Earl of Somerset, 1373–1410 ♦ ✠ ❁
3 c Cardinal Henry Beaufort, 1375–1447 ♦ ✠ ❁
3 d Thomas Beaufort, Duke of Exeter, 1377–1426 ♦ ✠ ❁
3 e Margaret Swynford, nun – no children
3 f Joan Beaufort – nine sons and six daughters

Sons of Joan Beaufort
3 f a Richard, Earl of Salisbury, died battle of Wakefield, 1400–60 ♦ ✠ ❁
3 f b Robert Neville, Bishop of Salisbury & Durham 140?–57 ♦ ✪ ❁
3 f c William, Earl of Kent, 1410–63 ♦ ✪ ❁
3 f d Edward, Baron Bergavenny, before 1414–76 ♦ ✪
3 f e George, Baron Latimer, 1407(?)–69 ♦ ✪ ❁
3 f f John Neville, died young ♦ ❁
3 f g Cuthbert Neville, died young ♦ ❁
3 f h Thomas Neville, died young ♦ ❁
3 f j Henry Neville, died young ♦ ❁

Daughters of Joan Beaufort
i Elizabeth de Ferrers, Baroness Greystoke, 1392–1434 – five sons
ii Mary (Margery, or Margaret) de Ferrers, Lady Neville, 1394–1458 – one son & one daughter
iii Eleanor Neville, Countess of Northumberland, *c.* 1397–1472 – seven sons and three daughters
iv Anne Neville, Duchess of Buckingham, 1405–80 – four sons
v Catherine Neville, Duchess of Norfolk, 1410–85 – one son and two daughters
vi Cecily Neville, Duchess of York, 1415–95 – eight sons and four daughters

Sons of Elizabeth de Ferrers
i a Ralph, 5th Lord Greystoke, *c.* 1408–87, d. Kirkham, Northumberland ✠ ♦
i b **THOMAS GREYSTOKE, b.** *c.* **1414, age, manner and place of death unknown**
i c **RICHARD GREYSTOKE, b.** *c.* **1418, age, manner and place of death unknown**
i d John Greystoke b. *c.* 1420, age at death unknown, but died in Spain ✠

i e William Greystoke, b. *c.* 1430, age at death unknown but died in Spain ✠
i f HENRY GREYSTOKE, b. *c.* 1424, age, manner and place of death unknown

Son of Mary (Margery, or Margaret) de Ferrers
ii a John Neville MP, Sheriff of Lincs., *c.* 1416–82, Althorpe, Lincs. ◆ ✠ ✪

Daughter of Mary (or Margaret) de Ferrers
ii b Joan (Jane) Neville, Lady Griffith, second wife of Sir Walter Griffith. This couple had no known children.

Sons of Eleanor Neville
iii a John Percy, b. 1418, died in childhood ◆ ✿
iii b Henry, 3rd Earl of Northumberland, 1421–61, died battle of Towton ◆ ✿
iii c Thomas, Baron Egremont, 1422–60, died battle of Northampton ◆ ✿
iii d George Percy, 1424–74 ◆
iii e Sir Ralph Percy, 1425–64 ◆ ✠ ✿
iii f Sir Richard Percy, 1426/7–61, died battle of Towton ◆ ✠ ✿
iii g William Percy Bp of Carlisle, 1428–62 ✪ ✿

Daughters of Eleanor Neville
iii h Joan Percy, 1415–75, a nun – no children
iii j Catherine Percy (Grey), Countess of Kent, *c.* 1423–75 – four sons
iii k Anne Percy, 1436–1522 – no sons, three daughters

Sons of Catherine Percy (Grey)
iii j a Anthony Grey, 1446–80, died naturally ✪
iii j b George Grey, Earl of Kent, 1454–1505 ◆
iii j c John Grey, 1455–84, died naturally ✪
iii j d Edmund Grey, 1457–84, died in Wales ◆ ✠

Sons of Anne Neville
iv a Sir Henry Stafford, 1425–71, Stafford ✠ ◆ ✿
iv b Sir John Stafford, Earl of Wiltshire, 1427–73, died naturally ✠ ◆
iv c Edward Stafford, *c.* 1428–84, Gwynedd, Wales ◆ ✠
iv d Richard Stafford, *c.* 1426–29, Wales ◆ ✠ ✿
iv e Humphrey, Earl Stafford, *c.* 1430–55, died first battle of St Albans ✠ ◆ ✿

iv f George Stafford, 1439–55 died first battle of St Albans ✠ ◆ ●
iv g WILLIAM STAFFORD, b. 1439, age, manner and place of death unknown

Son of Catherine Neville
v a John Mowbray, Duke of Norfolk, 1415–61 ◆ ✪ ✠ ●

Daughters of Catherine Neville
v b Joan Strangeways – one daughter
v c Catherine Strangeways – no children

Daughter of Joan Strangeways
v b i Cecily Willoughby, married Edward Sutton, Baron Dudley – six sons

Sons of Cecily Willoughby
v b i a William Sutton, 1489–1504, died Dudley, Worcs. ◆ ✠
v b i b John Sutton, Baron Dudley, 1494–1553, died London ◆ ✠ ●
v b i c Edward Sutton, 1497–1532, buried Dudley, Worcs. ✠
v b i d Thomas Sutton (known as Dudley), 1499–1549, died London ◆ ✠ ●
v b i e Arthur Sutton (Dudley?), Prebendary Lichfield Cathedral, 1505–1576 ◆ ●
v b i f Geoffrey Sutton, 1507–71, died/buried Dudley, Worcs. ◆ ✠ ●

Sons of Cecily Neville
vi a Henry, 1441–before 1445 ◆ ●
vi b Edward IV, 1442–1483 ◆ ✪ ✠
vi c Edmund, Earl of Rutland, 1443–60 ◆ ●
vi d William, 1447–before 1456 ◆ ●
vi e John, 1448–before 1456 ◆ ●
vi f George, Duke of Clarence, 1449–78 ✠ ✪
vi g Thomas, 1450/51–before 1456 ◆ ●
vi h RICHARD III, age, manner and place of death, manner and place of burial, physical characteristics, appearance, and social status all consistent with the Leicester bones

Daughters of Cecily Neville
vi j Anne, Duchess of Exeter – two daughters, no sons
vi k Elizabeth, Duchess of Suffolk – six sons
vi l Margaret, Duchess of Burgundy – no children
vi m Ursula – no children

Daughters of Anne Duchess of Exeter
vi j i Anne Holland – no children
vi j ii Anne St Leger – five sons

Sons of Anne St Leger
vi j ii a Thomas, Earl of Rutland, *c.* 1492–1543 ♦ ✪ ❀
vi j ii b OLIVER MANNERS, b. after 1493
vi j ii c ANTHONY MANNERS, b. after 1494
vi j ii d Sir Richard Manners, b. after 1495 & before 1510, d. 1551 ♦ ✪ ❀
vi j ii e JOHN MANNERS, b. after 1496

Sons of Elizabeth, Duchess of Suffolk
vi k a John, Earl of Lincoln, 1462–87, died battle of Stoke ♦ ✠
vi k b Edward, Archdeacon of Richmond, 1466–85 ♦ ✪
vi k c Edmund, Earl of Suffolk, 1471(?)–1513, executed at Tower Hill ♦ ✪ ✠
vi k d Humphrey de la Pole (in Holy Orders), 1474–1513 ♦ ✪
vi k e Sir William de la Pole, 1478–1539, died Tower of London ♦ ✠ ❀
vi k f Richard de la Pole, 1480–1525, died battle of Pavia, Italy ♦ ✠

The above list comprises Richard III himself and a total of 66 male relatives of the king in the female line – men who lived around the period defined by carbon dating of the Leicester Greyfriars bones (1475–1530). Of these 67 men, even if the age range is slightly extended beyond 30–33, there are only eight who cannot be excluded from possible identification with the Leicester Greyfriars bones. Thus the mtDNA evidence *alone* appears to be over 85% in favour of the identity of the bones as Richard III.

As has already been noted, of the eight men not excluded, only Richard III is known to fit the mass of other circumstantial evidence relating to the bones in question. In addition to social status, age at death, and a violent death, this circumstantial evidence includes: post-mortem injuries; twisted spine; a skull consistent with surviving portraits of Richard III; interment in the Franciscan Priory choir (high status location) but in a somewhat ignoble manner, and evidence of a diet upgraded towards the end of the life of the individual in question.

APPENDIX 2: THE PLANTAGENET Y-CHROMOSOME (EMAIL CORRESPONDENCE BETWEEN THE AUTHOR AND DR TURI KING OF THE UNIVERSITY OF LEICESTER, SEPTEMBER 2012)

On 21 September 2012, the current author wrote to Dr Turi King:

Turi, I think you already know that I began the historical/ genealogical research to find the mtDNA sequence for Richard III and his brothers and sisters, NOT directly in connection with Richard, but at the request of Belgian colleagues who were then studying possible bones of Richard's youngest sister, Margaret of York, Duchess of Burgundy.

Because in Margaret's case I was dealing with female remains I concentrated on the female line of descent (mitochondrial DNA). If I had then been dealing directly with Richard, I would also have sought a male line (Y-chromosome) sequence.

Actually, later I did investigate the male line DNA on a purely academic basis, and I asked for a sample from the most obvious all-male-line Plantagenet descendant – who then declined to give a sample. However, his answer might now be different (in view of the possible discovery of Richard's bones) – and anyway, I also have contact details for a number of other all-male-line descendants whom I have not yet approached, but any one of whom could provide a Y-chromosome sample.

So would you be interested in trying to get all-male-line DNA samples?

Dr King replied on the following day, saying that this was a good idea, and asking whether I would be happy for her to contact the male-line descendants under the banner of the University of

Leicester. I agreed, and later the same day I sent her the following list of names and addresses, together with a general genealogy showing the Somerset family's male line descent from the house of Plantagenet:

The addresses and other details given here are all taken from *Burke's Peerage* 1999, so I don't know whether you need detailed family trees for each individual, since the information is public knowledge.

Of course these addresses are some years old and may now be out of date!

The attached simplified family tree which I published in *The Last Days of Richard III* will explain the basic illegitimate descent of the Somerset family (the head of which is His Grace the Duke of Beaufort) from the medieval Beaufort family, Dukes of Somerset is well established (but – like all male lines of descent – open to possible paternity problems). As you can see, the Beaufort Dukes of Somerset were in turn illegitimately descended from John of Gaunt, Duke of Lancaster (son of Edward III and father of Henry IV). The 'Richard Duke of York', shown on this tree, was the father of Richard III

I contacted the Duke of Beaufort some years ago, at the same time as I contacted Joy Ibsen. However, the Duke then declined to give a DNA sample, and at that time – because I was working on possible remains of Margaret of York Duchess of Burgundy – a male-line sample was not actually required, so I didn't pursue it.

Because the Duke declined I haven't included him on this list – but you might possibly want to try him again – given the new circumstances.

1. Arthur Henry Somerset born 1926 married 1 daughter 3 sons. One son died young. No addresses for the two sons, both have children only the younger one has a son. The three children who grew up were all educated at the Queensland University [address redacted] Australia

2. Ronald Arthur Somerset born in 1940 he is divorced and only has one child. No address for his son [address redacted] South Africa

3. Robin Fitzroy Somersetborn 1930 1son 1daughter, no addresses for either
[address redacted] U.K.

4. William Plantagenet Somerset born 1934, married 2 sons, both married & one has son.
[address redacted] Australia. (No addresses for the sons.)

5. Charles Plantagenet Somerset born 1944 married 2 sons
[address redacted] Australia

6. William Michael John Charles Somerset – born in 1934, married 1 son.
[address redacted] U.K. (No address for the son.)

7. Stephen Raglan Somerset – married and has 2 daughters
[address redacted] Australia

8. Clement Charles Fitzroy Somersetborn 1956 married 1 son 1 daughter
[address redacted] U.K.

9. Henry Robert Fitzroy Somerset, born 1961
[address redacted] U.K.

& his father
10. David Henry Fitzroy Somerset, born 1930
[address redacted] U.K.

APPENDIX 3: SUGGESTED AMENDMENTS PROPOSED BY THE LOOKING FOR RICHARD PROJECT TEAM TO THE ARTICLE 'THE KING IN THE CAR PARK', AS PUBLISHED IN THE JOURNAL *ANTIQUITY*[1]

Re: antiquity.ac.uk_Ant_087_0519_ant0870519 – 'The King in the Car Park', the LOOKING FOR RICHARD PROJECT TEAM is very concerned about the following errors and omissions in this paper, and would ask you to correct them as indicated.

p. 520, para 1, lines 1 & 2, DELETE 'the culmination of the Wars of the Roses'. (The term 'Wars of the Roses' is a C19th invention. The battle of Bosworth was not the culmination of a war.)

p. 520, para 1, antepenultimate / penultimate lines: '...erected over the grave {INSERT REF.} (Edwards 1975: 8–9).

p. 520, para 2, line 1: after 'This paper reports' INSERT 'a preliminary summary of ...'

p. 520, para 2: AMEND 'initiated by Philippa Langley, a member of the Richard III Society' TO 'initiated by Philippa Langley, leader of the LOOKING FOR RICHARD PROJECT'
(Philippa was not operating as an independent member of the Richard III Society, but as the leader of a project team called LOOKING FOR RICHARD, formally founded in 2009, but based on work dating back to at least 2003.)

p. 520, para 3 line 2: AMEND 'collaboration between ... an amateur group (the Richard III Society) and ...' TO 'collaboration between ... a specialist research group (LOOKING FOR RICHARD) and ...'

(The Grey Friars Project was a specialist research project initiated by LOOKING FOR RICHARD – this should not be described as an amateur group – because it contains at least TWO academic historians. The Richard III Society was not directly involved except in that it provided part of the funding.)

p. 520, para 3, line 4: for 'specialists' substitute 'archaeologists'

p. 520, para 3, lines 5–6: for 'non-specialists' substitute 'non-archaeologists'; delete 'in academic research'

p. 520, para 3, lines 8–9: for 'amateurs' substitute 'others'; for 'in this case the non-specialists played a role' substitute 'in this case the specialists played a leading role' (since LFR led the way on this specific project in terms of years spent on prior academic research)

p. 520, para 4 line 1: AMEND 'For the Richard III Society ...' TO 'For the LOOKING FOR RICHARD PROJECT ...'.

p. 520, para 4 line 4: AMEND the term, 'non-specialist partners' TO 'specialist partners' (since LFR had spent years of research on this specific project.)

p. 521, para 1 line 1: AMEND '... (ULAS), commissioned to carry out the research ...' TO
'... (ULAS), commissioned as contractors to carry out an archaeological investigation of the locations identified by the LOOKING FOR RICHARD researchers ...'

p. 521, para 1 line 8: AMEND 'non-specialist partners' TO 'specialist partners' (see above)

p. 523, para 1 AMEND ' ..."here lies the body of Richard III sometime King of England" (Baldwin 1986:22)' TO ' ..."here lies the body of Richard III some time King of England" (Wren 1750: 144; Strange 1975: 6)'

p. 523, final para, lines 1–2: AMEND TO READ A GPR survey undertaken by the Looking For Richard Project in 2011 failed to reveal ...modern services (Austrums 2011 for Philippa Langley).'

p. 531, para 1 – DELETE 'Baldwin 1986:21' (The relevant source is Polydore Vergil.)

p. 536, last para – 'The genealogical Link between two modern day descendants' {INSERT REF}(Ashdown-Hill, 2007: 194)

p. 537, para 2, AMEND the term, 'non-specialist partners' TO 'specialist partners' (see above).

p. 537, para 3, INSTEAD OF 'to some extent academic research questions coincide with the research questions of our non-specialist partners and the wider public, but they are not identical' SUBSTITUTE
'to some extent questions of academic archaeological research coincide with the interests of our specialist partners and of the wider public, but they are not necessarily identical'

Acknowledgements should read 'Thanks are due to the Looking For Richard Project, the University of Leicester, Leicester City Council, and the project's additional funding partners the Richard III Society, Leicestershire Promotions Ltd., and Leicester Adult Schools'

REFERENCES
ADD:

Ashdown-Hill, J. 2007. 'Margaret of York's Dance of Death – the DNA evidence', *Handelingen van de Koninklijke Kring voor Oudheidkunde, Letteren an Kunst van Mechelen*, 111, 193–207.

AUSTRUMS, R. 2011 (for Langley, P) Geophysical survey report.

Edwards, R. 1975. 'King Richard's Tomb at Leicester', *The Ricardian*, vol. III, no. 50, 8–9.

Strange, A. 1975. 'The Grey Friars, Leicester', *The Ricardian*, vol. III, no. 50, 3–7.

Wren, C. 1750. *Parentalia, or Memoirs of the Family of the Wrens.*

APPENDIX 4: CORRESPONDENCE WITH THE EDITOR OF *ANTIQUITY* REGARDING THE AMENDMENTS PROPOSED IN APPENDIX 3 (ABOVE)

On 30 July 2014 the current author wrote as follows to the editor of *Antiquity*:

> As you may be aware, FINDING RICHARD III – THE OFFICIAL ACCOUNT OF THE RETRIEVAL AND REBURIAL PROJECT has recently been published.
>
> I, and my colleagues, responsible for the research which led to our employment of ULAS to carry out the archaeology resulting in the rediscovery of King Richard III's remains, are very concerned at the errors contained in a report published by ANTIQUITY under the title 'The King in the car park' (pdf copy attached).
>
> We should be grateful, therefore, if you would now examine, and publish, the attached corrections and amendments to this article.

The editor responded initially with a suggestion that we should take up our concerns with the authors of the published article. Subsequently he informed us that, since articles accepted for publication in *Antiquity* always pass through a rigorous peer-review procedure prior to publication, it was seen as impossible to alter or correct an article in any way once it had been published.

APPENDIX 5: MISLEADING INTERPRETATIONS FROM LEICESTER

In addition to the errors mentioned in the main text, here are a few more terminological inexactitudes circulated by 'stakeholders' in Leicester:

The University of Leicester
'We led the search for Richard III.'

Actually the search was led by members of the Looking For Richard Project and the designation LFR was instituted in 2009. The University of Leicester did not become involved in the project until 2011, when Philippa Langley obtained the university's agreement to make its specialists available to the project in two areas: DNA analysis and Psychology; the last for a psychological study of Richard III commissioned by Langley in 2011. In terms of contribution of finances to the dig, Langley did not bring the university on board with funding until May 2012, when the university became a partner in the project.

Leicester Cathedral
'The suggestion that these arrangements are in breach of binding agreements made privately between the Looking for Richard Team and the University before the discovery of the remains has no legal credibility, as was fully demonstrated by the outcome of the judicial review and the High Court in May 2014 ... this former monarch of our realm is to be laid to rest in Leicester Cathedral, the mediaeval parish church of the city in which he was first buried in 1485.'

In reality the agreement was made between the Looking For Richard Project and ULAS, and formally signed off by Langley's lead partner, Leicester City Council, in her agreement with them; the council being the landowner who gave Langley permission to dig, and who also confirmed it would hold any exhumation licence.

The judicial review of 2014 had nothing to do with the Looking For Richard Project. It was a case brought by The Plantagenet Alliance.

Leicester was not a city in 1485.

Leicester Cathedral is not THE medieval parish church of Leicester. There are several surviving medieval parish churches in Leicester. However, the cathedral is mostly a nineteenth-century building, and a nineteenth-century institution.

Notes

Introduction

1. Modern English translated edition, C. Wolters, ed. *The Cloud of Unknowing*, Harmondsworth 1961 (1974), p. 89.
2. A. J. Carson, ed., *Finding Richard III – The Official Account of Research by the Retrieval and Reburial Project*, Horstead 2014.
3. For the claim of the King of Portugal, see J. Ashdown-Hill, 'The Lancastrian Claim to the Throne', *The Ricardian*, vol. 13, 2003, pp. 27–38. For the claim of the Earl of Warwick, see J. Ashdown-Hill, *The Dublin King*, Stroud 2015, p. 67.
4. http://en.wikipedia.org/wiki/Mohammad_Reza_Pahlavi (August 2014), my emphasis.
5. http://en.wikipedia.org/wiki/Mohammad_Reza_Pahlavi (August 2014).
6. See Carson, ed., *Finding Richard III – The Official Account*.

Part 1 – The Geography of Richard III

1 York – or Leicester – or ...?

1. A. R. Myers, ed., G. Buck, *The History of the Life and Reigne of Richard the Third*, (London 1646), Wakefield 1973, p. 7.
2. http://authorherstorianparent.blogspot.co.uk/2013/03/a-northern-lord-in-london-city-richard_27.html (consulted July 2014).
3. http://en.wikipedia.org/wiki/Peter_of_Castile (consulted September 2014). My emphasis.
4. Personal communication from Richard III's 18th generation niece, Vanessa Roe, descendant of George, Duke of Clarence, and one of the leaders of The Plantagenet Alliance.
5. J. Ashdown-Hill, *The Third Plantagenet*, Stroud 2014, p. 36.
6. Myers / Buck, *The History of the Life and Reigne of Richard the Third*, p. 7.
7. C. A. Halsted, *Richard III*, 2 volumes, London 1844, vol. 1, p. 421. According to Halsted, 'Berkhampstead [*sic*] remained in the family of York until that house became extinct, when it returned to the crown.'

8. C. Peers, *Berkhamsted Castle*, HMSO 1948 (1968), p. 5.

9. Ashdown-Hill, *The Third Plantagenet*, appendix 1.

10. P. A. Johnson, *Duke Richard of York 1411–1460*, Oxford, 1988, pp. 119–20.

11. A. L. Lamb, J. E. Evans, R. Buckley & J. Appleby, 'Multi-isotope analysis demonstrates significant lifestyle changes in King Richard III', http://www. sciencedirect.com/science/article/pii/S0305440314002428 (consulted September 2014).

12. P. M. Kendall, *Richard the Third*, London 1955, pp. 439–40 contests this, while J. Wilkinson, *Richard, the young King to be*, Stroud 2009, p. 68, accepts that the Duchess of York and her younger children dwelt at a Kentish manor held by the Duke and Duchess of Buckingham. Indeed, she specifies their residence as Tunbridge Castle.

13. See Ashdown-Hill, *The Third Plantagenet*, pp. 56–8.

14. Personal communication from Richard III's 18th generation niece, Vanessa Roe, descendant of George, Duke of Clarence, and one of the leaders of The Plantagenet Alliance.

15. J. Wilkinson, *Richard the Young King to be*, Stroud 2009, p. 104.

16. J. Ashdown-Hill, *The Third Plantagenet*, p. 95.

17. R. Edwards, *The Itinerary of King Richard III 1483–1485*, London 1983.

Part 2 – The Path to the Throne

1. The Act of Parliament refers to Eleanor Talbot as 'Eleanor Boteler' – often modernised as 'Eleanor Butler'. Boteler (Butler) was the surname of Eleanor's first (and deceased) husband. Similarly the act refers to Elizabeth Woodville as 'Elizabeth Grey', for precisely the same reason. But since in a historical context Elizabeth is usually known by her maiden name of Woodville, it is logical that in a historical context we should also normally refer to Eleanor by her maiden name of Talbot.

2. *Ostendebatur per modum supplicationis in quodam rotuli pergameni quod filii Regis Edwardi errant bastardi, supponendo illum praecontraxisse cum quadam Domina Alienora Boteler antequam Reginam Elizabeth dixisset uxorem, atque insuper quod sanguis alterius fratris sui Georgii, ducis Clarentiae, fuisset attinctus ita quod hodie nullus certus et incorruptus sanguis linealis ex parte Richardi, ducis Eboraci, poterat inveniri, nisi in persona Richardi, ducis Glocestriae. Quocirca supplicabatur ei in fine eiusdem rotuli ex parte dominorum et communitatis regni ut ius suum in se assumeret.* N. Pronay & J. Cox, *The Crowland Chronicle Continuations 1459–1486*, London 1986 (hereinafter *Crowland*), p. 160.

2 Richard, the Abnormal Prince

3. J. Gairdner, *History of the Life and Reign of Richard the Third*, Cambridge 1898, p. 3.

4. *Op. cit.*, p. 3, citing Rous p. 215.

5. The word 'monster' comes from the Latin verb *monstro*, meaning 'show', because a monster was regarded as sign, or portent. St Augustine, *De civitate Dei*, xxi. 8.

6. Quoted in P-G. Boucé, 'Imagination, pregnant women and monsters in

eighteenth-century England and France', p. 97 (in G.S. Rousseau and R Porter, eds, *Sexual underworlds of the Enlightenment*, Manchester 1987, pp. 86–100).

7. Shakespeare, *The Third Part of King Henry VI*, act 5, scene 6.
8. K. Park and L. J. Daston, 'Unnatural Conceptions: the study of monsters in sixteenth- and seventeenth-century France and England', *Past and Present*, no. 92 (1981), p. 25.
9. 'In many cultures, long hair was linked to male virility and strength and the magic powers of regeneration'. J. Fletcher, *The Search for Nefertiti*, London 2004, p. 102.
10. Gairdner, *History of the Life and Reign of Richard the Third*, p. 5.
11. *Op. cit.*, p. 5, my emphasis.
12. *Op. cit.*, p. 6, citing Rous, p. 218.
13. Cited in A. F. Sutton & L. Visser-Fuchs, '"Richard Liveth Yet": an Old Myth', *Ricardian*, vol. IX, no 117, June 1992, pp. 266–269 (p. 267). I am grateful to Annette Carson for drawing this article to my attention.
14. Compare Sutton & Visser-Fuchs, 'Richard Liveth Yet', p. 269, note 9, with K. W. Barnadiston, *Clare Priory*, Cambridge 1962, p. 63.
15. The present writer, whose research into Richard's burial was one important part of the evidence which led to the excavation of his grave site, recalls that on the day when the dig started, local people told him that the excavation was a waste of time and money because Richard's body had been dug up long since, and thrown into the River Soar. This was despite the fact that I had already demonstrated clearly, and in print, that stories about the exhumation of Richard's body were later nonsense. (For details see below.)
16. J. B. Russell, *Witchcraft in the Middle Ages*, Cornel University 1972, p. 217.
17. A. F. Sutton and L. Visser-Fuchs with R. A. Griffiths, *The Royal Funerals of the House of York at Windsor*, London 2005, pp. 117–22.
18. Edward IV's height might perhaps have been a trait inherited from his ancestor, Edward I, who was known as 'Longshanks'.
19. Often known in England as WAURIN, but this surname is a toponym, and the modern spelling of the town name in northern France from which it is derived is WAVRIN.
20. '*le roy Edouard avoit deux jennes frères, lun eagie de neuf ans et lautre de huit ans*', W. & E. L. C. P Hardy, eds, J. de Wavrin, *Recueil des Chroniques et Anchienne Istories de la Grant Bretaigne, à Present Nommé Engleterre*, Vol. 5, 1891, reprinted Cambridge 2012, p. 357.
21. C. Weightman, *Margaret of York Duchess of Burgundy 1446–1503*, Gloucester 1989, p. 168, citing H. Ellis, ed., E. Hall, *Chronicle* etc., London 1809, p. 472.
22. M. K. Jones, *Psychology of a Battle, Bosworth 1485*, Stroud 2002, 2003, p. 83.
23. F. Madden, 'Political Poems of the Reigns of Henry VI and Edward IV', *Archaeologia* vol. 29, 1842, pp. 318–47 (p. 334).
24. For a fuller exploration of the evidence regarding George's height, see Ashdown-Hill, *The Third Plantagenet*, pp. 61–2.
25. Ashdown-Hill, *The Third Plantagenet*, pp. 121–2.
26. *Daily Mail*, 17 September 2014, cited in the Richard III Society Yorkshire Branch Newsletter, October 2014, p. 2.
27. *The Spectator*, 25 May 2013, p. 55, Leanda de Lisle, review of C. Skidmore,

Bosworth and the Birth of the Tudors, London 2013. I am grateful to Annette Carson for drawing this to my attention.

28. Report of a talk by Buckley, published in the Richard III Society Yorkshire Branch Newsletter, October 2014, pp. 2–3. I am grateful to Dr D. Johnson for bringing this to my attention.

29. *ibid.*

30. T. Hearne, ed., *Joannis Rossi Antiquarii Warwicensis Historia Regum Angliae*, London 1716, p. 218.

31. I am grateful to Marie Barnfield for this transcription, *ex informatio* Annette Carson.

32. I am grateful to Marie Barnfield for this transcription, *ex informatio* Annette Carson.

33. Professor Foxhall's online CV implies a certain preoccupation with the issue of masculinity. Two of her four listed publications are called *Thinking Men: Masculinity and its Self-Representation in the Classical Tradition* and *When Men were Men: Masculinity, Power and Identity in Classical Antiquity*. I am grateful to Marie Barnfield and Annette Carson for drawing this point to my attention.

34. http://www.le.ac.uk/richardiii/history/meetrichard.html (consulted September 2014).

35. *e començó a pelear con tan gran vigor y esforçó tanto aquellos que le quedaron leales, que con solo esfuerçó se sostuvo gran pieça la batalla.*

36. Personal communication, citing E. M. Nokes and G. Wheeler, 'A Spanish account of the battle of Bosworth', *The Ricardian*, vol. 2, no. 36 (1972), 2; http://www.r3.org/richard-iii/the-battle-of-bosworth/bosworth-contemporary-tudor-accounts/ item III a) *A Castilian Report* DATE: Early 1486. AUTHOR: Diego de Valera, Castilian courtier (consulted September 2014).

37. See Ashdown-Hill, *The Third Plantagenet*, plates 1 and 2.

3 Sorcery and the Supernatural

1. J. Ashdown-Hill, *The Last Days of Richard III*, Stroud 2010 (2013), pp. 45–6.

2. J. Ashdown-Hill, *Royal Marriage Secrets*, Stroud 2013, pp. 26, 35, 36, 52.

3. P. W. Hammond and A. F. Sutton, *The Road to Bosworth Field*, London 1985, p. 14.

4. R. Davies, ed., *York Records of the Fifteenth Century*, London, 1843 (repr. Dursley, 1976), p. 223.

5. Polly Toynbee, 2009, quoted in Ben O'Neill 'A Critique of Politically Correct Language', http://www.independent.org/pdf/tir/tir_16_02_8_oneill.pdf (consulted July 2014).

6. O'Neill, *op. cit.*

7. D. Wain, *Live Science*, 3 September 2013, http://www.livescience.com/39392-king-richard-iii-roundworm-infection.html (consulted July 2014).

8. See, for example, J. Appleby, P. D. Mitchell, C. Robinson, A. Brough, G. Rutty, R. A. Harris, D. Thompson & B. Morgan, 'The scoliosis of Richard III, last Plantagenet King of England: diagnosis and clinical significance', *The Lancet*, 30 May 2014.

9. This is, in fact a Jewish tradition specifically negated by Christ (*John*, 9, vv.

1–3). Nevertheless, it persisted in the Christian thought of the Middle Ages and beyond.

10. Παραδείγματα.

11. See, for example, D. Lee, ed., Plato, *Timaeus and Critias*, Harmondsworth 1965.

12. J. B. Russell, *Witchcraft in the Middle Ages*, Cornel University 1972, pp. 113, 255.

13. The question of Richard's right to the throne is discussed below – see chapter 6.

14. D. Williams, *Deformed Discourse, the function of the Monster in Mediaeval Thought and Literature*, Montreal and Kingston 1996, p. 109

15. O. N. V. Glendinning, trans., J. Caro Baroja, *The World of the Witches*, Chicago and London 1965, figure 1.

16. J. Boardman, *Athenian Black Figure Vases*, London 1974, plate 238.

17. Glendinning / Caro Baroja, *The World of the Witches*, figure 2.

18. See R. S. Sylvester, ed., St Thomas More, *The History of King Richard III*, New Haven & London 1976, pp. 48–9.

19. Her marriage with William Shore had been annulled on the grounds that he was impotent. Her real name was Elizabeth Lambert. Incidentally, she later became known as 'Jane', but she never bore that Christian name in her lifetime. It was only bestowed on her much later – the invention of a playwright who wanted to put her on the stage, but who didn't know her real name.

20. A. & J. Nicoll, eds, *Holinshed's Chronicle as used in Shakespeare's Plays*, London 1927, 1955, p. 151.

21. *ibid.*

22. 'no man was there present, but well knew that his arme was ever such since his birth'. Nicoll & Nicoll, eds, *Holinshed's Chronicle as used in Shakespeare's Plays*, p. 152.

23. C. Given-Wilson *et al.*, eds, *The Parliament Rolls of Medieval England*, 2005, 9 Edw. IV.

24. πρὸς δὲ καὶ πεφύκαμεν / γυναῖκες ἐς μὲν ἔσθλ᾽ ἀμηχανώταται, / κακῶν δὲ πάντων τέκτονες σοφώταται. L. Méridier, ed., *Euripide, Le Cyclope, Alceste, Médée, Les Héraclides*, Paris 1925, p. 138, lines 407–09; P. Vellacott, trans., Euripides, *Medea and other plays*, Harmondsworth 1963, p. 29.

25. *dux Clarentie reus est factus, quod in regis mortem cum magicis et maleficis aspirasset.* C. A. J. Armstrong, ed., D. Mancini, *The Usurpation* [sic] *of Richard III*, Gloucester 1989, p. 62 (English translation J. A-H.).

26. *Crowland*, p. 145.

27. J. Haslewood, ed., *Mirror for Magistrates* vol. 2 (part 3), London 1815, pp. 226–43, 'George Plantagenet', attributed to William Baldwin, fl.1547.

28. A. & J. Nicoll, eds., *Holinshed's Chronicle as used in Shakespeare's Plays*, 1927, 1955, p. 138.

29. *Et quia erat quaedam prophetia, quod post E. id est, post Edwardum quartum, G regnaret, sub hoc ambiguo Georgius dux Clarentiae, medus amborum fratrum Edwardi et Ricardi regum, dux ob hoc Georgius peremptus est.* Hearne / Rous, *Historia Regum Angliae*, p. 215.

30. Russell, *Witchcraft in the Middle Ages*, p. 242.

31. A. H. Thomas & I. D. Thornley, eds, *The Great Chronicle of London*, London 1938, p. 236. There are several slightly different published versions

of this rhyme, which was pinned by William Colyngbourn on the door of St Paul's Cathedral in July 1484.

32. Russell, *Witchcraft in the Middle Ages*, p. 216.

4 Richard, the Serial Killer

1. I am grateful to Annette Carson for drawing my attention to this accusation.
2. It is possible that Edward's real father was Henry VI's cousin, Edmund Beaufort, Duke of Somerset. See J. Ashdown-Hill, *Royal Marriage Secrets*, Stroud 2013, p. 73 *et seq.*, and *The Third Plantagenet*, p. 38.
3. M. Jones, ed., *Philippe de Commynes Memoires*, Harmondsworth 1972, p. 196.
4. *y mourut et fut tué le dit prince de Gales, qui fut moult grand pitié, car it estoit beau jeune prince*, B. de Mandrot, ed., *Journal de Jean de Roye 1460–1483, connu sous le non de Chronique Scandaleuse*, vol. 1, Paris 1844, p. 259.
5. A & J. Nicoll, Holinshed's Chronicle as used in Shakespeare's Plays, London 1927, 1955, pp. 136–7.
6. C. L. Scofield, *The Life and Reign of Edward the Fourth, King of England and of France and Lord of Ireland*, 2 vols. 1923, reprinted 1967, vol. 1, pp. 586–7, citing Hist. MSS. Com., Report 12, app. 4, p. 4. [AC].
7. Nicoll, Holinshed's Chronicle as used in Shakespeare's Plays, p. 137.
8. R. A. Griffiths, 'Henry VI', *ODNB*.
9. Cited in W. J. White, 'The Death and Burial of Henry VI, part 1', *Ric.* 6 (1982–84), pp. 70–80 (p. 70). Warkworth's account was penned after July 1482. 21 May 1471 was indeed a Tuesday.
10. Warkworth as cited in Gairdner, *Richard the Third*, pp. 16–17.
11. *ibid.*
12. B. Wolffe, *Henry VI*, London 1981, p. 347.
13. H. Ellis, ed., *Three Books of Polydore Vergil's English History comprising the reigns of Henry VI, Edward IV, and Richard III*, 1844, pp. 155–6.
14. White, 'The Death and Burial of Henry VI, part 1', pp. 70–1.
15. Cited in White, 'The Death and Burial of Henry VI', part 1, p. 71. White argues that this is the most nearly contemporaneous account.
16. A. Breeze, 'A Welsh Poem of 1485 on Richard III', *Ric.* 18 (2008), pp. 46–53 (p. 47).
17. L. Visser-Fuchs, 'Edward IV's *Memoir on Paper* to Charles, Duke of Burgundy, the so-called "Short Version of the *Arrivall*"', Reprinted from *Nottingham Medieval Studies* XXXVI (1992), p. 223.
18. W. Shakespeare, *Henry VI, part 3*, act 5, scene 6.
19. Quote from Professor Macalister's report, in W. H. St John Hope, 'The Discovery of the Remains of King Henry VI in St George's Chapel, Windsor Castle', *Archaeologia*, vol. 62, part 2, pp. 533–42 (p. 536).
20. St John Hope, 'The Discovery of the Remains of King Henry VI', p. 537.
21. *ODNB*, R. A. Griffiths, 'Henry VI'.
22. J. Gairdner, ed., *Letters and Papers illustrative of the Reigns of Richard III and Henry VII*, 2 vols, vol. 1, London 1861, p. 68.
23. See J. Ashdown-Hill & A. Carson, 'The Execution of the Earl of Desmond', *Ricardian* 15 2005, pp. 70–93.

24. Armstrong/Mancini, *The Usurpation* [sic] *of Richard III*, pp. 62–3.
25. For a fuller account, see Ashdown-Hill, *The Third Plantagenet*, chapters 11–13.
26. See Ashdown-Hill, *The Third Plantagenet*.
27. The Crowland Chronicle actually gives two different accounts of the time of Buckingham's arrival, suggesting earlier that Buckingham met Richard in Northampton, *before* Earl Rivers arrived. *Crowland*, pp. 154–5. See also J. Ashdown-Hill, *Richard III's 'Beloved Cousyn'*, Stroud 2009, pp. 86–7.
28. *ODNB*, M. Hicks, Anthony Woodville, 2nd Earl Rivers.
29. ... *dominus comes de Rivers Antonius Woodvyle morte instante cilicio ad nudam carnem, ut diu ante usus fuerat, indutus est repertus, In tempore tamen incarcerationis apud Pontem-fractum edidit unum Balet in Anglicis, ut mihi monstratum est quod subsequetur sub his verbis:* [English text of poem] *et sic comites praerecitati adiudicati sunt ad mortem tanquam rei & coniuratores mortis Ricardi ducis Gloucestriae, tunc temporis Protectoris regni Angliae. Et sic innocentes propter id quod no excogitaverunt a tortoribus suis pacifice inimicorum crudeli tormentatione humilime se submisserunt.* Hearne / Rous, *Historia Regum Angliae*, pp. 213–14.
30. http://en.wikipedia.org/wiki/Henry_Percy,_4th_Earl_of_Northumberland (consulted September 2014).
31. J. G. Nichols, ed., *Grants, &c from the Crown during the Reign of Edward the Fifth*, London (Camden Society) 1854, p. 19 *et seq.*
32. H. Pease, *The Lord Wardens of the Marches of England and Scotland*, London, 1912, p. 138 *et seq.* I am grateful to Annette Carson for drawing this to my attention.
33. *ODNB*, M. Hicks, Anthony Woodville, 2nd Earl Rivers.
34. 'The death of Anthony Earl Rivers is dated 20 June (instead of 25 June) in inquisitions post mortem of 1486 [footnote: *Inq. P. M. Henry VII*, I, No. 33 (2 Nov. 1486)]'. A. Hanham, *Richard III and his Early Historians 1483–1535*, Oxford University Press 1975, p. 29.
35. *ODNB*, R. Horrox, 'Hastings, William first Baron Hastings'.
36. A. Carson, *Richard III, the Maligned King* (hereinafter *R3MK*), Stroud, 2008, p. 28.
37. *Sed et privatarum voluptatum conscius ac particeps erat.* Mancini, pp. 68–9.
38. *R3MK*, p. 29.
39. *R3MK*, p. 27.
40. *R3MK*, p. 75.
41. Her sister was the Duchess of Norfolk; her uncle, the Earl of Warwick; her cousin by marriage, Sir Thomas Montgomery. Any of these could have introduced her to the king.
42. *R3MK*, p. 85.
43. J. Ashdown-Hill, *Eleanor, the Secret Queen*, Stroud, 2009, p. 37.
44. *ODNB*, Horrox, 'Hastings'.
45. *ODNB*, Horrox, 'Hastings'.
46. Armstrong/Mancini, p. 69.
47. Armstrong/Mancini, p. 69.
48. *R3MK*, p. 123, citing the *Great Chronicle*.
49. Mancini, p. 71; *Crowland*, pp. 154–5.
50. *Crowland*, pp. 154–5.

51. P. M. Kendall, *Richard the Third*, London 1955, p. 164.
52. Edwards, *The Itinerary of King Richard III*, p. 1.
53. *Crowland*, pp. 154–5.
54. Kendall, *R3*, p. 173.
55. *Crowland*, pp. 156–7.
56. *CPR 1476–1485*, p. 348.
57. 'In 1448 Stillington was appointed a commissioner to negotiate with Burgundy over recent breaches of a truce ... In 1449 he became a royal councillor, but ... his secular career during the 1450s remains obscure'. *ODNB*, Hicks, Stillington.
58. Stillington held the office of chancellor from 1467 to 1470 and from 1471 to 1473.
59. For full details see Ashdown-Hill, *Richard III's 'Beloved Cousyn'*, p. 9 *et seq.*
60. Hammond and Sutton, *The Road to Bosworth Field*, p. 103.
61. Hanham, *Richard III and his Early Historians*, pp. 24–9.
62. Hammond and Sutton, *The Road to Bosworth Field*, p. 105, citing R. Firth Green, 'Historical Notes of a London Citizen 1483–8, *English Historical Review*, vol. 96 (1981), p. 588. The extant copy of this account probably dates from the early sixteenth century, but is believed to reproduce earlier material: *R3MK*, p. 289.
63. *Crowland*, pp. 158–9.
64. *ex composito acclamat protector insidias sibi instructas esse, eosque cum armis latentibus venisse.* Armstrong / Mancini, p. 91, translation J. A-H.
65. Annette Carson's latest research (see the 2013 edition of *R3MK*) intimates that it was within Richard's powers as Constable of England – and acting under the Law of Arms – to convene an *ad hoc* trial of the 'drumhead courtmartial' variety and therefore due process could well have been followed.
66. Armstrong / Mancini, pp. 90–1.
67. P. Lindsay, *On Some Bones in Westminster Abbey: A Defence of King Richard III*, London 1934 (reprinted Bath 1969), pp. 36–7.
68. See J. Ashdown-Hill, *The Dublin King*, Stroud 2015.
69. P. Tudor-Craig, *Richard III* (catalogue for the National Portrait Gallery exhibition, June – October 1973), pp. 54–5 and appendix 4.
70. Hanham, *Richard III and his Early Historians 1483–1535*, p. 49.
71. J. J. Smith, *Essentials of Early English*, Oxford 1999, 2005, p. 115.
72. Personal communication from Marie Barnfield.
73. See, for example, the use of the word 'hadde' in the heralds' account of the 1476 Garter ceremonies at Windsor: '... Entred into the Chapter-house with the Soveraign and Knyghts of the Order; And thro the Chapter-house into the quier to evensonge, which donne they rode uppe to the Castle againe in their habitts according to the Statutes, and there hadde voyde of Espices &c'. I am grateful to Marie Barnfield for drawing my attention to this.
74. http://www.oed.com/view/Entry/67478?rskey=AV1wfu&result=1#eid (consulted September 2014).
75. Personal communication from Marie Barnfield.
76. '*Le Duc de Glaucestre ... feit mourir les deux fils dedans la tour de Londres, donnant à entendre aux peuples qu'ils estoient morts par accidant s'estans precipitez du hault du pont lequelentre dedans la tour*'. *Les Memoires de Mess Martin du Bellay, Seigneur de Langey*, Paris 1569, p. 6. Cited (briefly, with a

small error in the French spelling, and with no precise details of the source) in Gairdner, *Richard the Third*, pp. 125–6, footnote 2.

77. H. Ellis, ed., *Three Books of Polydore Vergil's English History: Comprising the Reigns of Henry VI, Edward IV and Richard III*, London 1844, pp. 188–9.
78. Ellis/Vergil, p. 184; my emphasis.
79. TNA, C81/1392/6, transcribed by R. C. and P. B. Hairsine and published in Hammond and Sutton, *The Road to Bosworth Field*, p. 145.
80. http://en.wikipedia.org/wiki/John_Rous_(historian) (consulted August 2014).
81. Gairdner, *Richard the Third*, pp. 194–5.

Part 3 – Richard's Religion

1. Lambeth Ms. 474, f. 183.

5 Catholic or Anglican?

2. 1958 edition, fifteenth impression, 1987, p. 63.
3. Gairdner, *Richard the Third*, p. 148: see below, chapter 7.
4. A. F. Sutton & L. Visser-Fuchs, *The Hours of Richard III*, Stroud 1990, 1996, p. 80.
5. J. Hughes, *The Religious Life of Richard III, Piety and Prayer in the North of England*, Stroud 1997, pp. 105–6.
6. Sutton & Visser-Fuchs, *The Hours of Richard III*, p. 80.
7. Hughes, *The Religious Life of Richard III*, p. 127.
8. Ashdown-Hill, *The Last Days of Richard III*, pp. 55–6.
9. *Verbum caro, panem verum verbo carnem efficit;/ Fitque sanguis Christi merum, et si sensus deficit,/ Ad firmandum cor sincerum sola fides sufficit.* Verse 4 of the hymn, *Pange, lingua, gloriosi Corporis mysterium*, setting out the Catholic doctrine of transubstantiation, written by St Thomas Aquinas (1225–74) for the Feast of Corpus Christi (translation J. A-H.).
10. Natasha Sheldon, 'Burying Richard III: Details of the Re-Interment and Tomb of 'The Last Warrior King' Revealed', 19 June 2014, http://decodedpast. com/burying-richard-iii-details-re-interment-tomb-last-warrior-king-revealed/10742 (consulted October 2014).
11. Some other European languages do not normally use this term. For example Italian translates 'Roman Catholic' simply as 'cattolico'; Albanian, as 'katolik', Icelandic, as 'kaþólsku'.
12. Letter from the Dean of Leicester to the *For Richard Group*.
13. In the fourteenth century some popes resided at Avignon instead of Rome, for political reasons.
14. See, for example, Richard's acknowledgement of papal jurisdiction in respect of his marriage to a relative, in chapter 8, below.
15. E. Duffy, *The Stripping of the Altars*, London 1992. I am grateful to Mark Goacher for reminding me that not everyone agrees with Duffy's point of view.
16. If there were not administrative and theological differences between these two groups, presumably they would be one.
17. E. Peacock, ed., *Instructions for Parish Priests by John Myrc*, London 1868 (reprinted 2005), p. 13.
18. http://en.wikipedia.org/wiki/Wycliffe's_Bible (consulted October 2014).

19. Personal communication from the Bishop of Leicester to the author, 16 March 2013; my emphasis.
20. Leicester Cathedral's *Brief for Architects*, first draft, 2 March 2013, 'Avoiding pastiche and the cult of "St. Richard"'.

Part 4 – The Monster King

6 Richard, the Usurper

1. http://www.royal.gov.uk/historyofthemonarchy/kingsandqueensofengland/theyorkists/richardiii.aspx (July 2014). However, Edward IV was called a usurper by Henry VII's historian, Bernard André: http://www.philological.bham.ac.uk/andreas/ (consulted August 2014).
2. http://www.thefreedictionary.com/usurper (August 2014) my emphasis.
3. The British Monarchy website does define Richard III as a usurper, not only in the entry under his own name, but also in its account of the accession of Henry VII.
4. Gairdner, *Richard the Third*, Appendix, note II, pp. 338–9.
5. Isabelle of France, widow of Edward II; Alice Salisbury (Perrers), mistress of Edward III.
6. Armstrong / Mancini, pp. 62–3. This is not to suggest, however, that she had been aware of the problem at the time when their secret marriage took place, in 1464.
7. Armstrong / Mancini, pp. 76–9.
8. J. Ashdown-Hill, 'The Elusive Mistress: Elizabeth Lucy and her Family', *Ricardian* 11 (June 1999), pp. 490–505 (p. 498).
9. In my book, *Eleanor, the Secret Queen*, I suggested that, after the battle of Towton, Edward IV returned south by an eastern route and may have secretly married Eleanor in the Norwich area, in April 1461. This was based on the fact that a document was issued in Norwich in the king's name in that month. However, it is now clear that Edward's journey south did not include Norwich. On his way back to London the new young king actually rode via Coventry, Warwick and Daventry. At the start of the second week of June, travelling between Warwick and Daventry, Edward IV passed close by Eleanor's manors of Fenny Compton and Burton Dassett.
10. *ODNB*, M. Hicks, 'Robert Stillington' (2004).
11. For the relevant original source material, see Ashdown-Hill, *Eleanor the Secret Queen*, pp. 192, 195, 205–7.
12. Surprise has sometimes been expressed that Stillington took no action earlier. However, he was not in a position to take any action in respect of the marriage itself (only Eleanor, as the wronged party, could have cited Edward IV before the church courts). What Stillington did in 1483 was not to question the *marriage*, but to question the right to the throne of Edward V.
13. J. Ashdown-Hill, *Eleanor, the Secret Queen*, Stroud 2009.
14. See, for example, C. A. J. Armstrong, ed., *The Usurpation of Richard the Third*, Oxford University Press 1969, reprinted Gloucester 1989.
15. W. Smith, ed., *A Latin-English Dictionary*, eighth edition, London 1868, p. 1164.
16. *et inaudito dictus Richardus protector, vicesimo sexto die praefati mensis*

Junii regimine regni sub titulo regii nominis sibi vendicavit, seque eodem die apud magnan aulam Westmonasterii in cathedram marmoream ibi intrusit. Crowland, pp. 158–9.

17. See Carson, *R3MK* (2013 edition), p. 284.
18. My earlier assessment of this point in *The Last Days of Richard III*, p 84 (2010 edition – p. 85, 2013 edition), was incorrect.
19. http://www.philological.bham.ac.uk/andreas/ (August 2014).
20. Gairdner, *Richard the Third*, p. 91.
21. Henry VII's Act of Parliament of 1485: *Rolls of Parliament*, vol. 6, p. 289.
22. *statim duxit in uxorem praeclaram dominam Elizabeth, filiam et heredem regis Edwardi IIII*. Hearne/Rous, *Historia Regum Angliae*, p. 218; my emphasis.
23. S. B. Chrimes, *Henry VII*, London 1972, 1987, p. 66.
24. H. C. Maxwell-Lyte, ed., *The Registers of Robert Stillington, Bishop of Bath and Wells 1466–1491 and Richard Fox, Bishop of Bath and Wells 1492–1494*, Somerset Record Society, 1937, p. xiii.

7 Richard, the Tyrant

1. Hammond and Sutton, *Richard III: the Road to Bosworth Field*, p. 135.
2. Gairdner, *Richard the Third*, p. 144.
3. *op. cit.*, p. 145.
4. *ibid.*
5. *ibid.*
6. *ibid.*
7. *ibid.*, citing Harl. MS 433, no. 1548.
8. *op. cit.*, pp. 145–46.
9. *op. cit.*, p. 148.
10. *op. cit.*, p. 149.
11. A. Carson, 'Notes Towards the Definition of a Tyrant', *Ricardian Bulletin*, December 2013, pp. 43–5.
12. D. Seward, *Richard III – England's Black Legend*, Harmondsworth 1997, p. 55.
13. C. Skidmore, *Bosworth and the Birth of the Tudors*, p. 207.
14. R. Horrox, 'Preparations for Edward IV's Return from Exile', *The Ricardian*, vol. VI, no. 79, pp. 124–7.
15. W. E. A. Axon [*recte* Axton], *The Black Knights of Ashton*, Manchester 1870; K. M. Briggs, *A Dictionary of British Folk Tales*, 4 vols, 1970, Part B, vol. 1, pp.47–9.
16. J. G. Wedgwood, *History of Parliament, Biographies volume 1439–1509*, London 1936, p. 26.
17. Skidmore, *op. cit.*, p. 207.
18. Carson, *op. cit.*
19. H. Ellis, ed., R. Fabyan, *The New Chronicles of England and France* (*c.* 1516), London, 1811, p. 671.

8 Marriage Mythology

1. W. H. Prescott, *History of the Reign of Ferdinand and Isabella*, 2 vols. New York 1837, vol. 1, p. 434, item 41, citing Diego Enriquez Castillo, *Crónica*

del Rey Don Enrique el Cuarto, cap. 136. I am grateful to Jonathan Hayes for drawing this to my attention.

2. Ferdinand the Catholic, heir to the throne of Aragon, succeeded to the throne of Sicily in 1468.

3. *E luego por remediar el peligro é daños que podrian recrescer, si los dichos reynos é señoríos no tuviesen quien adelante legitimamente en ellos subcediese, fue acordo por vuestra Excelencia é por los Grandes, é Perlados [Prelados] é caballeros de su Corte é muy alto Consejo, que segun las leyes y ordenamientos que cerca de lo semejante disponen, se viese con diligencia quál matrimonio de quatro que á la sazon se movian del Príncipe de Aragon, Rey de Secilia, é Rey de Portugal, é del Duque de Berri, é del hermano del Rey de Inglaterra parescia mas honrado á vuestro corona Real, é mas cumplidero á la pacificacion y ensanchamiento de los dichos vuestros reynos.* D. Enríquez del Castillo, *Crónica del Rey D. Enrique El Quarto De Este Nombre*, Madrid 1787, p. 252.

4. Ashdown-Hill, *The Third Plantagenet*, p. 99.

5. Ashdown-Hill, *The Third Plantagenet*, p. 73.

6. Ashdown-Hill, *The Third Plantagenet*, pp. 94–5; p. 124, note 11.

7. *Crowland*, p. 60.

8. *Crowland*, p. 133.

9. Gairdner, *Richard the Third*, pp. 19–20.

10. S. Cunningham, *Richard III, a Royal Enigma*, Kew 2003, p. 29.

11. A. Cheetham, *The Life and Times of Richard III*, London 1972, p. 94.

12. M. Barnfield, 'Diriment Impediments, Dispensations and Divorce: Richard III and Matrimony', *Ric* 17 (2007), pp. 84–98 (p. 84). I am grateful to Marie Barnfield for her valuable advice in respect of papal dispensations for marriages.

13. *Ricardus, dux Glouirestere [sic], laicus Lincolniensis diocesis, et Anna Nevile, mulier Eboracensis diocesis, cupiunt inter se matrimonium contrahere, sed quia tertio et quarto **affinitatibus** gradibus invicem se attinent, quare petunt cum ipsis dispensari. Item cum declaratoria super tertio et quarto.* P. D. Clare, 'English royal marriages and the Papal Plenitentiary in the fifteenth century', English Historical Review, vol. 120 (2006), pp. 1014–29 (p. 1028), my emphasis.

14. *Dispensatio Pauli PP iii [sic for ii] de matrimonio contrahendo inter nobilem virum Georgium Ducem Clarencie & Isabellam filiam nobilis viri Ricardi Nevill Comites Warwici, licet ipse Georgius & Isabella secundo & tertio & tertio & quarto **consanguinitatis** gradibus coniuncti sunt, Ac etiam licet mater ipsius Georgij eundem Isabellam de sacro fonte levavit. Datum Rome apud sanctam Petrum pridie Idus Martij Anno 1468 7° Edwardi 4ti.* M. Barnfield, 'Diriment Impediments, Dispensations and Divorce: Richard III and Matrimony', Ric 17 (2007), pp. 84–98 (p. 89) citing Bodleian MS Dugdale 15, fol. 75. My emphasis.

15. M. Hicks, *Anne Neville, Queen to Richard III*, Stroud 2006, pp. 130–4.

16. The marriage of George and Isabel created an affinity between George and Anne, and an affinity between Richard and Isabel, but not an affinity between Richard and Anne. Barnfield, 'Diriment Impediments', pp. 85–6.

17. = annulment.

18. *tacendum non sit quod per haec festa Natalia choreis aut tripudiis vanisque mutatoriis vestium Annae, reginae, atque Dominae Elizabeth, primogenitae defunct regis eisdem colore et forma distributis, nimis intentum est unde et populus obloqui proceresque et praelati vehementer mirari videbantur,*

dictumque a multis est ipsum regem aut expectata morte reginae, aut per divortium cuiis faciendi sufficientes causas se habuisse arbitratus est, matrimonio cum dicta Elizabeth contrahendo mentem omnibus modis applicare. Crowland, p. 174.

19. Lamb *et al.*, 'Multi-isotope analysis demonstrates significant lifestyle changes in King Richard III', http://www.sciencedirect.com/science/article/pii/S0305440314002428 (consulted September 2014).

20. http://www.sciencedirect.com/science/article/pii/S0305440314002428 Abstract (consulted September 2014).

21. http://www.sciencedirect.com/science/article/pii/S0305440314002428 (consulted September 2014).

22. http://www.sciencedirect.com/science/article/pii/S0305440314002428 Conclusion (consulted September 2014).

23. http://www.sciencedirect.com/science/article/pii/S0305440314002428 (consulted September 2014).

24. Society of Antiquaries of London, *Salon* online newsletter, Issue 326, 22 September 2014.

25. C. Catling, 'From the trowel's edge ...', *Current Archaeology*, issue 296, November 2014, pp. 56–7 (p. 56).

26. Ashdown-Hill, *Richard III's 'Beloved Cousyn'*, p. 119.

27. M. K. Dale & V. B. Redstone, eds., *The Household Book of Dame Alice de Bryene of Acton Hall, Suffolk, September 1412 – September 1413*, Ipswich 1931, pp. 1–3.

28. M. Clive, *This Son of York*, London 1973, p. 274.

29. R. Horrox & P. W. Hammond, eds., British Library Harleian Manuscript 433, vol. 3, London 1982, p. 190 (f. 308v).

30. C. A. Halsted, *Richard III*, two volumes, London 1844, vol. 2, pp. 569–70.

31. See H. Ellis, ed., *Three Books of Polydore Vergil's English History comprising the reigns of Henry VI, Edward IV, and Richard III*, 1844, p. 215, P. Sheppard Routh '"Lady Scroop Daughter of K. Edward": an Enquiry', *Ric.* 9 (1991–93), pp. 410–16 (pp. 412, 416, n. 12) and J. Laynesmith, *The Last Medieval Queens*, Oxford 2004, p. 199. Cecily's Scrope marriage was annulled by Henry VII soon after his accession. He subsequently married Cecily to his own supporter, Lord Welles.

32. *R3MK*, p. 257, quoting Kincaid's edition of Buck's reported text of Elizabeth of York's letter.

33. Myers/Buck, p. 128.

34. *ibid.*

35. See *R3MK*, pp. 262, 264.

36. *Crowland*, pp. 176–7.

Part 5 – Legends of Richard's Last Days

9 The Inn and the Bed

1. For full details, see below, note 9.

2. For a more detailed account of this material, see Ashdown-Hill, *The Last Days of Richard III*, particularly chapter 6.

3. Edwards, *The Itinerary of King Richard III*, pp. xiv, 39.

4. S. E. Green, *Selected Legends of Leicestershire*, Leicester 1971, p. 21. Thomas Clarke was mayor of Leicester in 1583 and again in 1598: H. Hartopp, *The Roll of the Mayors of the Borough and Lord Mayors of the City of Leicester 1209–1935*, Leicester 1935, pp. 75–6, 80. The story of Clark(e)'s treasure was first written down in Sir Roger Twysden's 'Commonplace Book' in about 1650, and published in J. Nichols, *History and Antiquities of the County of Leicester*, London 1795–1811.

5. L. J. F. Ashdown-Hill, 'The client network, connections and patronage of Sir John Howard' (&c), unpublished PhD thesis, University of Essex 2008.

6. Speede's account is cited in J. Throsby, *Memoirs of the Town and County of Leicester*, Leicester 1777, p. 61, n. b.

7. F. Roe, *Old Oak Furniture*, London 1908, p. 286.

8. Throsby, *Leicester*, pp. 14, 62, n. b. The feet, which were cut off in the mid eighteenth century, measured six inches square and were two feet six inches in height.

9. http://www.dailymail.co.uk/news/article-2607033/Listen-voice-Richard-IIIs-ghost-Amateur-ghoul-hunters-record-spooky-sounds-bed-legend-says-spent-night-alive.html (consulted September 2014). My emphasis.

10. *ibid*.

11. Announcement of the University of Leicester Press Office, 13 January 2014, http://www2.le.ac.uk/offices/press/press-releases/2014/january/historic-image-of-king-richard-iii-at-blue-boar-inn-to-be-made-available-to-public (consulted September 2014).

12. http://www.le.ac.uk/richardiii/history/blueboarinn.html (consulted September 2014).

13. J. D. Austin, *Merevale and Atherstone 1485: Recent Bosworth Discoveries*, Friends of Atherstone Heritage 2004, section 21.

14. I am grateful to Philip French, curator of Leicester City Museums, for this information.

10 The White Horse and the Sleepless Night

1. Shakespeare, *Richard III*, act 5, scene 3. For full details regarding the received form of the horse's name, see J. Jowett, ed., *The Tragedy of King Richard III*, Oxford 2000, p. 336 and n. 43, also N. de Somogyi, ed., *The Shakespeare Folios: Richard III*, London 2002, p. 267, n. 90.

2. R. Horrox & P. W. Hammond, eds, *British Library Harleian Manuscript 433*, vol. 1, Upminster 1979, pp. 4–5.

3. See Ashdown-Hill, unpublished PhD thesis, regarding John Howard's stable, and Horrox & Hammond, *Harl. 433*, vol. 1, pp. 4–5 for Richard III's surviving horse list.

4. J. Speede, *The History of Great Britaine*, London 1611 (1614), p. 725.

5. See the case of Jeweyn Blakecote, *sortilega*, in J. Ashdown-Hill, *Mediaeval Colchester's Lost Landmarks*, Derby 2009, p. 161. Regarding the Richard III Bow Bridge prophecy, the location, at a water crossing, may perhaps be significant. With the substitution of begging for washing, 'there is a hint of the Irish/Scottish 'Washer at the Ford' folk motif. The Washer at the Ford is an Otherworld woman whose task it is to wash the clothes of those who are about to die': personal communication from Marie Barnfield.

6. *Crowland*, pp. 180–1.
7. Ellis/Vergil, pp. 221–2.
8. Crowland, pp. 180–1.
9. The true identity of the Crowland chronicler is much debated. He may not have been a single individual: A. Hanham, 'The Mysterious Affair at Crowland Abbey', *Ric.* 18, pp. 1–20.
10. http://www.luminarium.org/encyclopedia/sweatingsickness.htm (consulted March 2009).

11 The Last Mass and the Last Battle

1. J. Ashdown-Hill, 'The Bosworth Crucifix', *Transactions of the Leicestershire Archaeological & Historical Society* vol. 78 (2004), pp. 83–96.
2. *Crowland*, pp. 180–1.
3. BL, Add. MS 12060, ff. 19–20, as quoted in P. J. Foss, *The Field of Redemore*, Newtown Linford 1990 (1998), p. 54. See also R. M. Warnicke, 'Sir Ralph Bigod: a loyal servant to King Richard III', *Ric.* 6 (1982–84), pp. 299–303.
4. J.W. Verkaik, 'King Richard's Last Sacrament', *Ric.* 9, [1991–93], pp. 359–360.
5. My emphasis.
6. http://www.catholictradition.org/Eucharist/mass-h10.htm (consulted October 2014).

Part 6 – Richard III's Dead Body

12 Burial Myths

1. Gairdner, *Richard the Third*, p. 252.
2. Kendall, *Richard The Third*, p. 161; Sutton, Visser-Fuchs & Griffiths, *The Royal Funerals of the House of York at Windsor*, p. 11.
3. *Inter alios mortuos corpora dicto Richardi regis ... multasque alias contumelias illatas ipsoque non satis humaniter propter funem in collum adjectum usque Leicestriam deportato.* Crowland, pp. 182–3. It is possible (but not certain) that there is a gap in the text, as tentatively indicated.
4. *Interea Ricardi corpus, cuncto nudatum vestitu, ac dorso equi impositum, capite et brachiis et cruribus utrimque pendentibus, Leicestriam ad coenobium Franciscorum deportant, spectaculum mehercule miserabile, sed hominis vita dignum, ibique sine ullo funeris honore biduo post terra humatur.* Quoted in C. J. Billson, *Mediaeval Leicester*, Leicester 1920, p. 180. See also Ellis/Vergil, p. 226.
5. See, for example, A. F. Sutton & L. Visser-Fuchs, 'The Making of a Minor London Chronicle in the Household of Sir Thomas Frowyk (died 1485)', *The Ricardian*, Vol. X, No. 126, pp. 97–8.
6. TNA, C1/206/69 recto, lines 4 and 5.
7. Ashdown-Hill, *The Last Days of Richard III* (2010 edition), p. 97.
8. Ashdown-Hill, *The Last Days of Richard III* (2010 edition), p. 91.
9. Ashdown-Hill, *The Last Days of Richard III* (2010 edition), p. 51.
10. White, 'The Death and Burial of Henry VI' part 2, *Ric.* 6, pp. 106–17 (p. 112); Wolffe, *Henry VI*, p. 352. This first bay has subsequently become the site of the tomb of King Edward VII and Queen Alexandra. An alternative

possibility is that Richard III intended to be buried at York Minster, where he proposed – and actually began constructing – a very splendid chantry chapel.

11. For further suggestions regarding Richard III's thoughts on this subject, see J. Ashdown-Hill, *The Dublin King*, Stroud 2015, pp. 65, 87–9.

12. The precise relationship between the two bodies was first explained to Philippa Langley (who commissioned ULAS to carry out the Leicester Greyfriars excavation on behalf of the LOOKING FOR RICHARD PROJECT on the basis of this information) by Richard Buckley (one of the directors of ULAS) at a meeting in the spring of 2011. Subsequently, in the summer and autumn of 2013 this situation was confirmed by both of the ULAS directors, Patrick Clay and Richard Buckley. The status of ULAS as an independent business was again confirmed in court by the University of Leicester barrister during the Judicial Review on 13–14 March 2014. I am grateful to Philippa Langley for this information.

13. M. Morris, R. Buckley & M. Codd, *Visions of Ancient Leicester*, Leicester 2011, p. 57.

14. Ashdown-Hill, *The Last Days of Richard III* (2010 edition), pp. 92–3.

15. *op. cit.*, p. 111.

16. See also *op. cit.*, p. 100, and 2013 edition, plate 25 (Wingfield tomb image).

17. See for example *Ricardian Bulletin*, June 2013, 'Grey Friars reconstructed', p. i.

18. http://www.dmu.ac.uk/about-dmu/news/2014/july/dmu-brings-richard-iiis-priory-back-to-digital-life.aspx (consulted October 2014).

13 The Body in the River

1. A. J. Carson (ed.), *Finding Richard III – the Official Account*, Horstead 2014, p. 83.

2. C. Wren, *Parentalia, or Memoirs of the Family of the Wrens*, London 1750, p. 144.

3. Richard III Society, Barton Library, personal communication from S. H. Skillington, Hon. Secretary, Leicester Archaeological Society, to Saxon Barton, 29 October 1935.

4. Speede's story that all coins of the Emperor Caligula were destroyed is untrue.

5. From Speede, *History*, p. 725.

6. See Richard Corbet's *Iter Boreale* (c. 1620–25), cited in J. Ashdown-Hill, 'The Location of the 1485 Battle and the Fate of Richard III's Body', *Ricardian Bulletin*, Autumn 2004, pp. 34–5.

7. A. Wakelin, 'Is there a king under this bridge?', *Leicester Mercury*, 8 October 2002, p. 10. See below, chapter 14.

8. Speede, *History*, p. 725.

9. Carson (ed.), *Finding Richard III – the Official Account*, p. 83 (my emphasis).

14 The Mythology of Rediscovery

1. http://www.11kbw.com/app/files/PDFs/RichardIIIJudgment.pdf item 28, p. 6.

2. C. Ross, *Richard III*, London 1981, p. 226.

3. 'The Tomb of Richard III' by Bill White, *Ricardian Bulletin*, Winter 2007, page 45. I am grateful to Annette Carson for drawing my attention to White's letter.

4. Alex Dawson, *Leicester Mercury*, Thursday 2 March 1995. I am grateful to Sally Henshaw, Secretary of the Leicester Branch of the Richard III Society, for this and other cuttings from the *Leicester Mercury*.
5. Adam Wakelin, *Leicester Mercury*, Tuesday 8 October 2002, my emphasis.
6. Ben Farmer, *Leicester Mercury*, Wednesday 11 May 2005.
7. For full details of my work on this, see Carson (ed.), *Finding Richard III*, pp. 9–15.
8. Morris, Buckley & Codd, *Visions of Ancient Leicester*, p. 42.
9. Carson, ed., *Finding Richard III, the Official Account*, appendix 5, pp. 75–81.

15 The DNA Link

1. J. Ashdown-Hill, 'Margaret of York's Dance of Death – the DNA evidence', *Handelingen van de Koninklijke Kring voor Oudheidkunde, Letteren an Kunst van Mechelen*, 111 (2007), pp. 193–207.
2. *Koninklijke Kring voor Oudheidkunde, Letteren en Kunst van Mechelen*.
3. This attempt appeared to show that the remains found were not those of Margaret. Of course, when the results were published, it was made clear that the mtDNA sequence of Joy Ibsen had still to be confirmed if possible, at some stage, by a second source.
4. For the follow-up research on this front, see Ashdown-Hill, *The Third Plantagenet*, chapters 16 and 17.
5. *op. cit.*, p. 124.
6. But see Ashdown-Hill, *The Dublin King*, Stroud 2015.
7. M. Morris & R. Buckley, *Richard III The King under the car park*, University of Leicester 2013, p. 58.
8. http://www.nature.com/ncomms/2014/141202/ncomms6631/full/ncomms6631.html (consulted December 2014).

Part 7 Kudos, Fantasies and Profit

1. http://theandalucian.com/yahoo_site_admin/assets/docs/ANDALUCIANnov2013.34922435.pdf (consulted September 2014).

16 The post-2012 Leicester Edition of Richard III

2. Personal communications from Sarah Levitt, 24 and 25 March 2013.
3. Personal communication from Sharon Lock, 8 August 2014.
4. http://www.theguardian.com/uk/2013/mar/13/row-richard-iii-burial-site (consulted November 2014).
5. Personal communication from Canon Barry Naylor, then the acting Dean of Leicester, 17 March 2013.
6. Personal communication from the Bishop of Leicester, 16 March 2013.
7. I am grateful to Philippa Langley for this information.
8. Personal communication from the Bishop of Leicester, 16 March 2013.
9. Personal communication from Canon Barry Naylor, then the acting Dean of Leicester, 17 March 2013.
10. Personal communication from George Jones, 9 August 2013.
11. http://www.bbc.co.uk/history/people/king_richard_iii (consulted August 2014).

17 Images

1. Personal communication from Very Revd Vivienne Faull, 4 November 2011.
2. Communication from Very Revd Vivienne Faull, 9 October 2012.
3. Episode 1 of *The Black Adder*, BBC TV, 15 June 1983.
4. http://en.wikipedia.org/wiki/Blackadder (consulted October 2014).
5. H. Hacking, *Historical Cats*, London 2003, p. 24.

18 The Tourist Trade

1. London 1923 (reprinted New York 1977), p. 183.
2. http://www.dailymail.co.uk/sciencetech/article-2705502/King-Richard-III-3D-PRINTED-Computer-generated-plastic-replica-monarchs-skeleton-goes-display.html (consulted July 2014).
3. Curiously, the members of the Plantagenet Alliance (who were not ultimately allowed any say in the fate of Richard III's remains) were all much more closely related to King Richard than the then Lord Mowbray was to Anne Mowbray, Duchess of York and Norfolk, in the 1960s. Yet Lord Mowbray was allowed to determine the fate of the remains of his distant relative, Anne. Could this have been because he was a lord?
4. http://www.independent.co.uk/news/uk/home-news/leicester-cathedral-denies-it-is-cashing-in-on-richard-iiis-reinternment-9706943.html (consulted September 2014).
5. Statement from Leicester Cathedral issued 3 September 2014.

Conclusions

1. http://www.historyextra.com/news/richard-iii/richard-iii-worth-%C2%A345m-leicester-economy (consulted November 2014)
2. Modern English translated edition, C. Wolters, ed., *The Cloud of Unknowing*, Harmondsworth 1961 (1974), p. 63.
3. I am grateful to Mark Goacher for his comments on this – and other – subjects.

Appendix 1

1. I am grateful to Stephen Lark for his help with the preparation of this appendix.

Appendix 3

1. As can be seen from the email correspondence in appendix 4, these proposed amendments were prepared by the Looking For Richard Project Team in July 2014.

Acknowledgements

My sincere thanks go to Marie Barnfield, Annette Carson, Judith Champ, Mark Goacher, Sally Henshaw, Fr Paul Keane, Philippa Langley, Stephen Lark, and Dave Perry, who have all helped and advised me in various ways in respect of parts of my text. Any mistakes which remain are, of course, my responsibility. I should also like to thank the friends and relatives who have helped me through the difficult times during which this book was written.

Bibliography

MS & Unpublished Sources

L. J. F. Ashdown-Hill, 'The client network, connections and patronage of Sir John Howard' (&c), unpublished PhD thesis, University of Essex 2008

Lambeth Ms. 474

Richard III Society, Barton Library, personal communication from S.H. Skillington, Hon. Secretary, Leicester Archaeological Society, to Saxon Barton, 29 October 1935

TNA, C1/206

Books

Armstrong C. A. J., ed., Mancini D., *The Usurpation of Richard III*, Oxford University Press 1969, reprinted Gloucester: Alan Sutton 1989

Ashdown-Hill J., *Mediaeval Colchester's Lost Landmarks*, Derby: Breedon Books 2009

Ashdown-Hill J., *Eleanor, the Secret Queen*, Stroud: The History Press 2009

Ashdown-Hill J., *Richard III's 'Beloved Cousyn'*, Stroud: The History Press 2009

Ashdown-Hill J., *The Last Days of Richard III*, Stroud: The History Press 2010; 2013

Ashdown-Hill J., *Royal Marriage Secrets*, Stroud: The History Press 2014

Ashdown-Hill J., *The Third Plantagenet*, Stroud: The History Press 2014

Ashdown-Hill J., *The Dublin King*, Stroud: The History Press 2015

Austin J. D., *Merevale and Atherstone 1485: Recent Bosworth Discoveries*, Atherstone: Friends of Atherstone Heritage 2004

Axon W. E. A., *The Black Knights of Ashton*, Manchester: John Heywood 1870

Barnadiston K. W., *Clare Priory*, Cambridge: Heffer 1962

Bellay, M. du, *Les Memoires de Mess Martin du Bellay, Seigneur de Langey*, Paris 1569

Billson C. J., *Mediaeval Leicester*, Leicester: Edgar Backus 1920

Boardman J., *Athenian Black Figure Vases*, London: Thames and Hudson 1974

Boucé – see Rousseau

Brett S., *Blood at the Bookies*, London: Macmillan 2008

Briggs K. M., *A Dictionary of British Folk Tales*, 4 vols, London: Routledge & K. Paul 1970

Buck – see Myers

CPR 1476–1485

Caro Baroja – see Glendinning

Carson A. J., *Richard III, the Maligned King*, Stroud: The History Press, 2008

Carson A. J., ed., *Finding Richard III – The Official Account of Research by the Retrieval and Reburial Project*, Horstead: Imprimis Imprimatur 2014

Carter H & Mace A. C., *The Discovery of the Tomb of Tutankhamen*, London 1923 (reprinted New York: Dover Publications Inc. 1977)

Cheetham A., *The Life and Times of Richard III*, London: Book Club Associates 1972

Chrimes S. B., *Henry VII*, London: Yale University Press 1972, 1987

Clive M., *This Son of York*, London: Macmillan 1973

Commynes P. de – see Jones

Cunningham S., *Richard III, a Royal Enigma*, Richmond: The National Archives 2003

Dale M. K., & Redstone V.B., eds., *The Household Book of Dame Alice de Bryene of Acton Hall, Suffolk, September 1412 – September 1413*, Ipswich: W. E. Harrison 1931

Davies R., ed., *York Records of the Fifteenth Century*, London, 1843 (repr. Dursley, 1976)

De But A. – see Kervyn de Lettenhove

Duffy E., *The Stripping of the Altars*, London: Yale University Press 1992

Edwards R., *The Itinerary of King Richard III 1483–1485*, London: Richard III Society 1983

Ellis H., ed., R. Fabyan, *The New Chronicles of England and France* (*c.* 1516), London: Rivington *et al.* 1811

Ellis H., ed., *Three Books of Polydore Vergil's English History comprising the reigns of Henry VI, Edward IV, and Richard III*, London: Camden Society 1844

Enríquez del Castillo D., *Crónica del Rey D. Enrique El Quarto De Este Nombre*, Madrid: D. Antonio de Sancha 1787

Euripides – see Méridier; Vellacott

Evans G. R., ed., St Augustine, *City of God*, Harmondsworth: Penguin 2003

Fletcher J., *The Search for Nefertiti*, London: Hodder & Stoughton 2004

Foss P. J., *The Field of Redemore*, Leicester: Kairos Press 1990 (1998)

Gairdner J., ed., *Letters and Papers illustrative of the Reigns of Richard III and Henry VII*, 2 vols., vol. 1, London: [no named publisher] 1861

Gairdner J., *History of the Life and Reign of Richard the Third*, Cambridge: University Press 1898

Glendinning O. N. V., trans., Caro Baroja J, *The World of the Witches*, Chicago and London: Weidenfeld and Nicolson 1965

Green S. E., *Selected Legends of Leicestershire*, Leicester: Leicester Research 1971

Hacking H., *Historical Cats – Great Cats who have shaped History*, London: Hodder & Stoughton 2003

Halsted C. A., *Richard III*, 2 volumes, London: Longman, Brown, Green & Longmans 1844

Hammond P. W. and Sutton A. F., *Richard III: The* Road *to Bosworth Field*, London: Book Club Associates 1985

Hanham A., *Richard III and his Early Historians 1483–1535*, Oxford University Press 1975

Hardy W. & E. L. C. P, eds, J. de Wavrin, *Recueil des Chroniques et Anchienne Istories de la Grant Bretaigne, à Present Nommé Engleterre*, Vol. 5, 1891, reprinted Cambridge: University Press 2012

Hartopp H., *The Roll of the Mayors of the Borough and Lord Mayors of the City of Leicester 1209–1935*, Leicester: [no named publisher] 1935

Haslewood J., ed., *Mirror for Magistrates* vol. 2 (part 3), London 1815

Hearne T., ed., *Joannis Rossi Antiquarii Warwicensis Historia Regum Angliae*, London 1716

Hearne T. ed., *Liber Niger Scaccarii nec non Wilhelmi Worcestrii Annales Rerum Anglicarum*, vol. 2, London: Benj. White 1774

Hicks M., *Anne Neville, Queen to Richard III*, Stroud: Tempus 2006

Horrox R., & Hammond P.W., eds, *British Library Harleian Manuscript 433*, vol. 1, Upminster: Richard III Society 1979; vol. 3, London: Richard III Society 1982

Hughes J., *The Religious Life of Richard III, Piety and Prayer in the North of England*, Stroud: Sutton Publishing 1997

Johnson P. A., *Duke Richard of York 1411–1460*, Oxford: Clarendon 1988

Jones M. K., ed., *Philippe de Commynes Memoires*, Harmondsworth: Penguin 1972

Jones M. K., *Psychology of a Battle, Bosworth 1485*, Stroud: Tempus 2002, 2003

Jowett J., ed., *The Tragedy of King Richard III*, Oxford: University Press 2000

Kendall P. M., *Richard the Third*, 1955, reprinted London: Book Club Associates 1973

Kervyn de Lettenhove, Baron, ed., *Chroniques relatives à l'histoire de la Belgique sous la domination des Ducs de Bourgogne*, vol. 1, Bruxelles: F. Hayez 1870, Adrien de But, *Chroniques*

Laynesmith J., *The Last Medieval Queens*, Oxford: University Press 2004

Lee D., ed., Plato, *Timaeus and Critias*, Harmondsworth: Penguin 1965

Lindsay P., *On Some Bones in Westminster Abbey: A Defence of King Richard III*, London 1934, reprinted Bath: Cedric Chivers Ltd 1969

Losey F. D., ed., *The Complete Dramatic and Poetic Works of William Shakespeare*, Philadelphia & Chicago: Winston 1926

Mandrot B. de, ed., *Journal de Jean de Roye 1460–1483, connu sous le non de Chronique Scandaleuse*, vol. 1, Paris: Librairie Renouard 1844; vol. 2 Paris: Librairie Renouard 1846

Mancini D. – see Armstrong

Maxwell-Lyte H. C., ed., *The Registers of Robert Stillington, Bishop of Bath and Wells 1466–1491 and Richard Fox, Bishop of Bath and Wells 1492–1494*, Somerset Record Society, 1937

Méridier L., ed., *Euripide, Le Cyclope, Alceste, Médée, Les Héraclides*, Paris: Société d'Edition Les Belles Lettres 1925

More T. – see Sylvester

Morris M., Buckley R. & Codd M., *Visions of Ancient Leicester*, Leicester: ULAS 2011

Morris M. & Buckley R., *Richard III The King under the car park*, Leicester: ULAS 2013

Myers A. R., ed., G. Buck, *The History of the Life and Reigne of Richard the Third*, (London 1646), Wakefield: EP Publishing Ltd. 1973

Myrc J. – see Peacock

Nichols J. G., ed., *Grants, &c from the Crown during the Reign of Edward the Fifth*, London: Camden Society 1854

Nichols J., *History and Antiquities of the County of Leicester*, London 1795–1811

Nicoll A. & J., eds, *Holinshed's Chronicle as used in Shakespeare's Plays*, London: J. M. Dent & Sons Ltd 1927, 1955

Peacock E., ed., *Instructions for Parish Priests by John Myrc*, London: Early English Text Society 1868, reprinted Elibron Classics 2005

Pease H., *The Lord Wardens of the Marches of England and Scotland*, London: Constable & Co. 1912

Peers C., *Berkhamsted Castle*, HMSO 1948 (1968)

Plato – see Lee

Prescott W. H., *History of the Reign of Ferdinand and Isabella*, 2 vols. New York: A. L. Burt 1837, vol. 1

Pronay N. & Cox J., *The Crowland Chronicle Continuations 1459–1486*, London: Richard III and Yorkist History Trust 1986

Roe F., *Old Oak Furniture*, London: Methuen & Co. 1908

Rolls of Parliament, vol. 6

Ross C., *Richard III*, London:Eyre Methuen Ltd. 1981

Rous J., The Rous Roll, London 1859, reprinted Gloucester: Sutton 1980

Rous – see Hearne

Rousseau G. S. and Porter R., eds., *Sexual underworlds of the Enlightenment*, Manchester: University Press 1987

Roye J. de – see Mandrot

Russell J. B., *Witchcraft in the Middle Ages*, New York: Cornel University Press 1972

St Augustine, *De civitate Dei* – see Evans

St John, *Gospel* – see Wansborough

Sayers D. L., *Strong Poison*, London: Victor Gollancz Ltd 1930

Sayers D. L., *Have His Carcase*, London: Victor Gollancz Ltd 1932

Sayers D. L., *The Nine Tailors*, 1934, reprinted London: Hodder & Stoughton 1987

Scofield C. L., *The Life and Reign of Edward the Fourth, King of England and of France and Lord of Ireland*, 2 vols. 1923, reprinted London: Cass 1967

Seward D., *Richard III – England's Black Legend*, Harmondsworth: Penguin 1997

Shakespeare – see Losey

Skidmore C., *Bosworth and the Birth of the Tudors*, London: W&N 2013

Smith J. J., *Essentials of Early English*, London: Routledge 2005

Smith W., ed., *A Latin-English Dictionary*, eighth edition, London: John Murray 1868

Somogyi N. de, ed., *The Shakespeare Folios: Richard III*, London: Nick Hearn 2002

Speede J., *The History of Great Britaine*, London: H. Hall & J. Beale 1611 (1614)

Sutton A. F., & Visser-Fuchs L., *The Hours of Richard III*, Stroud: Sutton 1990, 1996

Sutton A. F. and Visser-Fuchs L. with Griffiths R. A., *The Royal Funerals of the House of York at Windsor*, London: Richard III Society 2005

Sylvester R. S., ed., St Thomas More, *The History of King Richard III*, New Haven & London: Yale University Press 1976

Thomas A. H. & Thornley I. D., eds, *The Great Chronicle of London*, London: George W. Jones 1938

Throsby J., *Memoirs of the Town and County of Leicester*, Leicester [printed for the author] 1777

Tudor-Craig P., *Richard III* (NPG exhibition catalogue) London: National Portrait Gallery 1973

Vellacott P., trans., Euripides, *Medea and other plays*, Harmondsworth: Penguin 1963

Vergil – see Ellis

Visser-Fuchs L., 'Edward IV's *Memoir on Paper* to Charles, Duke of Burgundy, the so-called "Short Version of the *Arrivall*"', Reprinted from *Nottingham Medieval Studies* XXXVI (1992)

Wansbrough H. ed., *The New Jerusalem Bible*, London: Darton, Longman & Todd 1990

Wavrin – see Hardy

Wedgwood J. G., *History of Parliament, Biographies volume 1439–1509*, London: H. M. Stationery Office 1936

Weightman C., *Margaret of York Duchess of Burgundy 1446–1503*, Gloucester: Sutton 1989

Wilkinson J., *Richard, the young King to be*, Stroud: Amberley 2009

Williams D., *Deformed Discourse, the function of the Monster in Mediaeval Thought and Literature*, Montreal and Kingston: McGill-Queen's University Press 1996

Wolffe B., *Henry VI*, London: Eyre Methuen 1981

Wolters C., ed.,*The Cloud of Unknowing*, Harmondsworth: Penguin 1961 (1974)

Worcester W., *Annals* – see Hearne

Wren C., *Parentalia, or Memoirs of the Family of the Wrens*, London 1750

ODNB

Griffiths R. A., Henry VI

Hicks M., Anthony Woodville, 2nd Earl Rivers

Hicks M., Robert Stillington

Horrox R., Hastings, William first Baron Hastings

Papers

Appleby J., Mitchell P. D., Robinson C., Brough A., Rutty G., Harris R. A., Thompson D. & Morgan B., 'The scoliosis of Richard III, last Plantagenet King of England: diagnosis and clinical significance', *The Lancet*, 30 May 2014.

Ashdown-Hill J., 'The Elusive Mistress: Elizabeth Lucy and her Family', *The Ricardian*, vol. 11 (June 1999), pp. 490–505

Ashdown-Hill J., 'The Lancastrian Claim to the Throne', *The Ricardian*, vol. 13 (2003), pp. 27–38

Ashdown-Hill J., 'The Bosworth Crucifix', *Transactions of the Leicestershire Archaeological & Historical Society* vol. 78 (2004), pp. 83–96

Ashdown-Hill J., 'The Location of the 1485 Battle and the Fate of Richard III's Body', *Ricardian Bulletin*, Autumn 2004, pp. 34–5

Ashdown-Hill J., & Carson A., 'The Execution of the Earl of Desmond', *The Ricardian*, vol. 15 (2005), pp. 70–93

Ashdown-Hill J., 'Margaret of York's Dance of Death – the DNA evidence', *Handelingen van de Koninklijke Kring voor Oudheidkunde, Letteren an Kunst van Mechelen*, 111 (2007), pp. 193–207

Barnfield M., 'Diriment Impediments, Dispensations and Divorce: Richard III and Matrimony', *Ric* 17 (2007), pp. 84–98

Breeze A., 'A Welsh Poem of 1485 on Richard III', *The Ricardian* vol. 18 (2008), pp. 46–53

Carson A., 'Notes Towards the Definition of a Tyrant', *Ricardian Bulletin*, December 2013, pp. 43–5

Catling C., 'From the trowel's edge ...', *Current Archaeology*, issue 296, November 2014, pp. 56–7

Clare P. D., 'English royal marriages and the Papal Planitentiary in the fifteenth century', English Historical Review, vol. 120 (2006), pp. 1014–29

Coldwells A., *St George's Chapel, Windsor Castle* guide book, 1993

Hanham A., 'Henry VI and his Miracles', *The Ricardian*, vol. 12 no. 148 (March 2000), pp. 2–16 [erroneously numbered pp. 638–52 in the publication]

Hanham A., 'The Mysterious Affair at Crowland Abbey', *The Ricardian*, vol. 18 (2008), pp. 1–20

Horrox R., 'Preparations for Edward IV's Return from Exile', *The Ricardian*, vol. 6, no. 79 (December 1982), pp. 124–7

Madden F., 'Political Poems of the Reigns of Henry VI and Edward IV', *Archaeologia* vol.29, 1842, pp. 318–47

Park K. and Daston L. J., 'Unnatural Conceptions: the study of monsters in sixteenth-and seventeenth-century France and England', *Past and Present*, no. 92 (1981),

St John Hope W. H., 'The Discovery of the Remains of King Henry VI in St George's Chapel, Windsor Castle', *Archaeologia*, vol. 62, part 2, pp. 533–42

Sheppard Routh P., '"Lady Scroop Daughter of K. Edward": an Enquiry', *The Ricardian*, vol. 9 (1991–93), pp. 410–16

Sutton A. F., & Visser-Fuchs L., '"Richard Liveth Yet": an Old Myth', *The Ricardian*, vol. 9, no. 117 (June 1992), pp. 266–9

Sutton A. F., & Visser-Fuchs L., 'The Making of a Minor London Chronicle in the Household of Sir Thomas Frowyk (died 1485)', *The Ricardian*, vol. 10, no. 126, (September 1994), pp. 86–103

Verkaik J. W., 'King Richard's Last Sacrament', *The Ricardian*, vol. 9, no. 119, (December 1992), pp. 359–60

Warnicke R. M., 'Sir Ralph Bigod: a loyal servant to King Richard III', *The Ricardian*, vol. 6, no. 84 (March 1984), pp. 299–303

White J., 'The Death and Burial of Henry VI, part 1', *The Ricardian*, vol. 6, no. 78 (September 1982), pp. 70–80

Newspapers & Newsletters
Daily Mail, 17 September 2014

Leicester Mercury, 2 March 1995; 8 October 2002; 11 May 2005
Ricardian Bulletin, Winter 2007, 'The Tomb of Richard III'
Ricardian Bulletin, June 2013, 'Grey Friars reconstructed'
Richard III Society Yorkshire Branch Newsletter, October 2014
Society of Antiquaries of London, *Salon* online newsletter, Issue 326
22 September 2014
Ricardian Recorder, August 2014
Spectator, 25 May 2013

Internet & Electronic Resources
Bernard André: http://www.philological.bham.ac.uk/andreas/ (August 2014)
Given-Wilson C. *et al.*, eds, *The Parliament Rolls of Medieval England*, 2005
Lamb A. L., Evans J. E., Buckley R. & Appleby J., 'Multi-isotope analysis
    demonstrates significant lifestyle changes in King Richard III',
http://www.sciencedirect.com/science/article/pii/S0305440314002428 (consulted
    September 2014)
E. M. Nokes and G. Wheeler, 'A Spanish account of the battle of Bosworth', *The
    Ricardian*, vol. 2, no. 36 (1972), 2.
http://www.r3.org/richard-iii/the-battle-of-bosworth/bosworth-contemporary-
    tudor-accounts/ item III a) *A Castilian Report* DATE: Early 1486. AUTHOR:
    Diego de Valera, Castilian courtier (consulted September 2014).=
O'Neill B., 'A Critique of Politically Correct Language',
http://authorherstorianparent.blogspot.co.uk/2013/03/a-northern-lord-in-london-
    city-richard_27.html (consulted July 2014)
http://en.wikipedia.org/wiki/Blackadder (consulted October 2014)
http://en.wikipedia.org/wiki/Henry_Percy,_4th_Earl_of_Northumberland
    (consulted September 2014)
http://en.wikipedia.org/wiki/John_Rous (historian) (consulted August 2014)
http://en.wikipedia.org/wiki/Mohammad_Reza_Pahlavi (consulted August 2014)
    http://en.wikipedia.org/wiki/Peter_of_Castile (consulted September 2014)
    http://en.wikipedia.org/wiki/Wycliffe's_Bible (consulted October 2014)
Sheldon N., 'Burying Richard III: Details of the Re-Interment and Tomb of
    'The Last Warrior King' Revealed', 19 June 2014, http://decodedpast.com/
    burying-richard-iii-details-re-interment-tomb-last-warrior-king-revealed/10742
    (consulted October 2014)
http://theandalucian.com/yahoo_site_admin/assets/docs/
    ANDALUCIANnov2013.34922435.pdf (consulted September 2014)
http://www2.le.ac.uk/offices/press/press-releases/2014/january/historic-image-
    of-king-richard-iii-at-blue-boar-inn-to-be-made-available-to-public (consulted
    September 2014)
http://www.11kbw.com/app/files/PDFs/RichardIIIJudgment.pdf (consulted July
    2014)
http://www.bbc.co.uk/history/people/king_richard_iii (consulted August 2014)
http://www.catholictradition.org/Eucharist/mass-h10.htm (consulted October
    2014)
http://www.dailymail.co.uk/news/article-2607033/Listen-voice-Richard-IIIs-
    ghost-Amateur-ghoul-hunters-record-spooky-sounds-bed-legend-says-spent-
    night-alive.html (consulted September 2014) http://www.dailymail.co.uk/

sciencetech/article-2705502/King-Richard-III-3D-PRINTED-Computer-generated-plastic-replica-monarchs-skeleton-goes-display.html (consulted July 2014)

http://www.dmu.ac.uk/about-dmu/news/2014/july/dmu-brings-richard-iiis-priory-back-to-digital-life.aspx (consulted October 2014)

http://www.historyextra.com/news/richard-iii/richard-iii-worth-%C2%A345m-leicester-economy (consulted November 2014)

http://www.independent.co.uk/news/uk/home-news/leicester-cathedral-denies-it-is-cashing-in-on-richard-iiis-reinternment-9706943.html (consulted September 2014)

http://www.independent.org/pdf/tir/tir_16_02_8_oneill.pdf (consulted July 2014)

http://www.le.ac.uk/richardiii/history/blueboarinn.html (consulted September 2014)

http://www.le.ac.uk/richardiii/history/meetrichard.html (consulted September 2014)

Wain D., *Live Science*, 3 September 2013, http://www.livescience.com/39392-king-http://www.luminarium.org/encyclopedia/sweatingsickness.htm (consulted March 2009)

richard-iii-roundworm-infection.html (consulted July 2014)

http://www.nature.com/ncomms/2014/141202/ncomms6631/full/ncomms6631.html (consulted December 2014)

http://www.oed.com/view/Entry/67478?rskey=AV1wfu&result=1#eid (consulted September 2014)

http://www.philological.bham.ac.uk/andreas/ (consulted August 2014)

http://www.royal.gov.uk/historyofthemonarchy/kingsandqueensofengland/theyorkists/richardiii.aspx (consulted July 2014)

http://www.thefreedictionary.com/usurper (August 2014) http://www.theguardian.com/uk/2013/mar/13/row-richard-iii-burial-site (consulted November 2014)

List of Illustrations

Unless otherwise acknowledged, images are owned by the author.

1. Richard III's Spanish great-great-grandfather, Pedro I, King of Castile (from a gold *gran dobla* of 1360, by courtesy of Luis Garcia, under GNU free documentation licence). Should this king be remembered as 'Pedro the Cruel' or 'Pedro the Just'? Was he the wicked ancestor from whom Richard inherited his evil character, or were the reputations of both kings ruined by usurpers who overthrew them?
2. Images of Richard as Duke of Gloucester, in about 1475. Left: the Barnard Castle Church image, courtesy of Margaret Watson. Right: the Wavrin image, a nineteenth-century engraving, after a miniature from the copy of his *Chronicle* which Wavrin presented to Edward IV.
3. The 'Paston' Portraits of Edward IV and Richard III, *c.* 1520, courtesy of the Society of Antiquaries of London.
4. The 'Broken Sword' portrait of Richard III, *c.* 1530, courtesy of the Society of Antiquaries of London.
5. Mohammed Reza Shah Pahlavi of Iran, from an Iranian 20 Rials banknote of 1969.
6. Eva María Duarte de Perón.
7. The probable comparative heights of Edward IV, George, Duke of Clarence, and Richard III.
8. Richard III seems to have resembled his father in terms of his features, as is shown by this comparison of his modern facial reconstruction (left, courtesy of the Richard III Society) with a portrait of his father, Richard, Duke of York (right, redrawn by the author after BL MS Royal 15 E VI, fol. 3).
9. Anthony Woodville, 2nd Earl Rivers (nineteenth-century engraving after BL MS. 265, fo. 6).
10. A caricature of William, Lord Hastings, in the guise of a pig, redrawn from a contemporary marginal illustration accompanying an account of his 1483 execution in the register of the Abbot of St Albans, © M. Hanif.
11. The Infanta Isabel of Castile (later Queen Isabel la Católica): in 1469 she was mentioned as a prospective bride of Richard, Duke of Gloucester.
12. The other women in the picture: Top left: Anne of Warwick (from the Rous

Roll); top right: Elizabeth of York (nineteenth-century engraving); bottom left: Isabel of Aragon; bottom right: Joana of Portugal (both redrawn by Geoffrey Wheeler, © G. Wheeler).

13. A nineteenth century imaginary engraving showing 'Edward (*sic*) Duke of York parting from his mother'.

14. A nineteenth-century imaginary engraving of the alleged murder of the 'Princes in the Tower'.

15. The Great Schism of 1054 had divided the Church into two parts. Richard III unquestionably belonged to the western, Catholic Church. He was in communion with Rome and faithful to the Pope.

16. The Talbots: Eleanor (centre – based on a facial reconstruction of the skull found at the Norwich Carmel), her sister, Elizabeth, Duchess of Norfolk (left – from Long Melford Church, Suffolk), and their father, the Earl of Shrewsbury (right – from his tomb effigy).

17. Facsimile of an autograph letter of King Richard III, reading 'My lorde Chaunceler we pray you in all hast to send to us a pardon under our Gret Seale to Sir Harry Wode preste &c & this shalbe yo[r] warrant Ricardus Rex'. A note at the bottom right reads 'M[aster] Skypton sped this forth with ex[pediti]on Jo Omcots'.

18. Elements of the Boar Inn mythology of Richard III. Left: a nineteenth-century engraving of the sixteenth-century Blue Boar Inn, Leicester; upper right: the alleged original inn sign – Richard III's White Boar emblem (from a modern banner made by Mary Talbot of the former Richard III Society Essex Group); lower right: allegedly the White Boar Inn sign was repainted as a blue boar, following Richard III's defeat at Bosworth.

19. Elements of the story of how fifteenth-century gold coins – assumed to be 'Richard III's royal treasure' – were found hidden in a bed at the Blue Boar Inn by the innkeeper's wife about a century after the battle of Bosworth. This was taken as 'proof' that Richard III had slept there.

20. Part of the ruins of Leicester Castle, where King Richard III is known to have stayed when he visited Leicester in 1483.

21. Richard III and White Surrey, a modern image, © Frances Quinn.

22. A nineteenth-century engraving of Sutton Cheney Church. The only connection between this church and Richard III stems from the 'Last Mass' myth invented by the Fellowship of the White Boar in the 1920s.

23. A tentative reconstruction of Richard III's royal tomb of 1495, commissioned by the author in 2007, © Geoffrey Wheeler.

24. The author's suggested appearance of the Leicester Greyfriars Church, first published in 2010, before the excavation of the site. The yellow pit now added beneath the last bay of the choir marks the site where Richard III's grave was discovered.

25. What the choir of the Leicester Greyfriars Church might have looked like today, if it had survived. A reconstruction based upon a photograph of the choir of the Norwich Blackfriars Church.

26. John Speede, a leading (if unintentional) Richard III mythologist.

27. John Speede's map of Leicester, *c.* 1610. The red triangle marks the Dominican Priory (Blackfriars) site, where Speede mistakenly sought (and failed to find) Richard III's gravesite – leading to his story that the body had been exhumed at the Dissolution. The green area is the real Greyfriars site, which Speede did

not mark or visit, but where Richard III's gravesite was still marked by an inscribed column in the first quarter of the seventeenth century.

28. The 'Body in the River' legend. Centre: a nineteenth-century engraving of the original Bow Bridge; right: the Victorian Bow Bridge Plaque erected by Mr B. Broadbent in 1856 (the arrow and circle show its original position); upper left: the author's new Bow Bridge plaque of 2005, erected through the Richard III Society and with the permission of Leicester City Council.
29. The author's discovery of Richard III's mtDNA as reported by the *East Anglian Daily Times* and the University of Essex *Wyvern* Magazine in 2005, © *East Anglian Daily Times*/Archant Suffolk.
30. Dr Turi King taking a DNA sample from Michael Ibsen on 24 August 2012, © M. Hanif.
31. Joy Ibsen's first DNA letter to the author.
32. Richard III as depicted on the Coventry Tapestry, *circa* 1500, courtesy of St Mary's Guildhall/Coventry City Council.
33. The 'Paston Portrait' (left, courtesy of the Society of Antiquaries of London) and the 'Leicester Portrait' (right).
34. Left: Richard III Sunglasses. Right: A bar of Richard III Chocolate. © M. Hanif.
35. The Bosworth Battlefield Centre Stone Coffin.
36. The Richard III 'Death Stone'.
37. Philippa Langley standing on the exact site of the alleged Richard III grave (actually a Saxon grave) at 70, George Street, Leicester, August 2012. © Philippa Langley.
38. Clearing the tarmac from the spot which proved to be Richard III's gravesite on 25 August 2012, © M. Hanif.
39. Recording the discovery of Richard III's grave and his remains, © M. Hanif.
40. A fifteenth-century brass, showing two corpses laid out with their hands crossed in roughly the same position as the hands of Richard III's remains.
41. The author carrying the remains of Richard III from the Greyfriars site in September 2012, © Riikka Nikko.
42. Richard III's gravesite after his bones had been removed. The yellow peg marks the position of his head, © M. Hanif.
43. The funeral crown commissioned for Richard III by the author and made by George Easton. The crown is set with rubies, sapphires, emeralds and turquoises upon enamelled white roses, and also with pearls.
44. The rosary donated by the author for burial with Richard III. The crucifix is a copy by George Easton of the 'Clare Cross', which may once have belonged to Richard III's mother.

Index

Acre, Joan of, ancestor of Richard III 24

André, Bernard 83, 197, 213

Anglican 64–67, 70, 132

Anjou, Margaret of, consort of Henry VI 40–41

Annaghdown, Bishop of – see Barrett, Thomas

Antwerp, Lionel of, Duke of Clarence 51

Appleby, Dr Jo 27–28, 119, 132, 189, 191

Aragon, Catherine of, consort of Henry VIII 65

Argentina 9–10

Arras, treaty of 102

Ashmolean Museum, Oxford 146

Ashton, Sir Ralph (the 'Black Knight') 88–89, 198

Aung San Suu Kyi 9

Aveiro, Dominican Convent of 131

Baldwin, David 141–42, 156, 183–84

Baptism 32

Barnet, battle of 41

Barrett, Thomas, Bishop of Annaghdown 46

bastard – see illegitimate

Bath and Wells, Bishop of – see Stillington, Robert

Beauchamp, Richard, Earl of Warwick 78

    Richard, Lord 35

Beaufort, Duke of – see Somerset family

    Edmund, 1st (2nd) Duke of Somerset 193

    Edmund, titular 3rd (4th) Duke of Somerset 41

    family 149, 173, 178

    Joan, Countess of Westmorland 97, 173

    John, Earl of Somerset 149, 173

    Margaret, Countess of Richmond and Derby, Lady Stanley 56

Bedford, Duchess of – see St Pol

    Duke of – see Lancaster, John of

Bellay, Martin du 58, 195

Berkhamsted Castle 15, 18

Berry, Adrian 141

Black Adder, The 159, 161, 205

'Black Knight', the – see Ashton

Bockenham, Friar Osberne, OSA 23

Bosworth, battle of 7, 8, 20, 31, 43, 65, 74, 83, 87, 92, 104, 110, 112–14, 117, 119, 120, 122–24, 126, 131–32, 142, 161, 163–64, 168–69, 182

Broadbent, Mr B. 137–38, 169, 217

Bryene household (Suffolk) diet of 102

Buck, Sir George 14, 15, 104

Buckingham, Duchess of – see Neville, Anne

    Duke of – see Stafford, Henry

    Rebellion, the 59

Buckley, (Dr) Richard 26, 135, 139,
    143–45, 149, 151, 191, 203
Burdet, Thomas 35–37, 46
Burgundy, Duchess of – see York,
    Margaret of
  Philip the Good, Duke of 17
Burma – see Myanmar
Butler family of Sudeley 36
  Lady – see Talbot, Eleanor

Calais 16, 17, 52
Cambridge 18
Camoys, Alice de, Lady Hastings 51
Canterbury, Archbishop of – see
    Morton, John
Carson, Annette 11, 28, 29, 88–90,
    190, 191, 193, 194
Castile, Henry IV, King of 91
  Isabel I, 'the Catholic', Queen of 91
  Isabel of, Duchess of York, great-
    grandmother of Richard III 14
  Pedro 'the Cruel', King of 14
Catesby, William 38, 52, 84, 99
Catholic 62–71, 102, 123, 124, 125,
    132, 155, 169, 216
Catling, Christopher 101–02
Chertsey Abbey 45, 93
Chrimes, Professor S. B. 84
Christmas 15, 92, 99–100, 104, 126
Church – see Anglican; Catholic,
    Orthodox
Clare Castle 18
  Priory 23–24, 132
Clarence, Duchess of – see Neville
    Isabel
  Duke of – see Antwerp, Lionel of;
    York, George of
  Margaret of, Countess of Salisbury
    (niece of Richard III) 135
  Philippa of 51
Clarendon Code – see Penal Laws
Clarke, Agnes – see Davy
  Peter 95–96, 98
  Thomas 111, 201
Cobham, Eleanor, Duchess of
    Gloucester 34–35
Commynes, Philippe de 41, 102
consecrated ground 70, 154

Corpus Christi Feast of 63, 69
  Guild 94
Crofts, Sir Richard 42
Crowland Chronicler, the 19, 35, 53,
    55, 82, 94, 99, 100, 119–20,
    123–25, 129

Daily Mail, the 110, 114, 163
Dalí, Salvador 160
Davy, Agnes (Clarke) 111–12
Desmond, Earl of – see Fitzgerald,
    James
Devil, the 25, 32, 38, 57
DNA 142, 146–50, 155, 171, 176,
    177, 179
Dissolution, the 135, 137, 139, 141,
    217
Donington-le-Heath Manor 113–15
Dorset, Marquess of – see Grey,
    Thomas
Dyer, Chris, FSA 101

Edward II 47, 197
Edward III 20, 35, 47, 51, 54, 149,
    178
Edward IV 14, 17, 18, 20, 24, 25, 28,
    34–37, 40–49, 51–54, 56–59,
    74–85, 87, 89, 91, 92, 96, 99,
    102, 103, 105, 129–31, 146, 153,
    161, 168, 175, 190, 197
Edward V 20, 47, 48, 49, 50, 53, 59,
    74–76, 78, 79, 140
  illegitimacy of 36, 54, 55, 76, 78, 80,
    81, 87, 103
Edward VI (son of Henry VIII) 66
Edward VII 202
Ely, Bishop of – see Morton, John
'England, Richard of' 57
Essex 18
euphemism 30
Evita (musical) 10
Exeter, Duchess of – see York, Anne of

Fabyan, Robert 90
Farmer, Ben 142
fasting 123
Fellowship of the White Boar – see
    Richard III Society

Fitzgerald, James, 8th Earl of Desmond
    46
Fotheringhay Castle 15–16
Foxhall, Professor Lin 8, 26–28, 191
France, Isabelle of, consort of Edward
    II 47
    Jeanne or Yolande of, potential
    consort of Edward IV 77

'G', prophecy of 36–37, 46
Gairdner, James 20, 23, 59, 62, 75, 83,
    87–88, 90, 94, 128, 167
Gaunt, John of, Duke of Lancaster 47,
    96, 107, 149, 178
Gellar, Sarah Michelle 31
Gloucester, Catherine of (illegitimate
    daughter of Richard III) 103
    Duchess of – see Cobham, Eleanor
    Duke of – see Lancaster, Humphrey
    of; Richard III
Gloucestershire 18
Goldwell, Dr James (later Bishop of
    Norwich) 92
Grey, Lady – see Woodville, Elizabeth
    Sir Richard 39, 40, 48, 49, 76
    Thomas, Marquess of Dorset 52
Guardian, The 8, 153, 154
Guy Fawkes Day 66

Hacking, Heather 161
Hall, Edward 36, 37, 86, 117, 118
Hanham, Alison 57–58
Hastings, Anne, Countess of
    Shrewsbury 52
    Lady – see Camoys, Alice de; Neville,
    Catherine
    Ralph 52
    William, Lord 39, 40, 42, 48, 50,
    51–55, 75
Henry IV 74
Henry V 20, 35
Henry VI 15, 20, 22, 35, 39, 40,
    42–45, 47, 48, 54, 59, 74, 77, 93
Henry VII 8, 10, 15, 20, 34, 39, 49,
    50, 56–59, 70, 74, 77, 80–81,
    83–85, 87, 99, 106, 112, 113,
    124, 126, 128, 129, 133, 154,
    161, 162, 168, 200

Henry VIII 39, 65–66, 70, 87, 135,
    140
Herrick, Robert 136
Hicks, Michael 96, 171
Holinshed, Ralph 33–34, 41–42, 44,
    93
Hours, Richard III's Book of 15, 16,
    62, 66
Howard, Sir John, Lord, later Duke
    of Norfolk 18, 51, 52, 102, 104,
    106, 118
Hylton, Walter 130

Illegitimate 17, 36, 55, 76, 77, 87,
    103–04, 106, 178
Iran 9
Israel 9

Jacklyn, Harriet 132
Jenkin, Bernard, MP 156

Kennedy, Maeve 8
Kent 16, 43, 181
King, Dr Turi 147, 148, 177, 178
kudos 7, 150

Lancaster, Duke of – see Gaunt, John
    of
    Humphrey of, Duke of Gloucester
    48
    John of, Duke of Bedford 48
Lancastrian 8, 16, 40–45, 93, 107, 149
Langley, Philippa 11, 27, 29, 31,
    64–65, 130, 138–39, 142–44, 156,
    158, 182–84, 203
Latin 8, 24, 26–28, 58, 68–69, 82, 189
Leicester 7, 18, 110, 112, 114, 116,
    117, 118, 129, 130, 136, 137,
    139, 142, 143, 145, 163, 167,
    169, 170
    Abbey 18, 111
    Bishop of 69, 70, 154
    Blue Boar Inn of 111–13, 115, 168
    Bow Bridge 118, 137
    Castle 18, 111, 115, 129
    Cathedral 64, 65, 69, 70, 71, 122,
    123, 125, 131, 153, 154, 159,
    160, 163–66, 168, 169

City Council 10, 79, 130, 138, 152, 153, 154, 158, 160, 184
  Dean of 64, 155, 159–60, 165
De Montfort University 134
Diocese of 63
Dominican Priory of 70, 132
Franciscan Priory of (Greyfriars) 24, 31, 70, 130, 132, 135, 138, 139, 143, 147, 154, 156, 172
Guildhall 115, 152
Mayor of – see Clarke, Thomas; Herrick, Robert; Soulsby, Sir Peter
Museum 142
  Richard III Visitor Centre 11, 18, 32, 79, 114, 153, 168, 169
  University of 7, 8, 26, 65, 70, 79, 114, 115, 117, 132–34, 141, 144, 147, 148–49, 152, 153, 155, 156, 158, 160, 169, 171, 178, 184
Leicester Mercury, the 141, 142
Leuven, Catholic University of 146–47
Levitt, Sarah 152
Lisle, Leanda de 26
London 17, 18, 25, 36, 42–45, 47, 48, 53–57, 75–76, 81, 86, 92–94, 101, 103, 105–06, 123, 140, 175, 176
Looking For Richard Project 11, 64, 79, 130, 143–45, 152, 153, 157, 158, 159, 171, 182–84, 186, 203
Lovell, Francis, Viscount 38
Low Countries 17, 25, 172
Lucy, Elizabeth – see Wayte
Ludlow 16, 53
  Castle 15, 21, 47

Macalister, Professor 44
Mancini, Domenico 35, 46, 51, 52, 55, 81–82
Markham, Sir Clements 43
Mary I, Queen 124
Mass (religious service) 63, 69, 123–26, 166, 168, 216
Mechelen (Belgium) 147, 184
Middle East 9
Middle English 58
Middleham Castle 17–18, 40, 53, 62, 99, 160
Mirk – see Myrc

Mitochondrial (mt) DNA – see DNA
monster 10, 14, 21–23, 38, 189
More, Sir (St) Thomas 33, 57, 87
Morley, Lord – see Parker, Henry
Morris, Matthew 144, 149
Mortimer, Elizabeth 51
  family, ancestors of Richard III 15
Mortimer's Cross, battle of 51
Morton, John, Bishop of Ely (later Cardinal Archbishop of Canterbury) 55–56
Myanmar 9
Myrc, John 68

Navarre, Joanna of, consort of Henry IV 35
Neville, Queen Anne, consort of Richard III 39, 40, 59, 92–96, 98–99
  Anne, Duchess of Buckingham, aunt of Richard III 16
  Catherine, Lady Hastings 51
  Cecily, Duchess of York, mother of Richard III 16, 25, 28, 95
  family 15, 173–75
  Isabel, Duchess of Clarence 95–98
  Ralph, Earl of Westmorland 97
  Richard 'the Kingmaker', Earl of Warwick 78, 96
newspapers – see *Daily Mail, Guardian, Leicester Mercury, Spectator*
Norfolk, Duke of – see Howard, John
Norris, Dr Foxley, Dean of Westminster 56
Northampton 14, 15, 16, 48, 53, 174, 180, 194
Northumberland, Earl of – see Percy, Henry
Nottingham 18, 110, 111, 113, 115, 118, 130, 135

O'Callaghan, Jonathan 163
Orthodox 65–66

Pahlavi, Mohammed Reza Shah 9
Papacy 65
papal dispensation (for marriage) 92–93, 95–99

'papist' 66

Parker, Henry, Lord Morley 124

Parliament 8, 35, 45, 74, 76, 81, 83, 85, 86

   act of 1484 8, 58, 74, 77–78, 79, 80, 84, 105–06, 153, 189

Pedro I, King of Castile, ancestor of Richard III – see Castile

Pembroke and Huntingdon, Countess of – see Gloucester, Catherine of

Penal Laws 66–67

Percy, Henry, 4th Earl of Northumberland 50, 53, 128

Perón, Eva María Duarte de 9–10

   Juan 9

   regime 9

Perrers, Alice – see Salisbury

pilgrimage 63, 66

Pleasaunce, Palace of (Richmond) 17

Pole, John de la, Duke of Suffolk (brother-in-law of Richard III) 133

'political correctness' 30

Pontefract Castle 49

Pope, the 65–69, 96, 196, 216

Portugal, Infanta Joana of (Richard III's intended second wife) 29, 105, 107, 131

'precontract', meaning of 80–81

'Princes in the Tower', the 39, 56–58, 153

   and see Edward V

prisoners 9, 42, 89

Protector of England, Lord 33, 48, 50, 53, 54, 55, 76, 79, 82

Ratcliffe, Robert 38

Real Presence of Christ, the (Catholic doctrine) 63, 67

Richard II 15, 20, 47, 74

Richard III, accession 20, 50, 58, 74, 79, 83–84

   appearance of 24–25, 30, 162

   bed(s) attributed to 112–15

   birth of 15

   body of 7, 11, 24, 128–30, 133, 139, 141–44, 153

   burial of 70, 115, 130–31, 132–34

   (alleged) coffin of 137, 140

   conception of 15, 21–22

death of 43, 65

   deformity of 21, 24, 29, 31–33, 37–38

   diet of 100–02

   (alleged) ghost of 114

   health of 24

   horses of (and see 'White Syrie') 117–18

   (alleged) insomnia of 119–21

   last Mass of 63, 123–26

   marriage(s) of 11, 29, 104–07, 131

Richard III Society, the 11, 71, 122, 123, 125, 138, 142, 143, 158, 160, 162, 163, 168, 169, 182–84

'Richard the Furred' 161–62

'Richmond, Henry, Earl of' – see Henry VII

Rivers, Earl – see Woodville, Antony

'Roman' Catholic – see Catholic

'Romish' 66

Ross, Charles 11, 140, 167

Rotherham, Thomas, Archbishop of York 55

Rous, John 13, 22–28, 29, 30, 37, 49, 50, 59, 73, 84, 86, 130

royal supremacy 67

Roye, Jean de 41

Rutland, Earl of – see York, Edmund of

St Albans, battle of 40, 174

St George's Chapel – see Windsor Castle

St Pol, Jacquette de, Duchess of Bedford 34, 78

Salisbury, Alice, mistress of Edward III 35, 197

   Countess of – see Clarence, Margaret of

Savoy, Bona of, proposed consort of Edward IV 77, 78

Shah – see Pahlavi

Shakespeare, William 10, 20, 22, 23, 24, 28, 29, 39, 40, 44, 63, 91, 92, 93, 99, 104, 109, 117, 118, 119, 159, 160, 161

Shrewsbury, Countess of – see Hastings, Anne

   Earl of – see Talbot, George

Smith, Emily Kent 110, 114

Somerset, Duke of – see Beaufort,
  Edmund
  family 149, 178
sorcery 21, 34
Soulsby, Sir Peter 138
Southwark 16–17
Spanish 14, 91, 92, 106, 160
Spectator, The 26
Speede, John 113, 136, 137, 138, 145
Stacey, John 35–36
Stafford, Henry, Duke of Buckingham
  39, 48–50, 53–54, 58–59, 75–76,
  88, 89, 194
Stanley, Lady – see Beaufort, Margaret
  Thomas, Lord, Earl of Derby 28, 56,
  121, 126
Stillington, Robert, Bishop of Bath and
  Wells 54, 76, 78–81, 85, 195, 197
Stony Stratford 48–49, 53, 75
Suffolk 18, 23, 102, 132, 134
  Duke of – see Pole, John de la
Sutton Cheney 114, 119, 122–23,
  125–26, 166, 168
sweating sickness 121

Talbot, Eleanor (wife of Edward IV)
  11, 36, 51–52, 54, 55, 77–78,
  80–81, 83–85, 153, 168, 189
  George, 4th Earl of Shrewsbury 52
  John, 1st Earl of 54
Tewkesbury Abbey 147
  battle of 41, 42, 93–94
Test Act – see Penal Laws
Thirty-nine Articles, the 66
Three Estates of the Realm, the 8, 74,
  76, 81, 87, 102, 105, 168
Time Team 142–43
titulus regius, act of 34, 85
transubstantiation, doctrine of 67, 69,
  196
Tudor 10, 26, 29–30, 34, 36, 39, 60,
  78, 94, 120, 126, 137, 160, 161,
  167
Tudor-Craig, Pamela 57

ULAS 132–33, 135, 139, 143–44, 154,
  158, 183, 185, 203
usurper 10, 14, 15, 57, 74–75, 77,
  81–83, 85, 86, 153, 168, 197

Vaughan, Sir Thomas 39–40, 48–49
Vergil, Polydore 43, 58, 119–20, 129,
  130, 132, 133, 184
Vespers (religious service) 123
Vulgate, the (Latin Bible) 69

Wakelin, Adam 141, 204
'Warbeck, Perkin' – see 'England,
  Richard of'
Warkworth, John 42–43, 193
Warwick, Earl of – see Beauchamp,
  Richard; Neville, Richard
Wavrin, Jehan de 25, 190
Wayte, Elizabeth (Lucy), mistress of
  Edward IV 77, 84–85
Webber, Andrew Lloyd 10
Westminster, Dean of – see Norris, Dr
  Foxley
  Edward of, Prince of Wales 39–42,
  44, 93–94, 96, 99
Westmorland Earl of – see Neville,
  Ralph
Weymouth, Dorset 41
White, Bill 140–41
'White Syrie' ('Surrey') 117–18, 168
Windsor Castle 45, 131, 160
witches 25, 33, 35, 38
  and see sorcery
Wolsey, Cardinal Thomas 83, 86–87, 90
Woodville Anthony, Earl Rivers 47,
  49–50, 52, 76
  coup of 1483, the attempted 47, 50,
  75, 79, 102
  Elizabeth, bigamous wife and
  consort of Edward IV 33–37, 46,
  47, 49–54, 75, 76–81, 84, 99,
  102, 105–06, 189
  family 18, 59, 75, 78, 83
Wycliffe, John 68, 69
'Wycliffe's Bible' (so-called) 64, 67, 68,
  69

Y-chromosome – see DNA
York 10, 14, 15, 17, 30, 48, 53, 54,
  87, 94, 105, 106, 130, 131, 164
  Anne of, Duchess of Exeter (sister of
  Richard III) 148, 171, 175
  Archbishop of – see Rotherham,
  Thomas

Cecily, Duchess of (mother of
Richard III) – see Neville
Cecily of (daughter of Edward IV)
104, 200
Edmund of, Earl of Rutland, brother
of Richard III 17, 90
Elizabeth of, consort of Henry VII
60, 84, 99, 104
George of, Duke of Clarence, brother
of Richard III 16, 17, 24, 26, 28
Isabel, Duchess of (great

grandmother of Richard III) – see
Castile
Margaret of, Duchess of Burgundy,
sister of Richard III 16, 24, 102,
146, 147, 177, 179
Richard, Duke of (father of Richard
III) 15, 16, 19, 24, 26, 28, 46, 95
Richard, Duke of (son of Edward IV)
57, 161
Thomas of, brother of Richard III
22, 24